玛丽亚   Maria Teresa Kucharek

1990.

Translated by Jiao Tielan
Editing and Rewrite: Xu Yaoping
Advisor: Barbara Guangde Yang
Layout: xu Kehong

QIGONG ESSENTIALS
FOR HEALTH PROMOTION

Jiao Guorui

China Reconstructs Press

CONTENTS

General Concepts of Qigong

Practising Qigong

Scientific Research on Qigong

Quiescent Qigong Exercises

Dynamic Qigong Exercises

Preface

Qigong, an invaluable component of traditional Chinese medicine, has its origin in ancient times. Unique to China only, Qigong has also become an integral part of the Chinese culture. Qigong masters and medical scientists have developed a theory from a wealth of experience accumulated from their clinical experience and practice of Qigong over many centuries.

Needless to say, Qigong exercise can produce a myriad of beneficial effects, of which the most common are preventing and curing diseases, strengthening the constitution, avoiding premature aging, and prolonging life. Lacking systematization and academic studies, however, Qigong as a prophylactic and therapeutic exercise still needs to be re-evaluated in order to further advance its development.

Since the New China was founded in 1949, the government has paid great attention to the practice of Qigong as a medical and health-care program. And yet, mysticism and superstition have distorted the image of Qigong as a branch of science. Charlatans, who remain active in society, have aroused deepened suspicion in society causing great damage to the credibility of Qigong.

The purpose of this book is to change the social attitude, eliminate mystification, assert the principle of Yin/Yang in traditional Chinese medicine (TCM), and summarize and explain the theory of Qigong as well as its practising methods.

The outline of this book is based on my lectures to the junior and senior classes as well as foreign students at the Beijing TCM

College in early 1960s. An abridged edition, which is entitled *Health-preserving Qigong Methods,* was published by the Shanghai Science and Technology Press in 1964. The complete book was printed in a series by Hong Kong's *Wenhui Daily.* As a revised edition with twice as much as the original content, the book was published by the Beijing China Trade Federation Press and the Beijing Qigong Research Association for limited circulation. This version is translated from the newest edition under the present title of *Qigong Essentials For Health Promotion* published by the Fujian People's Press.

Loyal to the principle of being "simple, effective, appropriate and reliable," this book is a detailed introduction of the fundamental methods of Qigong exercise. Over more than twenty years, I have received letters from both Chinese and overseas readers which, to my great regret, I have failed to answer. I am taking this opportunity to extend my apologies and sincere gratitude to them all. Once again, I am extremely thankful to the comrades for their contribution of many valuable documents and, more important, their devotion to the development of Qigong.

I am looking forward to your comments and suggestions.

Jiao Guorui

About the English Edition

This book is on science. It explains how human beings can promote health and prolong life through discovering and developing the physiological potentiality of the body. Modern scientific research measures and proves the effects of Qigong exercise in preventing disease, promoting health, resisting premature aging and prolonging life. In this sense, the development of modern sciences has brought the significance and vitality of Qigong science to light. This science can no longer be neglected, but has attracted increasing attention from academic and intellectual circles around the world.

In recent years, international exchange in this field has proliferated quickly. The need for translations of Chinese books on the subject has also grown. Encouraged by my friends, I have asked my daughter Jiao Tielan to translate *Qigong Essentials for Health Promotion* into English in order to let more people of the world benefit from Qigong, a science unique to the Chinese nation and well developed by the 4th century B.C. Now the English version is about to be printed, I would like to extend my sincere gratitude to all the friends whose generous help has made the fulfillment of this exciting and yet most challenging project possible. I also hope that readers will be frank with their criticism of the text and translation so that we will be able to perfect our work.

As an important branch of the science of the human body, Qigong exercise is closely related with many other fields. More important, **it not only is on effective methods of health promotion, but also is an outstanding scientific system and art.** Its main effects are promoting resistance to diseases, strengthening one's physique, preventing premature aging and prolonging life. It is connected with other scientific fields including acupuncture, moxibustion, massage, gerontology, convalescence management, social medical science, prophylactic athletics, martial arts, sports, body building, psychiatry, cultural cultivation, the fine arts including drama, music and dance, paranormal capability training and physical development. So Qigong is useful in many ways. It is also easy to learn and promote. As the material quality of life improves, people will find themselves increasingly in the need of better health during longer lives. **It is inevitable that Qigong will be socialized, globalized and modernized.**

During my lecture tour of Japan in 1985, I was asked by the press about the future development of Qigong. I predicted that China's Qigong will dominate the 21st century worldwide as a new health-promoting technique. Since then, several worldwide Qigong upsurges have occurred. I deeply believe that, as long as Qigong is done properly and conscientiously, more people will be able to mobilize and foster their physiological potentialities and build up resistance to disease, giving rise to a new phase in public health care. When more people have benefited physically and mentally from Qigong, I believe, the World Health Organization (WHO) will have another approach to realizing its goal of "Health Care for Everybody by the Year 2000."

May the Chinese science of health promotion through Qigong contribute more to the health of humankind!

Jiao Guorui

Calm the mind, avoid worrying about worldly cares, and *Zhen Qi* (Essential Qi) will be able to travel smoothly along the channels; concentrate your thoughts, and the body will not be invaded by diseases....

Some great masters in ancient times could marshal heaven and earth, controlling *Yin* and *Yang*. They breathed essential Qi, stood quietly, and concentrated their minds on what they wanted. The spirit and body joined in flawless unity.

--A Theory of Congenital Qi from
the Plain Questions Section of Internal Canon of Medicine

A door hinge will never become insect-riddled. Rhythmic movement regulates Qi, promotes digestion and blood flow and guards against disease.

--Hua Tuo

General Concepts of Qigong

I. The Significance of Qigong

Qigong, an outstanding cultural legacy of ancient China, is also an important part of traditional Chinese medicine (TCM). Qigong is a prophylactic method which is unique to China. The aim of Qigong exercise is preventing and curing diseases, strengthening the constitution, avoiding premature aging, and prolonging life. The main characteristics of Qigong include the training of Essential Qi in the human body, which integrates mental activity with body postures and respiration. Therefore, Qigong has been highly regarded as an important method of treating diseases and extending life.

Historically, Qigong has always been widely used in China for medical purposes. It is also applied in Taoist and Buddhist physical exercises. The methods include Jinggong (Quiescent Exercise), Donggong (Dynamic Exercise) and Jing-Donggong. The types of movements include those emphasizing gentle force, strong force, internal exercise, external exercise, treatment of diseases and prophylaxis.

In the fields of medical treatment and prophylaxis, Qigong is different from other physical treatment therapies, and the term Qigong typifies this uniqueness. Qi refers to the body's physiological functions. Qigong experts call it Internal Qi or Dantian Qi (mainly from the visceral organs), which generates life. Gong refers to Gongfu (practising skill). Therefore, Qigong is a kind of self-training method by which the practitioner uses the initiative to train the body and mind, providing holistic training for self-reliance, self adjustment, body building, prophylaxis, curing diseases, invigorating and strengthening the constitution, resisting premature aging, and prolonging life.

In prophylaxis and treating diseases, Qigong exerts its effects on the body through its required movements, postures, regulation of respiration, and control of thought, building up the constitution and strengthening bodily resistance. For instance, the constitutions of those prone to catch colds can be effectively improved through regular daily Qigong exercise. This physical training can improve the holism and ameliorate symptoms. In disagreement with this theory some Qigong experts emphasize only certain parts of the body; others consider Qigong to be effective only for functional diseases. But it has been proved that Qigong is also effective in treating some diseases with organic changes, such as ulcers. Therefore, as long as Qigong is properly practised, therapeutic effects will be achieved and the duration of illness and recovery can be shortened.

Qigong is effective in treating some chronic diseases, especially hypertension, coronary heart disease, ulcers, neurasthenia and bronchitis. However, it is unrealistic to think of it as a cure-all. No therapeutic method is interchangeable with another, each having its merits. Qigong can reduce severity of disease and promote earlier recovery without any special equipment. So it is highly desirable to employ Qigong clinically.

Qigong is also effective for body building. People who are experts at the exercise usually experience its benefits of improved digestion and respiration and cardiovascular and nervous system. It improves sleep quality, relieves fatigue, strengthens one physically and mentally, enhances physical stamina and thus improves working efficiency. Of course, recovery from disease, consolidation of therapeutic effects, and health depend on a variety of factors. Although Qigong is an effective method of health care, it is not enough to practice it alone. We must also strike a proper balance between work and rest and regulate the diet.

Qigong also brings anti-aging and life-prolonging effects. In ancient times, people believed that Qigong was the the method for curing diseases and prolonging life. According to historical records, Hua Tuo, a famous doctor of the Three Kingdoms period (A.D. 220-280), invented the Frolics of Five Animals (Wuqinxi) exercises. He persisted in practising them. As a result, he looked young at the age of one hundred. This youth-preserving effect is verified by the aged who have practised long-term Qigong exercise. Most octogenarians and nonagenarians who persist in Qigong exercise are spirited with normal blood pressure, good vision and hearing, ringing voices, sound teeth, and can sleep well, walk with firm strides, are resistant to heat, and seldom suffer from diseases; they differ greatly from those taking little exercise. So Qigong contributes greatly to geriatrics.

In ancient times Qigong was regarded as the key to immortality. This is impossible, because aging is an objective law. The purpose of undertaking Qigong is not to attain immortality by closing the eyes and idling time away, but to build up physical stamina to avoid premature aging so that one can always be alert and vigorous and contribute more to mankind.

Some people believe that some mystery is involved in Qigong exercise, making it very difficult to master. This is wrong. Qigong consists of scientific knowledge. Guided by people with rich experience in Qigong exercise, one can expect to master it step by step according to the rules and regulations. As long as it is conscientiously and persistently practiced, it can be mastered and will benefit health, work and study.

II. The Origin and Prospects of Qigong.

As a prophylactic method, Qigong has a history which can be traced back to remote antiquity. Historical records indicate that people used a dance to direct body movements and regulate Qi and breathing in order to cure diseases in Yao times 4,000 years ago. *The Spring and Autumn Chronicles* by Lu states, a long long time ago, at the beginning of Tao Tang Tribe times, people became ill due to stasis of body fluids (Yin), which was actually clogging caused by dampness disease resembling rheumatism. So they were urged to do a dance exercise which relieved stagnation. At that time there was a deluge with clogging of rivers and flooding with cold, damp weather over a long period.

In the Warring States Period (770-222 B.C.), the scholar Laozi, 6th century B.C., suggested a method of health preservation by regulating respiration (Chui Xiu Yangsheng). His contemporary, Zhuangzi, carried it further and said, "Inhaling and exhaling helps to rid one of the stale and take in the fresh. Moving as a bear and stretching as a bird can result in longevity." At that time, people carved the 45-ideograph Qigong formula for making Qi flow on jade girdle pendants in pictures as well as characters (Fig.1). It goes: To make Qi flow freely one must be smooth and steady. In this way, Qi can be preserved and extended deeply

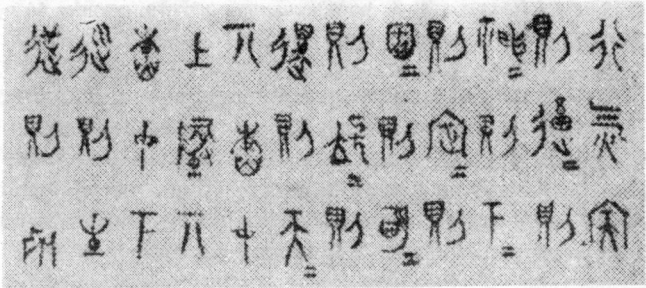

Fig. 1
Patterns carved on an ancient jade ornament illustrate Qi movement.

throughout the body. Flowing downward, it is consolidated This stimulates Qi proliferation which will carry it up to the sky (to of the head). The base of the sky is above, the foundation of earth extends into the depths. If you abide by this principle, you will lead a long life; otherwise, you will die. It is obvious that long-term practice had enabled the people of that period to develop a Qigong theory. An unearthed relic, Dao Ying Xing Qi Fa (Method of inducing Free Qi Flow) painted during the Western Han dynasty (206 B.C.- A.D. 24), shows Qigong exercises through pictures. Ten of the 44 pictures of females and males show imitation of animal movements. The internal canon of medicine, Huangdi Neijing devotes many chapters to detailing the origin, application, classification, and theory of Qigong. This includes ridding the mind of worries, controlling or concentrating thought, breathing exercise, muscle toning, swallowing the saliva to preserve it, bringing into play the body's physiological forces and stimulating circulation. Doctor Hua Tuo (2nd century) was

15

Fig. 2

Ui-guiding Diagrams, a silk book unearthed in 1979, includes 44 original drawings about Qigong in the Western Han dynasty.

not only a master of surgery, herbal medicine and acupuncture, but also famous for his knowledge of health preservation. His theory of prophylaxis emphasizes exercise. His words on this subject have become a famous motto: "The door hinge in an inhabited home will never be insect riddled. Rhythmic movement aids digestion and blood circulation, promoting health." He invented Qigong exercises imitating the movements of five animals -- the tiger, dear, bear, monkey and bird, inspired by his predecessors' experience. This Frolics of Five Animals are especially good for unclogging the channels and collaterals, dispelling diseases, limbering the extremities and promoting longevity. They are widely practiced by Chinese, enriched by family variations.

The literature shows that Qigong was traditionally expounded in most classics of past dynasties covering history and philosophy. Famous physicians in ancient China were usually adept at both healing and exercises for health preservation. Qigong is also alluded to in the following medical works: *General Treatment, Etymology and Symptomatology of Diseases* (Zhu Bing Yuan Hou Lun, 610 A.D.) by Chao Yuanfang of the Song dynasty; *Treasured Remedies for Emergencies*, mid-seventh century by Sun Simiao in the Tang dynasty; *On Conservation of Health* (Sheshen Lun) by Liu Wansu (1120-1200) in the Jin dynasty; *Clinical Experience of Rumen* (Rumen Shi Qin) by Zhan Zihe (1156-1228); *Medical Secrets of the Orchid Chamber* (Lan Shi Mi Gang) by Li Dongyuan (1180-1251); *A Medical*

Supplement of Ge Zhi Yu Lu by Zhu Danxi (1281-1358); and Li Shizhen, a very famous medical scientist of the Ming dynasty mentioned Qigong in his *Textual Research on the Eight Extra Channels* (Qi Jing Ba Mai Kao; 1578 edition), stating that changes in the channels anc collaterals can be perceived by noting the physiological reactions during quiescent Qigong. Shen Jinao, an outstanding doctor of the Qing dynasty, devoted exclusive chapters in his book, *The Shen's Experience on the Conservation of Health* (She Shi Zun Shen Shu) to the treatment of disease through Qigong exercise. He also proposed 12 principles of movement and described therapeutic Qigong. Qigong also can be applied in Wushu (Chinese martial arts) as the basic exercise with its emphasis on comprehensive training of posture, the mind, Qi and force. The book *A Formula for Thirteen Movements of Taiji Boxing* (Taiji Quan Zhi San Shi Xing Gong Jue) says, "Why do we practise Qigong? Because it provides a longer life."

In other countries of the world, there are also some physical training methods similar to Qigong. For instance, the Indian Yoga exercise has been introduced to Western countries since long ago. But it was only considered to be a part of an oriental philosophy without any scientific value. So it was not widely accepted. In recent years, the effects of Yoga exercise have been proved by modern scientific apparatus arousing wide interest. Nowadays people have recognized the harm of drug- induced diseases, and medical specialists have been seeking new cures without using drugs, or with small dosages of medicine if necessary. In these circumstances interest in Qigong, one of the recommended natural methods, has developed rapidly. In 1909, an American suggested a "gradual relaxing exercise be practised for prophylaxis. This method is like Relaxing Qigong Exercise. In 1955, the American scientist used the oscillograph to record muscular relaxation. It is reported that the relaxation method is effective in treating fatigue, angina, hypertension, neurasthenia, mental depression, Graves's disease, and chronic infectious diseases. Experimental research programs on Qigong have been established at many universities throughout the world, including the University of Europe in Switzerland, the University of California in the United States, the Institute of Physiology and Psychology of New York State University, Bourbeck Academy of

Science in Britain, and the People's University in West Germany. Qigong has been successfully applied in sports training. In the Soviet Union a training method similar to Qigong is a required course for senior athletes to raise their achievement level. A number of scholars in different countries have researched Qigong for geriatrics. Early in the 7th century during the Tang dynasty, Qigong was introduced to foreign countries.

For over several thousand years, the Chinese people have accumulated rich clinical experience and theoretical knowledge of Qigong. More than 100 books form the ancient, classical literature on Qigong have been published. In addition, there are numerous methods handed down within families for generations. All these form a precious legacy.

Since 1949, the Party and government have organized the most comprehensive research on Qigong as a scientific field. Clinical practices have proved it to be effective for treating certain kinds of complicated chronic diseases. Laboratory research using modern scientific apparatus has demonstrated Qigong's usefulness in preventing and treating diseases. The Conference on Qigong held in Beijing in 1979 drew great attention in Chinese medical circles and strong support from the leaders of the departments involved. According to some recent reports, Qigong research will soon have a major impact on the development of TCM theories in such basic areas as Yin/Yang, the five elements, visceral manifestations, channels and collaterals, Qi and blood, and the activity and nature of Qi. It will contribute to the medical theories on geriatrics, health care, physical culture, paranormal training and understanding of the functions of the human body. It is safe to predict that even greater attention will be drawn toward Qigong research in the near future.

III. Two Case Histories

The history of Qigong goes back at least 4,000 years. At a 1959 meeting on Qigong's medical effects more than 2,000 cases of gastric and duodenal ulcer were reported. Here I would like to present two cases in which Qigong showed its therapeutic effects.

The first case involves myself. Having started practising martial arts as a child, I had always been in good health. I was not interested in my health. When I began my medical studies, I did not notice the "Tu Na, Dao Yin" methods of expiration, inhalation and induction of Qi's free flow to cure stasis. Stasis is the cause of disease according to TCM. I did not believe in Qigong, for it seemed to simple to cure diseases.

Later, I led a very irregular life, taking supper late, wolfing food whether it was cold or hot, and my appetite and digestion weakened. Still, I did nothing and refused medical attention. As a result, my mental powers weakened, allergic- rhinitis developed. I was plagued by dizziness and my eyesight blurred. Although I took medicine, my condition did not improve.

In 1958, after a bad cold which exacerbated my chronic conditions, severe stomach pains interfered with my work. It was then that I began to pay attention to treatment. My symptoms were dizziness, severe headaches and stomachaches, dryness of and pain in the eyes, and exhaustion. What I experienced was described in TCM as "the body's feeling as heavy as mud from spleen disorder." Suffering from such diseases, the patient usually can feel the following reactions: They are susceptible to cold, lost sense of taste, bad appetite, nausea from acid stomach, and stomach pains felt throughout the lumbar and coastal regions. Sometimes I could not sleep. My weight dramatically decreased from 63 to 49 kilograms. The TCM diagnosis was dysfunction of the spleen and stomach; the Western medical diagnosis was duodenal ulcer and neurasthenia. Even after treatment with Chinese herbs, Western medicine and physiotherapy, my condition did not improve. At someone's suggestion, I decided to give Qigong therapy a try.

Lacking confidence in the exercise, I was merely driven to do it by the fear of my illness. I joined a group of less sick practitioners. The curative effects began to show very quickly after only 10 days of practice. My symptoms began to alleviate. My stomach symptoms, lumbago, drowsiness and others all improved significantly. After three months of practice, all the symptoms other than dizziness and eye pains were gone. Especially striking was that my fatigue and severe allergic rhinitis disappeared. My ulcer pains vanished on the very first day of Qigong exercise and I felt encouraged to continue. Now 20 years have passed and my diseases have never recurred. From personal experience, I came to believe that Qigong is a simple but very effective therapy.

The second case involves a foreigner. In 1946, when he was 60 years old, he left the hospital after he had given up on ineffective treatment. He had four injections of camphor a day. The doctor told his family that he might live no longer than one month. However, he miraculously lived 12 more years. How come? The diagnosis was arteriosclerosis, angina, TB, and emphysema. Three days after leaving the hospital, he entered another hospital. In addition to the diseases above, the diagnosis there was coronary sclerosis, cardiosclerosis, mitral insufficiency, asthma, chronic gastritis, chronic hepatitis, arthritis, and impotence. Failure of treatment and unimaginable pains left him hopeless. So he tried Qigong therapy.

After persistent Qigong exercise, he recovered. During his last decade or so, he took no nitroglycerin at all, and his symptoms gradually disappeared. He even looked young for his age.

Some readers long to know about Qigong as to how it cures diseases. The answer is unexpectedly simple: the abdominal respiration method similar to that of the Thirteen Prophylactic Postures. Yet it is not a cure that shows effects easily, not that the method is difficult to learn, but that it is too simple to believe. Therefore, patients are often reluctant to exercise conscientiously and persistently. As some foreign patients say, "The greatest difficulty about this exercise is to practise step by step and day to day.

From these two cases we can see the tremendous potentialities of the human body. If its physiological forces are fully mobilized, they will greatly strengthen the body's own resistance and play a major role in preventing and curing diseases, including some seemingly incurable ones. The theory of the physiological diseases is attracting more and more attention in world medical circles. It points out that most medical efforts are aimed at detecting external causes of diseases only. Research on how to increase and mobilize the body's own defenses has just begun in recent years. Our findings prove that Qigong is very effective in mobilizing the body's own resistance. How to enhance this effect remains an important topic open to discussions.

IV. The TCM Understanding of Qigong

Why and how does Qigong prevent and cure diseases and strengthen the body? This complicated problem needs systematic and comprehensive expounding.

The human body is a complicated organism. It exists by constantly unifying contradictions within itself and with the external world. While it exists in the universe, metabolism is going on inside it, each viscera at its own rate. Gases form, food is digested, Qi and blood circulate, saliva secretes, waste material is discharged, the PH changes, and spiritual activity influences metabolisms, all happening continuously in response to the growth of life. TCM regards such physiological changes as results of fluctuations and changes in the flow and function of Qi which circulate throughout the body through channels and collaterals. Qigong, a psychopneumatological exercise, drills posture, respiration and focus of the mind in order to unclog the channels and collaterals and re-establish body equilibrium. This improves the dynamic equilibrium of Yin and Yang, harmonizes Qi and blood, dredges the channels and collaterals, and fosters vitality and Essential Qi.

Effects of Dynamic Equilibrium Between Yin and Yang The TCM theory of Yin/Yang refers to the unity of the two opposites - - Yin and Yang, which depend on each other but also oppose each other. Yin and Yang are the source of each other and, under certain conditions, are opposites. Female is Yin and male Yang; Cold is Yin and hot Yang; the heart, lungs, kidneys, spleen and liver are Yin, and the stomach and bowels Yang; internal is Yin and external Yang; quiet is Yin and movement Yang, and so on. Unity means Yin and Yang are inseparable: With no high there is no low; no external, no internal; no upper viscera, no bowels; no cold, no heat; no activity, no quietude, and so on. Under the right conditions, they change into their opposites. For example, chills cause fever and fever leads to chills; Yin overflux unbalances the natural equilibrium, causing deficiency of Yang diseases and vise versa. And so on ad finitum, as long as life continues. Yin and Yang always depend on each other. With Yin alone, there would be no birth; with Yang alone, there would be no growth. Therefore, humans must maintain the Yin/Yang equilibrium in order for the body to function normally. If the balance is lost, illness or even death may ensue. Keeping fit is to keep in relative balance. Since Yin is quiescence and Yang movement, Qigong practitioners must observe the Yin/Yang relation. During Jinggong (quiescent exercise), it is important to keep the exterior quiescent while propelling Qi along the channels and collaterals; when practising Dynamic Qigong, it is important to keep the thoughts concentrated, thus remaining quiescent while carrying out body movements and propelling Qi. So, there is movement in Quiescent Qigong, and quiescence in Dynamic Qigong. This is the ancient philosophy of dialectical materialism applied in TCM.

Role of Qi and Blood Qi and blood play a major role in maintaining life. If Qi and blood circulate freely, the organism stays healthy; if they are blocked, disease ensues. So free, unimpeded flow of Qi and blood is most important. Qigong mainly trains the free flow of Qi. How does Qi influence blood? The TCM theory is, Qi guides blood flow, and Qi circulation causes blood circulation; Qi stagnation causes blood stasis. Another TCM theory holds that Qi should be regulated before blood circulation can be invigorated. If Qi goes on the wane, blood circulation will get stagnant. To warm blood, Qi must be warmed first. Warmed Qi will cause blood to warm up. Vigorous Qi produces blood. So the TCM treatment of blood diseases includes medication for synergism. As Qigong therapy trains Qi, it also fortifies blood. This theory is proved by the clinical results and experiments to be described below.

The Effects of Dredging Channels and Collaterals TCM holds that the channels and collaterals distribute Qi and blood throughout the body. If these passages are unobstructed, Qi and blood flow freely and normally. But if they are obstructed, disease will occur. Dredging channels and stimulating blood circulation are accomplished by Qi flow or channel and collateral Qi, to be specific. After practising Qigong a while, Qi can be felt circulating inside the body. When Qi passes through a disease affected area, blood circulation is stimulated and salivary secretion increased. With the quiescence of concentrated thoughts during Qigong exercise, awareness of Qi circulation is enhanced. These sensations and physiological changes show that Qigong is effective in dredging the channels and collaterals. (Qi can be felt as warmth, tingling, prickling, a flow, soreness, coldness, distention, burning, an ant crawling, throbbing, etc. -- Editor).

Effects of Cultivating Essential Qi Essential Qi (Zhen Qi) is also called Yuan Qi -- Original or Source Qi. TCM holds that Zhen Qi is the power source of all body movement. *Ling Shu of Internal Cannon* states: Its sources are heaven and earth, so air water and food nourish this Qi through the biochemical processes Qigong trains and strengthens Qi. The practice with basic skills can generate vigorous Qi which produces sensations during exercise and maintains its vitality afterwards. Persistent Qigong exercise helps maintain dynamic Yin Yang equilibrium, Harmonizes Qi and blood, dredges the channels and collaterals, cultivates Qi, increases resistance to diseases, strengthens the constitution and prolongs life and youth. (Qigong exercise should be a lifetime habit. -- Editor)

V. Clinical Therapeutic Qigong

In recent years, systematic medical observation has proved that Qigong therapy is satisfactory in treating various chronic diseases. It enhances curative effect and reduces the duration of treatment, especially in some chronic diseases which need cures

Clinical experience shows that Qigong is particularly effective in hypertension, gastric or duodenal ulcer, chronic hepatitis, chronic indigestion, gastroptosis, neurasthenia, TB, chronic bronchitis, chronic bronchial asthma, senile lumbago, toxemia of pregnancy and pelvic inflammation. It also reduces the pain of delivery. Qigong definitely ameliorates many diseases. It is still in the research stage as a therapy for chronic nephritis, silicosis, glaucoma, rheumatic heart disease, angina, neural paralysis, myasthenia gravis, cirrhoses and tumors. Although we have some clinical experience, many problems remain to be solved.

Qigong Therapy and Hypertension Hypertension is a common disease which occurs easily in the aged and middle aged. In Beijing, Shanghai and other cities, comprehensive observations have been conducted on Qigong therapy. Scientists believe that Qigong is suitable for hypertensives in all stages of the disease. By observing 185 hypertensives, the Shanghai Hypertension Research Institute found that the overall effective cure rate was 71.1 percent, including a markedly effective rate of 41.7 percent after one year. The 50 patients using the depressor in coordination with TCM medicine yielded no noticeable difference from another group of 67 on depressors only. The 68 cases on combined treatment with depressors and Qigong therapy, Group A; had markedly better results than Group B which was on depressors only. The A group had a total effective rate of 92.6 percent, including markedly effective rate of 72 percent, after one year of treatment. After two years of treatment, the A group's total effective rate was 94.1 percent with a 67 percent markedly effective rate, while Group B had a 64.2 percent total effective rate, and a markedly effective rate of 22.4 percent, after one year. After two years of treatment, the B group's total effective rate rose to 63.3 percent with markedly effective rate of 26.6 only.

A monthly average diastolic pressure lower than 90 millimeters was considered normal. Group A had 85 percent of the cases normal after one year of treatment, and 83.9 percent after two years of treatment. But Group B had only 47.7 percent normal after one year of treatment, and 45.9 percent after two years of treatment. The reduction in blood pressure was more obvious in the Qigong practitioners after exercise than after rest. After Qigong, patients with heart or kidney diseases improved with most returning to work.

Based on these results, many medical personnel realized that Qigong helps to consolidate the cure. Consolidation of a cure for ideopathic hypertension is the crux of the problem, lifetime medication being the norm.

Qigong Therapy in Gastric and Duodenal Ulcers

Gastric and duodenal ulcers are common. Many cities in China are achieving good results with Qigong. In 1959, 2,288 cases were reported at a meeting on Qigong. The Qigong Research Group of PLA Convalescent Hospital No.31 reported that 100 cases receiving Qigong treatment resulted in a curative rate of 96.8 percent. The niche shadows disappeared within 90 days. The Qingdao Convalescent Hospital observed 150 cases and reported that the disappearance rate of the niche shadow of gastric ulcer was 86.2 percent and the disappearance rate of the niche shadow of duodenal ulcer was 93.7 percent. After Qigong practice, five cases of complex ulcers with niche recovered. More than 80 percent of the patients increased their body weight. The Qigong Department of Tianjin Workers Convalescent Hospital No.1 reported 515 cases, including 230 with histories of five to 10 years' illness. After Qigong therapy (average inpatient treatment lasted 72.7 days) 500 (97.09 percent) went back to work. The patients in the non-Qigong group gained an average 1.1 kilograms while the average increase in the Qigong group was 4.4 kilograms and the cure rate was 70.8 percent versus the 15.27 rate in the non-Qigong group.

Zhao Liming, a TCM specialist from Harbin, reported use of complex Qigong therapy to treat 1,278 ulcer cases. Of the 190 cases of gastric ulcer, 154 recovered, 34 improved, and 2 were ineffective. Of the 955 cases of duodenal ulcer, 742 cured, 202 improved, and 11 were ineffective. For the whole group, the recovery rate was 77.4 percent, improved 20.9 percent and no effect 1.7 percent; in 82 percent the niche disappeared. Of the 175 cases under long-term clinical observation, disease recurred in 59 cases including two who persisted in Qigong exercise, 13 practising it on and off and 54 who gave it up. This indicates that keeping up Qigong exercise is very important in preventing recurrence.

Qigong Therapy in Gastroptosis Gastroptosis-related functional disorder requiring treatment is usually caused by reduction in muscle tension. Zeng Qingyuan of the Harbin Sun Island Workers' Convalescent Hospital reported use of Qigong therapy to treat 80 cases, in which 75 had X-rays taken before and after treatment. After Qigong therapy was applied in coordination with Taiji Boxing, 63 cases recovered, 12 cases improved markedly, four improved and one was not effective. In treating these cases of gastroptosis, the Qigong therapy also improved the gastric-peristalsis as well as gastric muscle tone and raised the stomach fundus. There were 31 case4s with the low limit of stomach between 5 and 6 centimeters under the crista- line anterior superior; 21 cases between 7 and 3 centimeters; 14 cases between 8.5 and 9 centimeters; nine cases between 11 and 12 centimeters. After Qigong treatment, in 60 cases the low limit of stomach returned to the normal position (about 5 centimeters under the crista line); 12 cases between 5 and 6 centimeter; three cases between 7 and 8 centimeters. Qigong treatment raised the low limit of stomach by 8 to 9 centimeter in seven cases; 6.5 to 7.5 centimeter in five cases; 4.5 to 6 centimeter in 21 cases; one case received no effect. For the whole group, the low limit was raised by an average of 4.5 centimeter.

Qigong Therapy in Neurasthenia Neurasthenia is common in mental workers. Qigong is an effective therapy in most such diseases. Fang Qixing of the PLA Convalescent Hospital No.33 reported that, of the 84 neurasthenia cases receiving Qigong treatment, 53 recovered. Most of the 84 had been hospitalized and treated by various methods, but had shown neither marked nor stable effects. After Qigong therapy for half a month to one month, most patients looked healthy again, regained their spirits, strength and good memory, increased their body weight, sleep quality improved and were well enough to resume work. Symptoms of dizziness and headache disappeared. Li Zongran of the Tianjin Cadres Convalescent Hospital reported using Qigong as the pivot of a comprehensive treatment for neurasthenia in 120 cases. Six cases had one year disease histories, 15 two years, 10 three years, 12 four years, 20 five years, 53 6-15 years, and four over 20 years. After treatment symptoms disappeared in 81 and the rest improved. Qigong therapy in this comprehensive treatment helped eliminate the main symptoms of prostration, fatigue, headache, dizziness, insomnia, palpitations, poor appetite, nervousness, shortness of breath, nightmares and hypomnesis. Very few people are Qigong resistant.

Qigong Therapy in TB Shanghai TB Hospital No.2

reported using Qigong therapy with TCM medicine to treat 357 TB cases. A two-month period of Qigong practice was required of all in the series, of whom 324 had infiltrative TB. To further divide the cases according to severity of disease, 63 were classed invasive stage, 51 spreading stage and 242 starting absorption stage. All took anti-TB medication continuously over long periods. Qigong therapy--Quiescent Neiyanggong was the key type used with auxiliary prophylactic exercises and relaxing exercise for emergency--and combined Western and TCM medicine including local injection were used. X-rays showed that 283 improved; 73 achieved no effects, and one worsened. Of the 357, 180 had lung cavities. After treatment these cavities sealed in 27 percent of the cases and shrank in 36.7 percent, a 63.8 effective rate. Of the same group, 62 showed no change in lung cavity, including 46 with lung cavity histories of more than one year and a negative phlegm TB bacteria rate of 55.2 percent. Of the 77 cases with high ESR, 48 (62.3 percent) normalized after treatment. This hospital believes that Qigong therapy is positive, safe, and helpful in improving the holism. Qigong added to comprehensive treatment yields better results than drugs alone. The hospital's experiment also proves the safety of treating active stage TB with Qigong. About 114 of the 357 cases were in the active stages, including the invasive and spreading stages. After two months of treatment, 93.8 percent of the 114 cases improved with none deteriorating. So Qigong is more effective in active TB cases. The Tianjin Cadres' Convalescent Hospital used Qigong in a comprehensive therapy to treat 30 TB patients with cavities. After five months of therapy, the cavity had sealed in 25 and shrunk in the other five. The doctors believe that although Western and TCM medicines are the main methods of treating TB cavity, Qigong aids recovery through toning the cerebral cortex and body function.

Qigong Therapy in Liver Disease The Tianjin Cadres' Convalescent Hospital used a comprehensive medication and Qigong therapy to treat 100 patients with liver disease, including 49 hepatitis cases, 34 chronic hepatitis cases, four cases of hepatitis-related complex syndrome cases, one persistent hepatitis case, and 12 cirrhosis cases. After being treated for one month and a half, 33 of the 49 cases recovered, 13 improved, and three showed modest improvement. Out of the 34 chronic hepatitis cases, 15 recovered and 16 improved markedly. Of the four cases of hepatitis-related complex syndrome, three recovered and one markedly improved. Of the 12 cirrhosis cases, seven improved markedly, seven improved markdly, three showed modest improvement and one was not affected. In liver disease, Qigong practice usually improves the appetite, alleviates abdominal distention, improves flatus, normalizes defection, relieves fatigue, hepatomegaly and splenomegaly and clears and calms the mind. Some patients impatiently forcing themselves to practise deep abdominal respiration during Qigong exercise occasionally aggravate pain in the liver. But correcting their Qigong method can make the pain vanish.

Of the 80 cases of hepatomegaly treated with Qigong, 33 achieved liver size normalization and 41 reduced the size, a 92.5 percent success rate. Of the 17 with splenomegaly, symptoms disappeared in seven and reduced in six, a 76.5 percent success rate. Comprehensive therapy with Qigong is obviously more effective than medicine alone.

Qigong Therapy and Heart Disease Most reports are on Qigong therapy of functional heart disease. Treatment of organic heart disease is reported little. The Beidaihe Qigong Convalescent Hospital reported using Qigong therapy to treat 19 cases of rheumatic heart disease and three of sinus tachycardia. Both patients and doctors verified the effectiveness of the therapy. Palpitation was slowed in all cases, atrial fibrillation disappeared in one, ECG strain disappeared in one, heart murmur was eliminated in 31.8 percent and reduced in in 40 percent, three enlarged hearts with lung congestion were alleviated, and three cases were cured of sinus tachycardia.

Shi Xiunong of the Baoding Convalescent Hospital Cardiovascular Department in Hebei province reported the use of Qigong therapy in treating 12 cases organic heart disease, including five rheumatic heart disease, two hypertensive heart disease, two syphilitic heart disease and one congenital heart disease. The therapy includes a three-month course of Qigong practice. In cases of abnormal heart function of heart failure, TCM medicine was also used. Most patients received good effects or began to receive curative effects at the end of one course of treatment. Some did not receive effects until the second course and only one showed no effects. The curative effect is most obvious in cases of arrhythmia. After Qigong practice, symptoms disappeared in some cases of persistent coupled rhythm, and systolic pressure and strong heart beat ameliorated in some cases of syphilitic heart disease. Generally speaking, Qigong is effective in treating congenital heart disease because the exercise helps regulate Qi and blood circulation, strengthening resistance to colds and thus reducing danger of heart failure.

Liang Guocai of the Shanghai Thorax Hospital has also reported the use of Qigong therapy in heart disease. He reports that the patients were divided into a selective group of 35 cases and a non-selective group of 18 cases. The clinical diagnosis of the selective group is: nine cases of coronary sclerosis, four hypertensive heart disease, 13 rheumatic heart disease, three congenital heart disease, three paroxysmal tachycardia, two corpulmonary heart disease, and one cardioneurosis complex with tachycardia. The diagnosis of the non-selective group is: 10 cases of rheumatic heart disease, two hypertension and hypertensive heart disease, one coronary sclerotic heart disease, two paroxysmal tachycardia, and one cardioneurosis. Qigong exercise in these conditions may be done lying down or sitting up. It features body relaxation, natural respiration and concentrating the mind at Dantian. The exercise should last at least one month under a doctor's supervision.

After Qigong therapy, in the selective group of 35 cases, the number of heart attacks decreased in eight, blood pressure dropped in nine hypertensives treated simultaneously with ·Western and TCM medicine, symptoms disappeared or were controlled in seven with paroxysmal tachycardia and one ventricular premature contraction, five showed obvious analgesia of postoperative thoracic wound pains, and three chronic heart failure cases improved. After combining Qigong therapy with Western medication, average ventricle pressure dropped from 40 to 24 millimeters in a case of congenital auricular septal defect complicated by pulmonary hypertension, one cardiophrenia complicated by tachycardia normalized after two years of Qigong practice. The results of Qigong therapy in the non-selective group are: 16 cases improved markedly, and two improved slightly. Doctors of the Shanghai hospital believe that Qigong effects on heart disease is significant. Generally, Qigong therapy has the following effects: calming the mind, harmonizing Qi and blood, toning the cardiovascular and nervous systems, lowering metabolism and energy consumption, lightening the heart load and lung load and enhancing the function of all the organs. This helps strengthen resistance against colds and other ailments. Therefore, heart disease caused deterioration.

Qigong Therapy in Bronchial Asthma Shanghai People's Hospital No. 6 reported the use of Qigong therapy in treating 107 cases of severe bronchial asthma. All the cases had been treated with Western medication and some had been treated by several methods, such as umbilical cord implant, hemolysis, incision, folk prescription, and acupuncture. But the disease recurred. After Qigong therapy was added to Western and TCM medication, acupuncture, physiotherapy, or folk prescription, the curative effects were marked. The Shanghai hospital recommends the following methods in specific situations: Use mainly Western medicine in acute attacks; otherwise use Qigong as the main therapy if the patient has mastered Qigong exercise or physiotheray and TCM medicine if the patient has not mastered Qigong. For stabilization, Qigong should be the main method supplemented with physiotherapy and TCM medicine. During clinical observation for three to 10 months after treatment, all the patients went through at least one hitherto disease prone season. Of the 107 cases, treatment in 34 percent was markedly effective, 32 percent improved, and 4 percent had no effects. The doctors believe that the Qigong exercise ability closely correlates with the curative effects. For example, of those who achieved marked effects, 31 were very good at Qigong, and among those who made obvious improvement, 22 were very deft at Qigong. Clinical observations also indicate that Qigong helps in significantly consolidating cures.

Qigong and Constipation Dr. Wang Shubin of Tangshan Qigong Convalescent Hospital has reported the use of Qigong in treating 126 cases of constipation. All the cases had complications, including 75 cases of duodenal ulcer, 24 gastroptosis, 22 gastric ulcer, three gastric resection and two hepatitis. Bowel movements occurred every two to three days only and once in more than 10 days. All recovered daily defecation after practising Neiyanggong, abdominal respiration, and focusing the mind on Dantian. The method featured lying sideways. After more than 10 days, this is changed to sitting posture and, in addition, Taiji (Shadow Boxing). Constipation disappeared in most cases after seven days. The doctors believe that Qigong treats the root of constipation, increases the tone of the bowel smooth muscle movement and activates bowel movement. The therapy also effectively improves digestive system function.

Qigong is a holistic exercise, although different methods may lay emphasis on particular parts of the body. The cure depends on improved conditions of the holism and so helps the patient recover fully. Qigong methods vary widely, and should be adjusted to the needs of each individual patient to be effective. Only when it is properly practised can Qigong bring about the desired results.

VI. Experimental Research on Qigong

Qigong can affect the complex mechanism of the human body in various ways. Qigong experts and doctors in the past have done much research and established many theories. Contemporary research has further proved that Qigong is a holistic exercise, which requires little of the environment but produces a positive effect on the functions of all body organs and systems or tracts.

Effects on the Respiration System The effect of Qigong is very obvious on the respiratory system because most people can deepen, prolong, invigorate and slow down their breathing after practice. Step by step, the practitioner can reduce his breathing from 10-20 times per minute to 4-5 times or even fewer. Recording demonstrates that the respiration of a practitioner is smoother than that of a non-practitioner. X-rays show that the up-down movement scope of the diaphragm's muscle is three to four times that of the ordinary. Clinical observations show that Qigong exercise can increase the difference in chest measurement by an average 2.8 centimeters and the length of breath stoppage at the end of expiration an average 18.4 seconds. The average value of maximum pulmonary ventilation is increased from 70.62 liters to 93.47 liters per minute, and the average value of vital capacity from 3,724 millimeters to 3,444 millimeters. According to one report, the amount of pulmonary ventilation decreased but breath dampness increased, the amount of oxygen decreased but the amount of alveolar carbon dioxide increased, both air metabolic rate and generated heat reduced dramatically. These changes are most obvious in practitioners who can enter into complete quiescence and are oblivious of their surroundings. Those who practise ordinary deep breathing do not experience these changes.

When Qigong practice is effective, oxygen consumption and carbon dioxide decrease. This indicates that Qigong increases alveolar ventilation by activating gas exchange. Reduction in the number of respirations does not cause shortage of oxygen but saves much biophysiological energy which otherwise would be consumed in more respiratory movement.

Effects on the Digestive System Qigong exercise invigorates and regulates digestion. Peristalsis is invigorated and regular after Qigong exercise Weak contractions are strengthened and strong movements reduced through exercise adjustment. After Qigong practice, gastrographic examination indicates that peristaltic wave is reduced in pace and symptoms disappeared in the ill. X-rays show that the up-and-down movement of the diaphragm muscles in the Qigong-practising group of patients were much larger on scale than in a comparison group which did not practise Qigong. The stomach fundus ascends with inhalation and descends with exhalation. The comparison group of patients also adopted abdominal respiration, without effect. The stomach fundus of a Qigong practitioner was found to be six times higher that of a non-practitioner. Neiyanggong (Internal Fostering Exercise) can effectively accelerate gastric and bowel evacuation. With improved gastrocolic function, removal of gastric gas and bowel residue can be much easier.

These Qigong-related changes prevent diseases of the gastrointestinal tract and premature aging. Qigong can also cause changes in the saliva ptyalin content. Clinical reports indicate that many TB patients' low saliva ptyalin normalizes after Qigong therapy. In some cases, only one course of Qigong exercise normalizes saliva ptyalin. However, proof of Qigong regulation of gastric juice acidity and pepsin is lacking.

Effects on Blood Function Qigong can dramatically change the peripheral blood picture. Measuring Qigong effects on blood shows that red and white cell counts increase in most practitioners after exercise. White cells increase an average 13 to 23 percent, usually more than the red cells. But the extent to these Qigong- related changes varies with the different methods of Qigong used and the practitioner's health conditions.

Increased white cell phagocytic ability is another marked effect of Qigong which can raise the phagocytic index of white cells from 40 percent before practice to over 90 percent afterwards. Shanghai TB Hospital No. 2 has reported that Qigong therapy helped 87 percent of the patients recover. This shows how Qigong builds resistance.

Effects on Cardiovascular Function Quiescent Exercise is particularly effective in slowing the heart beat. In contrast to non-practitioners, the electrocardiograph demonstrates that the practitioner's heart beat is slow and powerful. Because of this change, both the heart burden and oxygen consumption can be reduced. Qigong is also effective in changing the transparency of flood vessels. P32 tests prove that the Qigong practitioner's blood vessels are more transparent. This difference is attributed to vasodilation due to Qigong exercise. During Neiyanggong, when the practitioner deepens and cuts down the frequency of respiration, parallel changes appear in the curve of respiratory movement and blood volume. This means that the blood vessel contracts with inhalation and extends with exhalation--the blood volume in the vessels is related to the exercise method. Most people practising Neiyanggong or Relaxing Exercise can achieve blood vessel extension, with the latter producing the effect faster. But those who practise Three Circle Exercise While Standing usually find that their blood vessels tend to contract. In order to test the effect of Qigong on blood vessels, doctors used cold water to stimulate blood vessel contraction setting up conditioned reflex before they had patients practise Qigong. During Qigong exercise, they discovered, the patients' blood vessel showed little or no counteractive reflex. This indicates that the sympathetic nerve center is inhibited. Other experiments have discovered a close relationship between the Qigong effect on cardiac output with respiration. Examinations by electromagnetic ballisto-cardiography show a slight increase in cardio-output while the patient inhales, and a decrease while exhaling. Since the duration of inhaling is longer than exhaling, cardiac output can be reduced. Another example is the use of Qigong therapy in rheumatic vascular disease. Qigong can significantly reduce pulmonary pressure, of which the effect is better than intravenous injection. Comparing the Relaxing Exercise with simple resting, we found differences in the average blood pressure of 10 cases. After simple resting, the systolic pressure dropped 8 millimeters but the diastolic pressure did not. After Qigong practice, the systolic pressure dropped 18 millimeters and the diastolic dropped 16 millimeters. Comparing Relaxing Exercise effects with natural sleep, we found very similar differences. The drop in systolic pressure was greater with medication than with Relaxing Exercise, but the drop in diastolic pressure is larger after Qigong than with depressor medication. Comparison between Relaxing Exercise and another Qigong method, which requires focusing the mind on Dantian, shows that Relaxing Exercise causes a slighter drop in blood pressure. It is shown that many hypertensives' diastolic pressure dropped 20 millimeters after a single round of Qigong practice. This effect, however, does not occur in practitioners with normal blood pressure. So, the effect of Qigong on blood pressure is related not only with the practice method, but with the practitioner's physiological and pathological condition as well.

Effects on Metabolism It has been proved that a practitioner's gas metabolism is reduced when he enters the quiescent state of Qigong, but change in the quantity of oxygen consumption varies with the posture of practice. Lying down while doing Qigong exercise can reduce gas metabolism to the minimum level required by the human body ordinarily, which is lower than simply lying. The sitting posture can reduce the consumption of oxygen to the level before the exercise, much lower than the minimum level. But Qigong in the standing posture can cause a slight increase in oxygen consumption.

As to brain oxygen consumption, tests of oxygen content in the blood of the internal jugular vein show that Qigong exercise can bring about marked changes. After Qigong practice, only one third of the oxygen contained in the returning blood was consumed. This indicates that Qigong can significantly reduce the metabolism of brain blood sugar. Another example of how Qigong affects metabolism is in the change in body temperature after Qigong practice. The skin temperature can be raised during the exercise. The sitting posture raises the temperature most, the prone posture next, and the standing least. Under given conditions the skin temperature varies in different parts of the body, from the lowest in the extremities to the medium in the chest to the highest in the forehead. Skin temperature throughout the body, especially that of feet, can be raised during prone exercise and cross-legged exercise. Cross-legged exercise causes the greatest change. Internal Fostering Exercise can raise the skin temperature of the head, hands, chest and abdominal areas, but not of the feet. In ulcer patients, 10 minutes of exercise can raise the skin temperature of the back of the hands and feet to that of the front of the chest. The temperature remains high for 10 minutes after the exercise is finished. Based on clinical experiments, Qigong effects on the skin temperature is closely related to the exercise method, disease and deftness at the exercise.

Effects on Secretions The Endocrine hormones play an important role in metabolism, growth, reproduction, and physiological function. Qi is the body's physiological functions. Qigong exercise propels and invigorates Qi. Therefore, it influences endocrine hormones, too. Motion mainly depends on nerve regulation and nerve and body liquid regulation. Clinical observation shows that some bronchial asthma patients with deficiency of kidney Yang recovered normal ketone levels 24 hours after Qigong exercise. Patients who have practised Qigong for over a year experienced reduced ketone 17 in the urine even if they stopped practising just one day. So people tend to believe that the curative effect of Qigong in bronchial asthma is probably achieved by improving the function of the adrenacortex.

Effects on the Nervous System Function Qigong can produce obvious effects on the function of the nervous system, especially the cerebral cortex. According to eletroencephalographic records, the state of Qigong quiescence is inhibitory. Observation of two groups demonstrated general differences. The non-practicing group showed no obvious change in the electroencephalgraphs after simply sitting for half an hour quietly. The Qigong group began to show an increasingly strong alpha wave only five minutes after entering quiescence. The wave returned to the original state 10 minutes after the exercise was completed. Encephalgraphs demonstrate gradually increasing relation in aged Qigong practitioners, suggesting cerebral cortex inhibition during quiescence. This shows Qigong's protection of the cerebral cortex.

Take the knee reflex as an index. As practitioners enter quiescence, the knee reflex is weakened or disappears as during sleep. This suggests that skeletal muscle movement is inhibited. The conditioned reflexes of the second signal system are also affected. The reflexes of the practitioners stimulated by sound, skin or language hints after they entered quiescence were dulled, or they even did not react. In another experiment, an electronic chronaximeter was used to observe muscle movement changes caused by Neiyanggong. During Qigong quiescence, the muscle changes were related with cerebral cortex movement analyzing organ. In other words, the muscle chronaxy increases as inhibition extends to the movement analyzing organ. Although this organ becomes inhibited, this does not affect the function of the body. Some doctors have experimented with a Qigong and non-Qigong group in measuring plasma CAMP levels. Group I simply rested while Group II practised Qigong. Little change was discovered in plasma CAMP in Group I, but Group II showed obvious changes, which indicates that some internal organs were carrying on active movement. Therefore, quiescence is different from simple rest. It activates movement and benefits metabolism, though both are outwardly quiet states. Also reflecting nervous system function are the changes in electric potential and skin conductance. Modern medicine attributes changes in skin electric potential to internal organ movement or central nerve system, and to relation between the skin and the internal tissue, blood supply, sweat gland activity and metabolism controlled by the nervous system in the region. Therefore, determination of skin electric potential is helpful in explaining Qigong-related changes in the nervous system. Electric potential is raised in the area where the mind is focused during Relaxing Exercise and drops in other areas. This parameter returns to its original state immediately after practice. But those who receive no obvious curative effects usually do not show such changes.

Qigong helps stabilize the skin's electric potential. When drop occurs, the curve is similar to that caused by amytal medication. During Qigong, skin conductance drops gradually and does not rise until after the exercise is completed. In the 12 original channels, Qigong balances occupant electric conductance by raising or lowering it. The bioelectric current that passes the Zhongwan point tends to move toward the negative pole during sleep more obviously in practitioners than in non-practitioners. The effect of Qigong on the skin's electric potential is related with respiration. One report states that, when practitioners regulate their respiration and focus the mind in a state of quiescence, the skin's potential changes with the breathing rhythm. At each interval between inhalation and exhalation, there is an increase in the difference in electric potential. Qigong quiescence differs from natural sleep, sitting or simple rest. Because Qigong can turn the body from consumption to storing, the body can enter a state of regulation, repairing and reconstruction, which has positive effects on treatment and prevention of diseases and strengthens the constitution. Further studies are needed to show the mechanisms of Qigong quiescence and propulsion of Qi, the body's physiological functions.

VII. Qigong and Geroncomia

Geriatrics is a broad science covering all aspects of aging which emerged at the beginning of this century and gradually developed into an independent field only after the 1950s. Today, it is drawing attention widely as a new subject in clinical medicine.

When a person becomes aged or nearly aged, the health starts to decline, the body getting feeble and resistance decreases, much due to lack of exercise. Some people suffer deterioration before becoming aged. This is called premature aging. All these people face the challenge of senile diseases, such as hypertension, ateriosclerosis, chronic bronchitis, senile lumbago, and climacteric syndrome. Their working endurance and efficiency decrease, and some even lose the working ability entirely. Ironically, it is in this period that a person is most experienced and competent. For this reason, preventing and treating senile diseases and premature aging is a major task for medical workers and a means of saving society from tremendous waste.

After birth, humans go through the process of growth, maturation and aging. The body's physiological features change constantly with the advancement of age. When the human being reaches the aged period of its life, its hair, skin, bones, muscles, ears, eyes, teeth, internal organs and nervous systems are also gradually changing and the functions of Qi and blood as well as the channels and collaterals through which vital energy travels also begin to fail. Therefore diseases of senility start invasion, including coronary bronchitis, heart disease, heart- and-lung disease, hypertension and bronchitis. The cardiac muscle and artery of the aged become susceptible to sclerosis, and other organs atrophy and tend to congest. In order to carry on blood circulation and clear up congestion, the heart has to work so hard that it often enlarges. A common senile disease of the cardiovascular system is arteriosclerotic hypertensive heart disease. Lung function degenerates, coastal cartilage hardens and loses elasticity while the thoracic muscles atrophy, weakening lung-thorax expansion. This physiological change plus weakened resistance makes it easy for the aged to catch colds. When the elastic tissue of the air sacs atrophy, the aged suffer pulmonary emphysema or bronchitis; when their digestive system weakens, they contract chronic gastro-colic diseases, such as senile indigestion and constipation. Degeneration of bones and muscles will cause pain and obstruct movement, and nervous system degeneration, especially in the cerebral cortex, resulting in functional disorders.

According to TCM, growth in the young causes Qi to move downward, permeating the channels in the feet, and Yuan Qi

(Source or Original Qi) is waxing. When the person ages, the body fluids start to deteriorate and Qi begins to ebb. In consequence, the five organs, lungs, heart, kidneys, spleen and liver weaken. The head feels heavy and the feet light, which makes the walk shaky. These symptoms indicate that QI is excessive in the upper part of the body but deficient in the lower part, or that both Yin and Yang are becoming deficient.

According to TCM theories on Yin/Yang and the channels and collaterals, the upper body is Yang and the lower body Yin. All the Yang channels converge in the face; the ribs and feet are the sources of Yin. Excess in upper body means deficiency of Yin in the lower body which allows the Yang to rush upwards. Either Yin deficiency or Yang excess will unbalance the dynamic Yin/Yang equilibrium which is symbolized by coordination between the heart and kidneys, giving rise to the symptoms of aging. This explains why health preservation through Qigong exercise are of special importance for the aged.

Premature aging is discussed in the *Plain Questions Section of the Internal Canon of Medicine*. The book states: To keep Yin/Yang equilibrium, one must understand the Seven Damages and Eight Benefits; without this understanding, premature aging will occur. The book devotes much space to dealing with the waxing and waning of Yin and Yang, the cause of birth, growth, reproduction and premature aging. Doctors in ensuing centuries vary greatly in their interpretations of this theory. Li Nianer of the Ming dynasty says in his book, *Essentials of the Internal Canon of Medicine* (Nei Jin Zhi Yao): Seven is a Yang number and Eight Yin; damage is reduction and benefit growth. Neither Yang should be reduced nor should Yin grow, otherwise diseases will occur. Understanding the Seven damages and Eight benefits can help keep them balanced. Another book, *Footnotes to the Internal Canon of Medicine's Plain Questions* (Huang Di Nei Jing Shu Wen Ling Shu Zhu), by Zhang Zhicong of the Qing dynasty, states that because Yang often goes to excess, it needs losing; because Yin is often in deficiency, it needs to benefit. *Internal Canon of Medicine: On the Ancient Theory of Heavenly Essence* (Shu Wen: Shang Gu Tian Zhen Lun) states; If one knows and obeys the law of the relative waning and waxing of Yin and Yang in the human body, Yin/Yang balance can be maintained. If not, premature aging will ensue. As we understand, a person must follow the law of Yin/Yang in order to regulate the process of growth, maturation and reproduction and prevent premature aging. For example, early marriage, excessive sexuality or frequent pregnancy will all cause premature aging. To prevent premature aging, one must regulate his or her sexual behavior, control pregnancy and carry out family planning. Since Yang tends to flux, males after maturity at 16 should not overindulge in sex. After female maturity at 14, Yin waxes and wanes monthly. The waning and waxing should be balanced and regulated.

Early medical scientists and Qigong experts laid great emphasis on the body's balance of Yin and Yang, and heart and kidneys. They believed that no disease occurs if Yin and Yang are kept at equilibrium, that the heart is the monarch of organs and the kidneys are the root of Original Qi (Yuan Qi) as well as the basis of inborness. Much research has been done on TCM theory. A TCM classic, *A Thousand Golden Remedies: Qi Circulation* carries this teaching; "Exhale stale Qi through the mouth, inhale fresh Qi with the nose, slowly calm the mind and then practise Chanshi (one method of Buddhist Quiescent Exercise). In a while, you will feel Original Qi traveling beyond the Dantian acupoint to Yongquan acupoints." *Health Preservation* (1606 edition) states: Protecting the essence of life, training Qi and cultivating the spirit are methods for acquiring longevity. *A Medical Supplement to Ge Zhi* (1347 edition) states that regulating respiration and the spirit form a basic curative method. *Bao Pu Zi* (A.D. 341 edition) says, "Expertise in Qi training can help cultivate the interior of the body, preventing invasive diseases." *The Later Han Dynasty Chronicle: Folk Remedies* quotes the ancient master of medicine Hua Tuo as saying, "Rhythmic movement helps digestion, promotes blood circulation and prevents diseases."

Most early medical scientists believed in keeping equilibrium of Yin and Yang. This theory requires the correct combination of quiescence and activity. It regards the kidneys as the source of congenitality and the spleen as the basis of postnatality. The theory also holds that old age features excess of Yang in the upper body and its deficiency in the lower body. Therefore, training is particularly important in guiding Qi downward, strengthening the Dantian area and, most important, foster Original Qi in the lower body. When Qi and strength are substantial in the lower parts, the body feels agile, the mind is clear and the gait is steady. For this reason, martial arts require 70 percent of training being focused on the lower body and 30 percent on the upper body. In Qigong practice for the aged, the goal of establishing insubstantiality in the upper body and substantiality in the lower body should always be kept in mind.

Mastering the key points and correct methods of Qigong practice produce many positive effects which can be sensed by the practitioner. They include increase in saliva secretion, moistening of dry eyes, clearing the mind, intestinal health, flatus production, slight perspiration, and a sensation of warmth flowing like a stream through the whole body. All these effects make the practitioner feel comfortable and reflect internal movement activated through Qigong exercise. We believe that the comfortable sensation during Qigong practice is due to the vibration of muscles including viscera muscles, smooth blood circulation, soft, even and deep respiration, and gentle, rhythmic responses to internal movement reflected by the nervous system.

Qigong exercise has many methods designed to achieve specific effects. For instance, a certain method can stimulate saliva secretion. Scientific research in recent years has established the relationship between the endocrine believed to come from the same source as saliva. In the aged, functional deficiency of salivary gland endocrine is likely to occur. Collecting salivary gland endocrine has a limited possibility of improving this situation. Qigong may become a much needed new method of regulating salivary gland endocrine, and preventing and treating senile diseases, judging from its increase of saliva secretion.

A survey has shown that Qigong helps the elderly keep fit. Most of the aged surveyed had practised Qigong for a long time and were in good health. Their average blood pressure was normal, 140/64 millimeters. Nearly 93 percent had normal hearing and 92.8 percent had good memories. A comparative group of elderlies who did not practise Qigong showed similar average blood pressure of 144/82 millimeters, but 24.5 percent of them had hypertension, 50 percent had normal vision, only 33.5 percent had normal hearing and 35.2 percent had lost their working ability. After doing Qigong exercises five months, 51.7 percent of the second group recovered some of their working ability and all experienced obvious physiological improvement. Comprehensive Qigong therapy can cure or ameliorate senile diseases. Beside clinical value, Qigong adds a new perspective to gerontology.

VIII. Strengthening Resistance, Dispelling Diseases, Prevention and Treatment

Building up resistance and dispelling diseases is a major principle of TCM theory and has guided medical practice throughout the Chinese history. Qigong, as an exercise or therapy, is an important approach to this tenet. Before explaining this principle, it is necessary to give a brief introduction to the human body and its basic physiological functions.

The body is a complex organism. It consists of many systems- -bones, muscles, respiration, digestion, waste disposal, nerves, organs such as the heart, liver, spleen and lungs and tissue. Being unique in function, these parts do not work independently. They all function under the unified direction of the nervous system, especially the cerebral cortex. Because the cerebral cortex has this function and keeps adjusting the whole body to its environmental conditions, people sometimes call it the body's Supreme Headquarters.

The TCM Explanation of Body Functions TCM states that the body consists of bones, five viscera and six organs. It functions as an entity through a system of communicating channels and collaterals. Although all of them have their individual functions, the 12 organs must always cooperate with each other. The heart commands all functions of the body and keeps adjusting the body to its environment. The concept of the heart as the monarch of all organs originated about 2, 000 years ago in China. It shows that our ancestors had an understanding of the body's holistic functions in relation with its environment, though modern science regards the cerebral cortex as the supreme headquarters.

TCM attributes the functional activities of human organs to the movement of the body's Yin (matter) and Yang (function) which form a unity of opposites. The unity of contradicting Yin and Yang is always changing. They adjust to each other and inhibit each other. And the development of this unity keeps the functional movement of the organs active and in equilibrium. TCM calls this state the balance of Yin and harmony of Yang. As long as balance and harmony exist, the body functions normally. When Yin or Yang is in excess, the body's functions are disturbed and diseases occur. When Yin or Yang unbalances, the unity of these opposites is lost and Original Qi disappears disrupting body functions. According to Engles, life is biological, and things are independent entities as well as a part of other things. It exists in matter and in a process of producing and solving contradictions. If this process stops, life comes to an end. So this process is also true of organ function. The organs are independent are yet rely upon cooperation. When this process is disturbed, diseases will occur; when the disturbance goes beyond a certain limit, body function will cease.

How is the process disturbed and what gives rise to a disease? The causes are numerous, of course. But generally all diseases are caused by pathogens. TCM divided all the pathogens into three categories--the internal, the external and the miscellaneous. The external causes include cold, heat, damp, dryness and infection; the internal mainly refer to emotional causes and anxiety; the miscellaneous causes are mainly related to living habits such as food, fatigue, drink and sleep. If we regard the normal condition of the body as internal factors, then they are the conditions for external pathogenic factors. Not all pathogens can cause disease, because disease depends on two conditions. First, it depends on the body's resistance and vulnerability to the pathogen. Therefore, TCM only recognizes the body's internal deficient conditions as the cause of disease. The external cause provides the condition and affects the body through the internal cause, which is the basis of disease. Healthiness and illness is the relation of cause and effect. When pathogens (Xie Qi) invade the body, the body's resistance (Zheng Qi) will pit itself against them. If Zheng Qi gains ascendancy, the disease is prevented or ameliorated. If Xie Qi wins, the disease will occur or worsen. In treating a disease, we should pay attention not only to the external cause, but also to strengthening the patient's resistance and dispelling diseases.

We have proved the importance of increasing resistance and dispelling disease as a method of treating diseases and consolidating cures. Only when Original Qi is fostered, can the patient resist pathogens and enjoy good health. Unfortunately, both doctors and patients often pay attention to dispelling disease only, neglecting the increase of resistance. There are many ways of strengthening resistance, but in the long run, Qigong is one of the few most effective methods of curing and preventing disease and prolonging life. Qigong differs from most simple physical exercises. It tones the holism, dredging the channels and collaterals and is self-training.

Practising Qigong

I. An Outline of Qigong Exercise

There are myriads of ways of Qigong exercise, each with its own features and effects, which differ according to posture, method, form, style and purposes.

(I) Postures: Lying, Sitting, Standing, Walking

1. Lying Down Posture This posture can be assumed in two ways, lying on the back or on the side (see illustration). It is suitable for a person with weak constitution and at certain stages of severe illness. A patient with insomnia, for example, can adopt the lying posture before going to sleep. One lying prone posture named "Upturned Tail" particularly fits patients with visceroptosis.

2. Sitting Down Posture This can be assumed with several variations, sitting without back support or with back support and with the legs crossed or not. The sitting posture is most commonly adopted by patients with modest deficiency of vitality. It includes both quiescent and dynamic exercises. One method, "the Posture of Sitting With a Leaning Back" actually falls between the sitting and prone postures and mainly suits persons with poor health.

3. Standing Posture Patients assuming a standing posture outnumber those using the prone or sitting postures. This posture can be divided into many kinds which owe their own names to the different requirements. They include the "Standing Exercise," "Training Mixed Original Qi" and "Bronze Bell." Some exercises with the standing posture sometimes allows the arms to move, such as the "Benefiting Tendons," and "Eight Elegant

Movements." Therefore, the standing posture includes both static and dynamic exercises.

   4. Walking Posture All methods of Qigong exercises requiring leg movements fall into the walking posture category. This includes simple and complex leg movements, which may feature soft or strong force, slow or quick steps, beautiful patterns or forceful gestures, powerful, simple or blunt steps. This posture is diverse, therefore interesting, and meets many needs of the practitioner. Some methods in this category are called Step Exercises, such as Tiger Steps, Crane Steps, Deer Steps, and Marsh-crossing Steps. They are all easy to learn and very effective.

(II) Methods

   1. Body-regulating Method In ancient times, this category laid emphasis on the body postures during practice. It is divided into the quiescent and dynamic methods and can be practiced in the prone, sitting, standing or walking postures. Each exercise has its own characteristics of respirtation and focusing the mind.

   2. Breathing Methods Under many names in ancient times, this category emphasizes the training of respiration. It consists of the quiescent and dynamic exercises and can be practiced in all postures, which require different ways of focusing the mind.

   3. Mind-focusing Methods Also called Heart-regulating methods in ancient times, this category is divided into quiescent and dynamic exercises and uses different postures, which varies with the different methods of respiration.

   All these three categories of methods form an entity within which they are related, restrain and influence one another. In practice, they are not separable. Even the Relaxing Exercise cannot exclude breathing and mind-focusing methods. These methods can be categorized into their different functions in practice. The body posture is the starting point, breathing is the key, and the mind provides guidance. Because the mind guides the body posture and breathing, its activity is decisive in Qigong practice.

(III) Forms: Internal and External

1. Internal Exercise Neigong (Internal Exercise) emphasize the training of the body's internal functions. As quiescence trains Internal Qi, Qigong masters in past centuries grouped all exercises featuring quiescence into the internal exercise. But the truth is not so absolute as they thought. Some quiescent exercises, such as Standing Exercise, are most effective in training the body for Qigong.

2. External Exercise Waigong (External Exercise) includes all the exercises which emphasize the external functions of the body. Early masters held that movement was the only method of training the external, but they were also too absolute to be completely correct. Some external exercises have great effect on the body's internal organs.

Experience tells us that quiescent exercise can also adjust the posture to Qigong requirements, and dynamic exercises can help improve internal organ function. They cannot be separated. But quiescent exercises mainly train the internal organs, and dynamic exercises mainly shape the body to Qigong requirements. We suggest the practitioner combine both exercises rather than neglect either of them.

(IV) Styles: Quiescent, Dynamic and Quiescent-Dynamic

1. Quiescent Exercise Jing Gong includes all Qigong exercises that forbid any motion of the trunk and limbs. The Relaxing Exercise, Foster the Internal, and Standing Exercise are all variations of this style. Among these exercises, some emphasize mind focusing, others stress the posture or breathing. It can be divided into the prone, sitting, and standing positions.

2. Dynamic Exercise Dong Gong includes all Qigong exercises which require motions of the trunk and limbs. Examples are the Health Preserving, Shadow Boxing, Frolics of Five Animals and Mt. Ermei Standing. Most dynamic exercises feature standing and walking postures. But sometimes, as in the Eight Elegant Movements, it can be done in the sitting posture. For clinical purposes, it can be done prone.

3. Quiescent-dynamic Exercise Jing Dong Gong is a style which combines static and dynamic methods. It requires quiescence before movement and then the combination of both. This produces a diversity of effects. It has been spread widely at home and abroad. Because of superstition, there are prejudice and misunderstandings which make popularization of this style a difficult task, and so research is sorely needed.

The line of division betweer quiescent and dynamic exercises is whether the legs and feet move during practice. Quiescent exercises feature motionless posture and direction of the cerebral cortex into a relatively quiet state. With Qi moving inside the body, this style is described as being externally still but internally active. The quiescence, therefore, refers to the external appearance only, and the motion is the flow of Qi and internal organ movement; the motion of the dynamic style refers to the external movement of the body and its quiescence is in the mind. In practicing quiescent exercise, we should pay attention to the motion covered by the stillness and during dynamic exercise, we should seek the mental quiescence which underlies the motion. Although both styles are interwoven, they have their own effects. Specifically, although the quiescent style is designed to affect the body, mind and Internal Qi mainly for health preservation, it also helps strengthen the constitution. Although the dynamic style focuses the mind and trains Internal Qi, cures diseases and strengthens the constitution, it mainly trains the extremities, tendons and bones. Therefore, the choice of a style should depend on the health of the practitioner. The general principle is to practise both styles alternately. The Dynamic-Quiescent Exercise has its own features.

(V) Purposes

According to the practitioner's needs, Qigong can be divided into the following categories: disease treating, prophylactic, force building, acupuncture and massage, martial arts, performing arts, combat, sports, special skill training and so on. The methods, requirements, and key points vary with he purposes of exercise.

Varying as it is, all Qigong has these commoii features-- posture, respiration and mental activity. Dynamic and quiescent exercises form two basic styles, but their methods and postures are interchangeable and cooperative. All variations of these two styles form a list of methods to suit all ages, physical constitutions, diseases and practice purposes. This makes Qigong differentiate from most physical exercises.

II. Qigong Applicability

As a self-training exercise, Qigong, if practised correctly, can cure diseases, improve weak constitutions, preserve health and increase working endurance and efficiency.

Generally speaking, although the practitioner trains the body by improving physiological functions through Qigong, the effect is holistic. Because the approach to invigorating the constitution is self-training, self-building, self-nourishing and self-regulating, Qigong has fewer limits to its use than most other exercises. And respiration regulating, mind focusing and calming, and soft and rhythmic movement in Qigong exercise are beneficial to health in all circumstances.

As a therapeutic exercise, Qigong can play a positive role in enhancing medical curative effects, shortening duration of treatment and permanently preventing recurrence of some chronic deceases. Qigong is satisfactory as a part of many comprehensive therapies for many diseases. Examples are hypertention, gastric duodenal ulcer, chronic bronchitis, chronic enterogastritis, indigestion, gastroptosis, neurasthenia, TB, bronchitis, bronchial asthma, senile lumbago, toxemia of pregnancy, chronic pelvic inflammation, and pain-free delivery. Qigong can also be used to accelerate the effects of acupuncture anesthesia. In addition, it has been reported several times that Qigong therapy has been successfully applied in treating diabetes, mellitus, primary glaucoma and cirrhosis. In recent years, Qigong has been used to treat some cancers. On the whole, Qigong is becoming an important part of many therapies for chronic diseases.

Analysis of Qigong effects proves that it is curative for certain diseases, and helpful in others. It can be the major cure for some diseases at certain stages, but simply beneficial for the same diseases at other stages. Examples are ulcer at the active stage and asthma at the beginning stage, regardless of the nature of the effect, Qigong, through enhancement of self- training and self-regulating abilities, can increase resistance, accelerate recovery and consolidate permanent cures.

Diseases that are considered improper for Qigong probably have not been treated with the correct type of Qigong exercise. The method should be selected according to the patient's health condition. Patients in emergencies or with mental disorders, of course, should abstain from Qigong for a time until expert advice is available. Unstable or extremist subjects should not conduct mind focusing unless with special advice from an expert.

III. Essentials of Qigong Exercise

Even though there is such a variety of Qigong exercises, each with its own features and requirements, the general principles for all of them are the same: combination of relaxation, inward peace, natural movement, flow of Qi, integration of movements, quiescence, flexibility in the upper body and stability in the lower body, a moderate amount of exercise, and exercising in an orderly way.

(I) Combined Relaxation, Inward Peace and Natural Movement

First, Qigong relaxation entails the extremities and the whole body as well as a relaxed mental state. But it does not entail listlessness, slackness, and rigidity. If a position becomes uncomfortable, adjust it.

Second, the quiescent state achieved by reflex conditioning is relative inward peace. While conscious, the brain continues working without stop. To relieve fatigue and restore energy, the brain needs to be in a quiescent state. However, this quiescence differs from the state of sleep or other kinds of rest because it requires a clear, focused mind. In this condition, active self-regulation and restoration of energy is going on. The quiescent state of Qigong does not mean complete stoppage of mental activities, but a state of relative quiet. There is a synergistic relation between relaxation and quiescence, each promoting the other, so equal attention should paid to both.

Third, natural movement is another important aspect which we should bear in mind. During the entire course of exercise, the posture, respiration and mind focusing should be done naturally and easily. Nothing should be forced.

(II) Mental Activity and the Flow of Qi

Qi (vital energy) includes the Qi obtained through respiration and the Internal Qi of the Dantian area. Qigong practitioners breathe deeply and promote Qi flow. So, the flow of Qi and direction of the thoughts are coordinated. When Qigong exercise is carried out, respiration should be conducted slowly and naturally by mental direction, just like a silkworm spinning silk-- gently and constantly. While cultivating Internal Qi, one must coordinate the mind and respiration in order to influence Internal Qi movement. This process is aimed at perfect integration of mental and Qi activities, guiding Qi slowly and smoothly with mental direction.

(III) Integration of Dynamic and Quiescent States

Dynamic state refers to movement of the body and the internal flow of the Qi, the former being regarded as external movement and the latter internal movement. Quiescence here includes motionless body posture and mental quietude. The former is called external quiescence and the latter internal quiescence. The purpose of Qigong exercise is to promote and regulate physiological functions so as to keep a relative equilibrium between Yin and Yang, harmonize Qi and blood, remove obstruction of the channels and collaterals, cultivate Original Qi, eliminate pathogenetic factors and prevent premature aging. In other words, it is done to achieve self-promotion, self-regulation, self- repair and self-reconstruction. Internal quiescence is the prerequisite for practising Qigong ensuring the achievement of desired effects, as has been proved clinically and experimentally. As to the methods of Qigong exercise, some stress the dynamic state and other quiescence. But the integration of both states must be kept in mind, though individual conditions-- age, sex, physical constitution, disposition and health--are decisive factors in choosing either state of exercise. The procedure can be carried out as follows: Do dynamic exercise after practising quiescent exercise, or add quiescent exercise once or twice a day, or do dynamic exercise in the morning and static exercise in the evening; or perform mainly static exercise for a period of time, then give a new turn to dynamic exercise.

(IV) Flexibility in the Upper Body and Stability in the Lower Body

The upper body is the part above the umbilicus, while the parts below are the lower body. During Qigong practice, one should conduct Qi to the Dantian area to induce sensation in the chest and a plentiful feeling in the abdomen; Qi/breath should be rooted at Dantian so that one can acquire nimble motion of the upper body when Qi is firmly rooted at Dantian. With slight Qi deficiency and flexibility in the upper body there is nimble motion of the upper part, the head feeling clear and both hearing and vision improving. Sufficient Qi and stability in the lower body causes a feeling of plentiful energy and abundant Internal Qi. However, slight deficiency in the upper body and sufficiency in the lower body are based on sufficiency and stability in the lower body to be obtained by concentrating the mind on the lower part of the body. So, never concentrate on the upper body during Qigong exercise, relaxing and focusing on the middle or lower part of the body only. During maturation and aging, those who are not good at physical exercise are apt to have hypertension, heavy top feelings and unstable gait. Therefore, Qigong practitioners insist on conducting Qi downward and rooting it in the lower part of the body.

(V) Moderate Exercise

A moderate amount of exercise must be taken during Qigong exercise. If the amount is not sufficient, the exercise is less effective, whereas excessive exercise may produce side effects. Moderate exercise means limitation of movement. Everything in the universe has its limitations. For instance, food intake is necessary for maintaining life, but overeating is harmful to digestive system function despite the good quality of the food. For another example, recreation is beneficial to the health helping to relieve fatigue, regain physical strength and raise working efficiency. But it may increase fatigue when you indulge in it excessively to the point of unfavorably affecting your health and work. Hence, the following precautions: First, never force mind focusing; second, make the posture natural, flexible and comfortable rather than rigid; third, conduct abdominal respiration and circulation of Internal Qi naturally; fourth, make 20 minutes the limit for the duration of exercise in order to avoid tiredness, though it may be extended in treating disease or according to physical limits of the individual.

(VI) Proceeding in an Orderly Way

Qigong is a health-care exercise of which benefits appear gradually. Practitioners should guard against impetuosity and avoid rushing. Learners must first of all try to have an understanding of the principles, grasp the essentials and practise the exercise correctly and persistently. In this way, beneficial effects can certainly be achieved. Thorough basic training lays a good foundation. Impatience brings no benefits. A Chinese saying goes, "Pulling up rice shoots can't help their growth." We must bear in mind the maxim of "Well begun is half done."

IV. Qigong Effects

Qigong exercise may bring about some effects. Some of them are normal and some abnormal. Generally, as long as we have a correct understanding of the key points, observe the requirements and learn step by step, most of the effects are basically normal. If deviations occur they can be easily adjusted. Abnormal effects appear only through misunderstanding. The following is a list of effects divided according to normality and abnormality.

(I) Normal Effects

1. Warm Sensation in the Lumbar-sacral Region and Four Extremities When the mind is focused at the umbilicus, Qihai and Guanyuan acupoints, a sensation of warmth or heat is felt there, which may appear as a pocket of hot air or diffusing hot air and sometimes like a gush of warm water rippling and flowing inside the body. If the mind is focused at the Mingmen acupoint, the hot sensation can be easily detected in the lumbar-sacral region. Warmth or heat may also be felt in the feet and hands. After getting this sensation, you feel very comfortable. However, do not let it become too hot and try to control the heat by exhaling and diverting the mind a bit.

2. Slight Perspiration Practising Qigong, both dynamic and quiescent, may lead to perspiration. The amount of sweat should be controlled to a damp film on the skin, as if a wet towel has been used. After sweating, as all athletes do, protect yourself against the wind and cold, especially when practising outdoors in winter.

3. Increase of Saliva Secretion Saliva may increase during Qigong exercise. Sometimes, this is induced by softly clamping the teeth, or rolling the tongue vigorously. Saliva secretion may also increase markedly in the quiescent state without any motion of the teeth or tongue. If there is too much saliva, swallow it, which may add in digestion and disinfecting enzyme. Some people may feel the eyeball is moist with tears or tears dropping. These are also normal.

4. Accelerated Peristalsis of the Stomach and Intestines Accelerated peristalsis of the the stomach and the intestines may appear during the exercise, especially when deep abdominal respiration is instituted and the mind is focused at the umbilicus (Dantian), or Qihai acupoint. Practitioners not only may feel peristalsis, but emit borborygmus sound. These phenomena can also be experienced during evacuation of food, absorption of nutrients and eliminating flatus obstructing the intestinal tracts. This facilitates the bowel movement and is normal.

5. Improvement of Appetite and Increase in Body Weight Qigong exercise may improve the appetite and increase the weight of under-weight practitioners with poor appetites and malnutrition. However, no abnormal increase in food intake or body weight has been noticed in those who had good appetites before practice. In contrast, the body weight of those who are obese can be reduced through this exercise.

6. Better Sleep Quality This exercise can make some people sleep more deeply and therefore more restfully eliminating nightmares and increasing the speed of going to sleep. This improved quality of sleep can better relieve both mental and physical fatigue, promoting the recovery of physical strength and mental energy. These effects may be more obvious in light sleeper or those with insomnia.

7. Itching This may appear during Qigong exercise, just like a worm crawling on the skin. The itch can be reduced by rubbing the local area. But when resuming exercise, it may appear once again. If the sensation is not strong, ignore it, for it may disappear by itself in a minute. However, if the itch grows more and more unbearable, reduce it by diverting your mind from exercise. Some Qigong experts hold that this shows Qi being at the surface of the body, and the dredging of Qi passageways.

8. Slight Involuntary Muscle Vibration and Clicks in Joints Slight muscle vibrations may occur during Qigong exercise, and sometimes clicks may be emitted in the joints, even audible to other persons nearby. These are easily experienced during quiescence. In this state, all responses are clearly noticed. Experts deem that these phenomena show Qi invigoration.

9. Bright-eyed, Clear-headed and High-spirited Sensations Qigong exercise, both quiescent and dynamic, can make one feel bright-eyed, clear-headed and high-spirited. If the exercise is taken properly, such sensations can last quite a while afterwards.

10. Other Comfortable Sensations Qigong can also cause feelings of euphoria, perfect peace, complete relaxation, and refreshment.

All these normal effects can not be experienced by everyone. Occurrence of these effects depend on the internal condition of the individual. Therefore, if one does not achieve these effects, do not blindly search for them. And if they do appear, do not pay too much attention to them. The exercise should be done naturally.

(II) Abnormal Effects

1. Dizziness, Headache, Etc. Some people may feel dizziness, headache, heaviness, tiredness or distention in the head. These are caused by nervousness, over-tense focusing of the mind, and forced quiescence. One should relax mentally and physically by exhaling deeply.

2. Shortage of Breath or Suffocation These are mainly due to over concentration on respiration, tension in the upper body including the chest, shoulders and back, or forced stoppage of respiration in a blind search for deep, sustained respiration. They do not obey the principle of coordinating mental activities and the flow of Qi, but carry out the exercise wilfully, running counter to the requirements of relaxation, inward quiescence, natural movement and orderly procession. However, these phenomena can be easily eliminated by relaxing.

3. Upward Surge of Qi From the Lower Abdomen While exercising, some people may feel Qi running upward from the lower abdomen. Perhaps, Qi has not been stably fixed at the Dantian area. This can be overcome by fixing the mind on it. Do not place Qi too high. The practitioner should relax and avoid nervousness. If this is too difficult, focusing the mind and Qi to Dantian should be omitted. The main thing is to relax mentally and physically, to reach the state of quiescence through natural respiration. This method is called forgetting respiration. By doing this, other means of Qigong exercise can be done naturally. So the key is naturalness and relaxation.

4. Heaviness in the Trunk or Shoulders These sensations may be experienced in the exercise, which may be caused by forced, fast mental activities, or lack of coordination between mental activities and the flow of Qi. Tension in shoulder muscle may also give rise to the feeling of heaviness. If the sensation in the trunk is obvious, mental activities should be relaxed a bit. While the shoulders are heavy, they should be relaxed by mental direction or gentle rotation of the shoulders. Another type of trunk heaviness results from Qi movement and is normal, which feels comfortable and will leave the body limbering up again after a while. Alternating feelings of weight bearing and lightness due to Qi are comfortable.

5. Mouth Dryness and Scratchy Throat Generally, saliva secretion increases during exercise, but sometimes people may feel mouth dryness and scratchy throat. This is probably caused by breathing through the mouth or closing the mouth tightly. If mouth dryness is experienced often in the day, drink warm water before exercise.

6. Heartbeat Acceleration Quiescent Qigong exercise lowers or normalizes the heart rate. But occasionally, the heart rate is accelerated during exercise. This probably is due to nervousness, tension in the chest or unnatural respiration. To eliminate it, relax mentally and breathe naturally.

7. Abdominal Distention This may appear during or after Qigong exercise, excluding the comfortable, slightly distended sensation of warmth in the abdominal region. It is caused by forced deep respiration, compressing Qi downward or holding the breath. Relaxing and slowing the respiration will relieve this type of distention.

8. Insomnia Qigong usually promotes and deepens sleep. But sometimes it interferes with going to sleep or soundness of sleep. This manifests as sleepiness during Qigong practice and restlessness during sleep. As a result one can benefit neither from Qigong nor from sleep. In addition to nervousness or over excitement induced by the practice, this is caused mainly by confusing the quiescence of Qigong with sleep. To overcome this effect, one should bear in mind a clear distinction between the two states.

9. Drowsiness Feeling sleepy and sometimes actually falling asleep interfere with Qigong exercise. Quiescence should be a mentally lucent state of peace, which is quite different from sleep. Beginners, in particular, may feel the mental and physical tiredness from Qigong. Therefore, do not practise Qigong when feeling tired.

10. Swaying This is not encouraged during quiescent Qigong exercise. But some dynamic exercise requires sideways swaying of the body to induce Qi flow. When slight vibrations occur during exercise as a result of Qi activation, they are beneficial to health but should not be intensified. If this is caused by closing the eyes, open them and the vibration will stop.

Deviational aberrations are due to defects in the exercise. So beginners should be guided by an experienced coach.

V. Precautions for Qigong Exercise

(I) Precautions for Coaches:

1. Give the learners some pointers by lecturing on the basic knowledge of Qigong exercise, so that they have a correct understanding of Qigong and practise it in a proper way.

2. Explain the key points and precautions of Qigong exercise in the light of the problems which learners encounter. Stop in this way, correct their performance, and give full play to their initiatives in training.

3. According to different conditions of the learners and specific features of the Qigong method adopted by them, coaching can be done collectively or individually.

4. For those who have practised Qigong before, the coach must check on their original foundations, the Qigong exercise practised, the level of their understanding of the basics, and the key points of Qigong exercise. Coaching should be very specific.

5. Instruction is based on constant and careful observation in accordance with the practice, health conditions, and emotional state of the learners.

6. Arrange informal discussions according to the diseases

presented, methods of exercise, and progress of practice in order to exchange experience, build confidence and consolidate the progress already made. But do not mention normal or abnormal effects among novices to avoid side effects.

7. The coach must have full knowledge and be well versed in the methods being taught in order to have the foresight to correct any deviations in practice.

8. Pay attention to the problems which arise during exercise and sum up experience to improve the coaching quality and enhance the beneficial effects of Qigong exercise.

(II) Precautions for Learners

1. There should be a correct understanding of Qigong. All learners must grasp the key points of the exercise, obey the requirements, and be determined, optimistic and persistent in conquering the diseases. Above all, analyze what has been accomplished. One should have confidence in the exercise.

2. Beginners must be instructed by an experienced person and select suitable methods of Qigong in accordance with the health conditions of themselves. Never arbitrarily change to other methods of the exercise.

3. The basic skills must be mastered step by step. Do not get side-tracked by gimmick training.

4. The frequency and duration for exercise can vary according to the conditions of health, severity of the disease, and progress of practice. Generally speaking, for treating diseases, each session lasts 30 to 60 minutes, twice or three times a day (at the beginning, practise about 10 minutes each time, and then prolong it gradually). For Prophylaxis, 20 to 30 minutes each time, one to three times a day. If you have enough time, you can practise more, but stop before feeling tired. Quiescent Qigong exercises should be done in combination with dynamic Qigong exercise. And the exercise should be practised consistently as a part of the daily program. Curing diseases and building up the constitution

through Qigong is to better your work. So the frequency and duration of exercise should be arranged according to the principle of facilitating your work and treating illnesses.

5. The environment for Qigong practice should be relatively quiet with plentiful fresh air. Absolute silence is impossible to achieve. Therefore do not search for it. The quiescent state can only be achieved in quiet surroundings with good air circulation, or it will not be consolidated. The ability to subjectively eliminate external interferences should also be fostered for good results. A place with trees and flowers is more satisfactory for Qigong exercise. The burning sun in summer and cold wind in winter should be avoided during exercise. Sudden, violent noises and dazzling light should be avoided.

6. Do not exercise when too upset or quiescence can not be achieved. Arrange work and duties so they do not interfere with concentration. Defecate or urinate before exercise. The collar should be unbuttoned and waist band loosened.

7. Do not practise Qigong when feeling tired, hungry, overwrought, unhappy, or overfed. We should pay attention to mental cultivation and avoid rashness and anger. Do not search blindly for certain effects of Qigong. Patients with chronic diseases such as hypertension, coronary heart disease, pulmonary tuberculosis, hepatic diseases, ulcers and neurasthenia should stop sexual intercourse for about 100 days. And sexual intercourse should be moderated after recovery.

8. During menstruation women may continue practising Qigong, but not for too long or too strenuously. The location for focusing the mind should be a little bit higher than usual to avoid overflow of Qi and blood to the lower part of the body.

9. The three stabilities must be kept in mind when doing Qigong exercise. Body movements and circulation of Internal Qi should be stable at the beginning of, during and at the end of exercise.

10. Schedule time for Qigong exercise and live a well ordered

life. Besides Qigong exercise, one must pay attention to mental cultivation and plan for a full life including diet, rest, work, study, physical exercise, and recreation. In this way, one can lead a regular life which is beneficial to the health.

VI. Entering Quiescence

This is a major requirement of Qigong exercise. But how to achieve this is a common problem for beginners.

First of all, we must understand the quiescent state correctly. This state exists relatively as compared to the dynamic state. Fundamentally speaking, the physiological activities of human beings develop and change in the course of constant movement (the dynamic state). In other words, life is movement. The Chinese philosopher, Wang Chuanshan, who lived from the late Ming dynasty to the early Qing dynasty, said, the quiescent state is actually quiescent movement. It is not motionless. Therefore, quiescent Qigong exercise is essentially quiescent movement. So entering the quiescent state is entering a special state of movement.

What then is quiescence? Generally speaking, it is a special state of inward quietude. Some people think that, after entering quiescence nothing can be felt, and one even forgets one's existence. This is impossible. One should also avoid sleep during Qigong exercise. As we know, sleep is the most quiet state, during which the cerebral cortex rests. But even during normal sleep, the cerebral cortex sometime is activated to dream and dreaming is a mental activity. Entering quiescence during Qigong exercise is a directional exercise of mental activity during the awake state. In this state the brain is aware of changes in physiological functions inside the body and maximally eliminates interferences from both inside and outside the body, providing favorable conditions for the CNS to carry out active and automatic regulation of body functions. Some people feel like a frozen river melting during spring time after entering quiescence in which the whole body is completely relaxed and comfortable.

There are many methods for achieving quiescence. Those commonly used are focusing the mind on Dantian, focusing the mind on the surrounding objects, counting the respiration, listening to respiration, reciting silently the words of catch sentences or verses, thinking about the meanings of word, and listening to light music or simple, pleasing sounds. Rid oneself of worries and concentrate on something to relax the mind. Achieving quiescence is actually training mental activity. The beginner may select a personally suitable method and repeat it to consolidate it into a conditioned reflex. Once the conditioned reflex is established, entering quiescence is easy. Do not set too strict a criterion for yourself, because it may lead to nervousness, in which it is impossible to enter quiescence. One must be relaxed physically and mentally to enter quiescence and keep the method simple. If it is too complicated, it will interfere with the process. So, for beginners, two points are necessary: The posture should be comfortable and use only one method to induce quiescence. Listening to the respiration or focusing the mind at Dantian are good. If you feel uncomfortable due to your posture, adjust it slightly. Yet, the sound of respiration should be avoided during Qigong exercise. One should use Dantian (the umbilicus) to listen to the sound of respiration.

Scientific Research on Qigong

The effects of Qigong in preventing and treating diseases and strengthening the constitution have been proved through practice. However, its mechanism needs further research. In this chapter I will explain the main points of Qigong exercise, drawing on my own experience with it and clinical application of it in accordance with the rules of TCM and modern medicine.

I. The Effect of Mind and Consciousness in Qigong Exercise

As the saying goes, "Qigong depends on nothing but Xin Yi." Xin Yi refers to the mental and physiological activities, consciousness and thinking process. All mental activities are conducted by the cerebral cortex, a specialized material structure. Therefore, the training of mind and consciousness is actually the training of spirits and thinking. In other words, it is the training of the cerebral cortex, which is the superior part of the nervous systems. Because a person's conscious activities are conducted with the body, Qigong exercise is a positive exercise. According to many Qigong experts, one key point in training the mind and consciousness is concentration. This principle is embodied in many things related to Qigong practice. For example, use the mind instead of Qi; use Qi instead of force; if thought is concentrated, the consciousness is concentrated and so is the body's force. In this sense, thought is dominant, and mind over matters.

Actually Qigong is a special method for controlling physiological activities through psychopneumatological activities. Psychopneumatologically, Qigong exercise works on the physiological activities in two ways--through dynamic and quiescent movement. Both types of movement are guided by the mind--conscious activity.

Let us begin with dynamic movement. As is known, mental activity influences the physiological activity, such as those of the extremities, face, eyes, and tongue. The muscles of all these organs are voluntary muscles, through which various Qigong postures and methods are given physical forms. Through their tension, the muscles affect different corresponding physiological functions under the direction of the nervous system.

Parts of the body's physiological activities can not be fully controlled by the mind. But the mind can control and affect them to a certain extent. One obvious example is respiration. Its speed and depth can be controlled mentally.

The respiratory organs' movement is semi-voluntary. Qigong uses the mind to regulate lung rhythm, using the breathing rate, scope, strength and method to affect respiratory function and its related physiological activities through the nervous system. Apart from the voluntary and semi-voluntary muscles there are the involuntary muscles. Although the physiological activities of the involuntary muscles are controlled by all the laws governing voluntary muscles, they can be affected by the mind. The effect of Qigong on involuntary activity is achieved through training the voluntary and semi-voluntary muscles and focusing the mind in accordance with the type of Qigong practised. These three ways of training affect physiological activity through the mind and consciousness, typifying psychopneumatology. The following illustrates the mental (psychological) direction of physiological activity: focusing the mind at Dantian, focusing the mind along the channels of Qi circuits, counting the respiration or listening to it, focusing the mind by holding an imaginary ball, or walking through mud, focusing the mind to gain strength by symbolically pushing a mountain or pulling the tail of a running bull, and focusing the mind by silently reciting catch words, phrases, verses or mantras. These also illustrate using movement of thought to influence physiology. From the perspective of Qigong quiescence, the exercise should foster peace and quietude of the mind, to the get practitioner into a relatively quiescent state. Through active self-training in a conscious state, mental activity can be controlled in relative tranquillity and, at the same time, continue working on a simple plane, directing physiological functions.

So Qigong trains the mind and the spirit through certain conscious activities and methods to improve and regulate the physiological functions of the body. By this exercise, practitioners can prevent and treat diseases and strengthen their constitutions.

II. Dynamic and Quiescent States of Qigong Exercise

The two states form another key point of Qigong exercise. The dynamic state is divided into the internal dynamic and external dynamic aspects; the quiescent state can also be divided into the internal and external aspects. The internal dynamic aspect refers to the Qi movement inside of the body while the external dynamic aspect means the movement of the extremities. The internal quiescent aspect refers to the relative quietude of the mind during practice; the external quiescent aspect means the motionless posture.

The dynamic state is absolute and quiescent state only relative. Everything in the universe is developing and changing in incessant movement, and so is the human body. The process of dispelling staleness and absorbing freshness is a manifestation of the body's movement. To cite *Meditation and Questions* by Wang Chuanshan of the late Ming and early Qing dynasties, quiescence refers to tranquil movement, not stillness. Therefore, the dynamic state is basic and quietude a special form of movement. The essence of Qigong is to mobilize the body's functional activities and stimulate movement so as to maintain the equilibrium of Yin and Yang which adjust to and inhibit each other, harmonize Qi and blood, dredge the channels and collaterals and cultivate vitality and Essential Qi. However, the dynamic state of Qigong is different from ordinary movement. It is movement directed by special quietude of the brain. So the quiet mental state is the prerequisite for the dynamic state. During practice, if you cannot enter the quiescent mental state, you will not achieve the full effects of movement, which has been proven experimentally. For this reason, Qigong experts always pay attention to both the quiescent and dynamic states.

It should be noted that, after the practitioner enters the

quiescent mental state, the body's superficial activities seem to be still, its physiological activities continue being guided by special cerebral cortex quietude. The cerebral cortex is in quietude in one part, another part being directed by thought to restore energy and recover from diseases. Tests have demonstrated that Qigong can cause changes in dermal electricity reducing it in some areas and raising it in others. It has been proven that Qigong can raise the skin temperature on hand back and foot top (the places with lowest body temperature) to level with that of the chest. Patients with reduced ptyalin have normalized it through Qigong exercise. Just 30 minutes of Qigong exercise can significantly increase the saliva content of active ptyalin. Persistent Qigong exercise can strengthen the phagocytic ability of white cells to an index number above 90 percent. These examples show that the quiescence of Qigong can bring about physiological changes. In this state, the body's energy-consuming processes change to energy storation.

According to the TCM Yin/Yang theory, the dynamic state is Yang and the quiescent state Yin. Yin and Yang form a unity of two opposites which coordinate with, inhibit and spring from each other. As one ancient master said, "With Yin alone there is no birth, with Yang alone, no growth." Therefore, Qigong should combine Yin and Yang, the dynamic and the quiescent, the upward and the downward movements, and the right lateral and the left lateral or opening and closing movements. According to experience, two problems should be solved in order to achieve the correct dynamic and quiescent states of Qigong exercise. One is the choice of appropriate methods of training movement and quiescence, and the other is the linking of both states.

There are numerous methods available for dynamic and quiescent training. When doing the quiescent exercise, we should retain the dynamic exercise within the quietude (Qi should move. Editor); when doing the dynamic exercise, the cerebral cortex should be quiescent as the body moves. In practising dynamic-quiescent exercise, do the dynamic after the quiescent combining the features of both exercise. Specifically, dynamic exercise stresses movement of the extremities, and static exercise stresses that Qi circulation and mental direction lead to quiescence which starts from certain movements. Examples are the Eight Elegant

Movements and Taiji (shadow boxing). These exercises gradually concentrate and guide mental activity toward simple movement of the extremities, so that the mind calms down. Other methods start from a motionless posture and, after the cerebral cortex enters quiescence, proceed into dynamic exercise.

Generally speaking, dynamic and quiescent exercises can be combined naturally into one exercise, though the methods depend on the individual's constitution capability. For example, one can practise quiescent Qigong after finishing dynamic Qigong, or do dynamic Qigong exercises in the morning quiescent qigong exercises in the evening. Of course, one should choose the method of exercise to suit one's conditions.

Why must dynamic exercise be combined with quiescent exercise? Because they have different effects. While quiescent exercise trains the body's internal functions, dynamic exercise trains the external parts. As far as we combine the two exercises, we benefit from both types of exercise making Qigong practice the perfect exercise.

III. Qi and Qigong Exercise

Qi is a general concept of TCM. Take Qi inside the body for example. There are Zhen (Essential) Qi, Yuan (Original) Qi, visceral Qi, channel and collateral Qi and so on. According to the Yin/Yang theory, Qi of the Yin parts is called Yin Qi, and Yang Qi is of the Yang parts; judging by the depth, Qi on the surface is called Wei (defensive) Qi, and Ying (nutritious) Qi comes from inside the body; by the location, Qi in the upper part is called Visceral Qi or Lung Qi, Middle Qi or Gastric Qi is in the middle part, and Yuan (Original) Qi or Kidney Qi is in the lower part. Inborn Qi is called Congenital Qi and acquired Qi Postnatal Qi. Qi gathered from the sky (air) is called Celestial Qi and from the earth, Earthly Qi or Water-grain Qi.

Qigong experts pay special attention to the training of both Congenital and Postnatal Qi.

The inborn Qi is obtained at the earliest stage of life. As to its origin, there are two different explanations: One holds that

Congenital Qi refers to the essence or precondition for the formation of the fetus; the other says this Qi is the same as Original Qi which is acquired inside the mother's body.

The Postnatal Qi refers to the Qi acquired after birth. This Qi can be divided into Celestial Qi, the air we inhale, and Earthly Qi, of which water and grain form the source. Both kinds of Qi interact to nourish the human body.

Congenital Qi and Postnatal Qi are closely related, interact, and rely upon each other to form Zhen (Essential) Qi, the motivating power of life. While Congenital Qi serves as the foundation of life, Postnatal Qi is the indispensable source of materials for the body's vital activity. A persons life and activities are motivated by Congenital Qi and supplemented by Postnatal Qi. In Qigong exercise, equal attention should be paid to the training of both kinds of Qi. Some Qigong experts have stressed specific types of Qi, dividing the exercise into Congenital Qigong and Postnatal Qigong. Congenital Qigong trains Kidney Qi--Yuan Qi and Mingmen (an acupoint) Qi; Postnatal Qigong mainly trains Lung Qi and Gastric Qi--the respiratory and digestive systems.

QI INSIDE THE HUMAN BODY

Postnatal Qi

Congenital Qi

Celestial Qi — is acquired from inhaled air. It develops into lung Qi through respiration.

Earthly Qi — originates from food intake. It is also called the Qi of water and grain in the digestive system.

Essential Qi —— refers to the essence of life. It preconditions the formation of the fetus and is the initial motivating power of life.

Original Qi —— refers to the condition for acquirement during the fetus' formation. It is the foundation for postnatal development.

It becomes the material source of nourishment.

It becomes the motivating power of life.

The two different kinds of Qi interact forming the body's Essential Qi, the motivating power of life.

Among the various methods for Qi training, the following stress Congenital Qi: focusing the mind at Dantlan, focusing the mind at Qihai, focusing the mind at Mingmen, counting respiration and so on. All these are mind-focusing methods for training Internal Qi or Dantian Qi. Methods for training Postnatal Qi include tranquil respiration, deep respiration and abdominal respiration. These methods aim at training the respiratory system to improve respiratory and digestive system.

IV. Qigong Exercise and Internal Qi

Internal Qi refers to the internal movement of Qi along the channels and collaterals as evidenced by the Qi sensations felt during exercise. Such comfortable sensations in the abdomen, lumbar region, and four limbs feel like a warm flow. Internal Qi, therefore, describes that warm flow.

How is Internal Qi produced? First of all, Internal Qi is produced from material and thus should be regarded as a material phenomenon. As breathing, the practitioner's mental activity plays an important role in the formation of Internal Qi. Actually, focusing the mind is a process of affecting physiological activity through mental activity. It has more important effects than merely inducing the quiescent state, including focusing the mind at certain acupoints or on certain objects to avoid interruption by stray thoughts. Because mental activity is cerebral action, focusing the mind is cerebration. The area of focus is in the cerebrum. This center supplies bio- electricity to related organs and tissue. Scientific experiment has proved that bioelectric changes become more obvious with the strengthening of the mind-focusing ability. Dermal electricity grows in the area of focus and drops in other areas, though it returns to the original level immediately after exercise. This indicates that the metabolism of the related organs and tissues is changed by mental suggestion. Qigong experts say, "Where the attention is focused, there force will be." Internal Qi is fostered gradually by the mind. The warm, flowing property of Internal Qi shows bio-electricity in operation.

The effect of Internal Qi on the body accords with the TCM theories of Yin and Yang, Qi and blood and channels and collaterals. Internal Qi helps balance Yin and Yang, harmonize Qi and blood, dredge channels and collaterals, and nurture Essential Qi. There are individual variations in the speed of generating Internal Qi, some people developing it fast and others never feeling its existence at all. Therefore, practitioners should not hurriedly seek after the phenomena of Internal Qi.

V. Qi Transformation, Circulation and Function and Qigong Exercise

Qi transformation is a TCM concept which refers to the change of material and energy in the process of life. It is the physiological functions of human life. As long as life exists, the transformation of Qi will not cease. Material and energy absorbed from nutrition and inhaled from air are transformed into Qi in order to be used by the body. This includes the process of removing waste material. Life depends on the quality of Qi transformation.

The *Internal Canon of Medicine* describes life activity in these words: "Yin and Yang are the essentials of life. Yang breaks things down into Qi, and Yin synthesizes producing Qi form." (This shows the movement and quiescence of matter--Editor) and summarizes Qi transformation according to the Yin/Yang theory of TCM. A more specific explanation is provided in *Jing Yue's Anthology* by Zhang Zhongjing of the Ming dynasty: "Qi is the basis of life. Everything in the universe depends on Qi for change and development." The law of life movement and transformation known already in ancient times is now known as the effect of Qi transformation. The normal function of urination depends on the urinary bladder's normal Qi transformation. When Qi transformation of the urinary bladder become balanced, incontinence may occur among other symptoms. Digestion of food and circulation of blood depend on spleen Qi transformation. When spleen movement is disturbed, there is loss of appetite, fatigue, facial swelling, and swollen extremities, semi-liquid stool or blood in stool. Qi transformation is very important to the human body's normal functions.

From where does Qi transformation originate? According to TCM theory, the origin is in the Mingmen (Gate of Life) acupoint at the back of the waist between the kidneys. Zhao Xianke, medical expert of the Ming dynasty and author of *An Illustrated Book of Medical Practice*, said, "Mingmen dominates all twelve channels. Without it, the kidneys would be weak; the spleen and stomach can not digest food; the liver and gall would not give even the greatest general any energy to think and plan; the urine and feces would not be moved, and the heart would malfunction causing dizziness and endangering life. During the lantern festival, for example, many families hang at the gate a lantern with a candle surrounded by paper figures. When the candle is lit, the figures start revolving. As the flame gets stronger, they move faster; as it weakens or goes out, they slow down or come to a stop. The figures may remain on the lantern, but they are actually dead. This is Mingmen's role in Qi transformation." Qigong experts in old times regarded Mingmen as the motivating force of the body and paid special attention to its training during Qigong exercise.

TCM theory recognizes Mingmen as a part of the kidney function because the kidneys are viscera for liquid which store essence and control the fire of Mingmen. Kidneys are divided into Yin and Yang, water and fire, hence such names as Kidney Yin and Kidney Yang, Original Yin and Original Yang, and True Yin and True Yang. Kidney water is Kidney Yin, and Kidney Yang the fire of Mingmen. All internal organs rely on the nourishment of kidney water and the fire of Mingmen for growth and development. *Jingyue's Anthology* says, "The Gate of LIfe (Mingmen) is a sea of blood and essence; spleen and stomach are a sea of water and grain and are the most essential of the viscera. Mingmen is the root of Original Qi and houses water and fire; spleen and stomach gather the essence of nourishment from Postnatal Qi; Mingmen is the source of vital energy from Congenital Qi." These explanations have been proved by TCM clinical studies to reflect certain pathological conditions. For instance, a patient with deficiency of Yin will often have liver deficiency with hyponomesia, palpitation, and insomnia. It can also cause lung deficiency, with cough, high fever, night sweats and bloody sputum. The patient with deficiency of Kidney Yang is apt to suffer deficiency of Spleen Yang with liquid stools, or deficiency of Heart Yang with short breath, cold extremities, and spontaneous sweating. When these diseases occur, the TCM method of treatment features nourishing the kidneys and cultivating Yin in cases with Kidney Yin deficiency, or nurturing the kidneys and reinforcing Mingmen fire in cases of Kidney Yang deficiency. Another important Mingmen function is its reproductive role. Deficiency of Mingmen fire may lead to hypogonadism and impotence. On the contrary, if the Mingmen fire is excessive, hypergodaism will occur. The TCM method of treating excessive Mingmen fire is reinforcing the water and controlling the fire of the kidneys. Qigong exercise can produce good effects on both these types of diseases, no matter how serious.

VI. Essence of Life, Qi, Spirit and Qigong Exercise

All Qigong experts pay attention to this triad. As a saying form ancient times summarizes the early master's views, " There are three treasures in the sky, which are the sun, the moon and star constellations; there are three treasures on earth, which are water, fire and wind; there are three treasures in the human body, which are essence of life, Qi and spirit." They regarded essence of life, Qi and spirit as the most important material and function of the body.

Essence of life here refers to the essence of all material things which are indispensable to life. According to *Plain Questions*, a person's essence is the origin of life. Essence originates from two sources, the inborn essence which stimulates life and growth, and the postnatal essence which comes from air, water, and grain to nourish physiological activity. Essence can be divided into general essence and specific essence. General essence refers to the essence of the viscera--the body's main organs--which is absorbed from air, water and grain by the lungs and stomach through Qi transformation. Specific essence refers to the reproductive essence stored in the kidneys; it is the essence of the five Yin viscera and nourishes the Congenital Qi. *Ling Qu Canon: Channels and Collaterals* states: "Inborn essence comes form the parents at the earliest stage of life while the fetus takes shape. The fetus acquires Qi and blood from the mother from which the brain, bones, tendons, skin and hair develop." *Health Preservation*, by Tao Xuanjing of the Liang dynasty, points out, "The way of health preservation is treating the essence as a treasure." Essence and sperm are one word in Chinese meaning the same thing. Qigong experts are careful about their sex lives. Control of sex is important for people with weak constitutions or chronic diseases.

As essence, Qi can be divided into general Qi and specific Qi. Specific Qi refers to the air inspired and general Qi refers to Essential or Original Qi which is the body's physiological functions. The two kinds of Qi are very important in Qigong exercise. *Zhuang Zi: Roaming North* states, "Life comes into being because Qi is amassed; when Qi is scattered, the person dies." I wish to re-stress the importance of Qi as the motivating power of life and that attention to the training of Qi is of major importance in practising Qigong exercise.

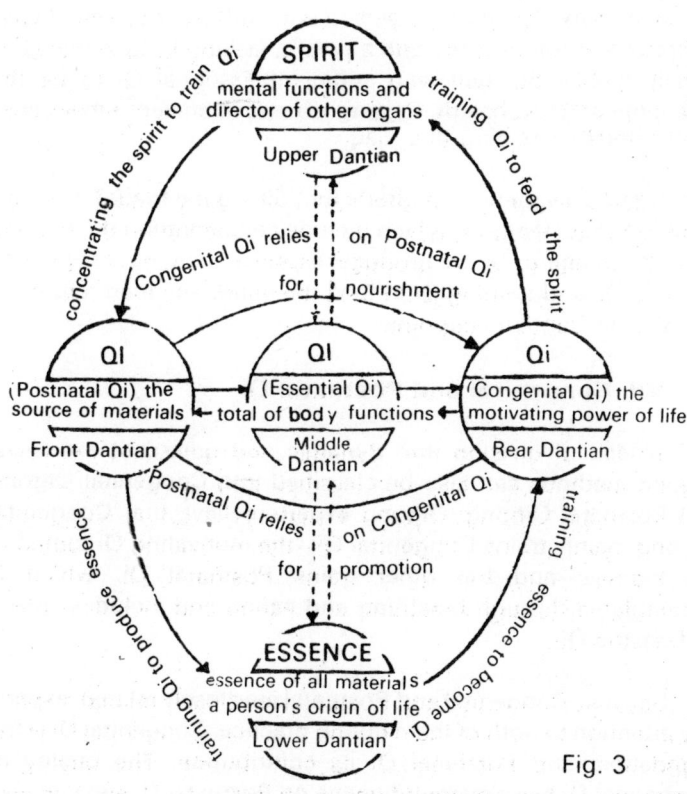

Fig. 3

The spirit refers to a person's mental activity. It is one's mental functions, the guide of life activities. *Plain Questions* states, "The heart (mind in Chinese) is the director of other organs." TCM theory acknowledges a close relation between a person's mental activity and the functions of the five Yin viscera which feed it energy. Mental activity is unique to humans and reflects the objective world as well as one's analysis of it. Therefore, the training of mental activity is a major approach to Qigong exercise.

Although there are differences among essence of life, Qi and spirit, they are closely related, influencing, changing and relying on one another through mutual coordination. Qi springs from the essence of life. The production of essence relies on Qi, and Qi is the source of energy and material foundation for the human body's mental activity. Therefore, a person with sufficient Essential Qi is vigorous and full of spirit, and a person lacking in Essential Qi is usually feeble. So, believing sufficient Essential Qi to be the guarantee of good health, Qigong experts in ancient times spent great efforts in training this triad.

There is a variety of methods for training the triad. They have some common features, which include concentrating the mind to train Qi, training Qi to produce essence, training essence to become Qi, and training Qi to feed the mind. The triad returns to the Middle Dantian acupoint.

VII. Congenital and Postnatal Qi

Instead of division into dynamic and quiescent exercises, Qigong methods can also be classified into Congenital Qigong and Postnatal Qigong. Qigong experts believe that Congenital Qigong mainly trains Congenital Qi--the motivating Qi rooted in the kidneys--and the other trains Postnatal Qi, which is accumulated through breathing and eating and includes spleen and gastric Qi.

Because Congenital and Postnatal are closely related, experts pay attention to both of them during practice. Congenital Qi is the foundation, and Postnatal Qi its contribution. The quality of Congenital Qi has a major influence on Postnatal Qi and can also be affected by the latter. For example, the physical constitution is inherited from the parents and decides the health of the fetus as in inherited diseases. But this influence is not absolute. Postnatal health is continually affected by one's life activities. People with congenital deficiency can improve their health through proper training and nourishment. Some congenital diseases can now be cured with the development of medical science. So postnatal training and nourishment are very important to growth and health.

The relation between congenital quality and postnatal development is described in *Jingyue's Anthology*: "Those who have excellent congenital condition and good nourishment can expect to strengthen their constitutions; if they are ill-nourished, their constitutions will weaken. Those who have poor congenital condition but good nourishment can expect to strengthen their constitutions; if they do not become good at training and nourishing themselves, they will get worse." So physical exercise is vital in preventing and treating diseases, improving weak constitutions, avoiding premature aging and prolonging life.

VIII. Posture, Breathing Methods and Mental Activity in Qigong Exercise

Posture, respiration and focusing the mind are three basic methods of Qigong exercise. There are innumerable methods varying in form, requirements and function. Generally, Qi flows in the body by circulating up, down, leftwards and rightwards. Posture, respiration and focusing the mind are interactive, promoting and restraining one another. Direction of Qi flow, respiration and posture are to be discussed in detail.

(I) Mind Focusing and its Effects on Qi Movement

Focusing the mind is one way of training the mind. The mind directs matter by directing Qi flow. It is the key to starting any movement in Qigong exercise.

Besides, directing the mind into quiescence to influence Qi, mental direction of Qi flow moves it up, down, leftwards and rightwards.

The region of mental focus also makes a difference on the movement. With the naval (Middle Dantian) as the focus, the mind can guide Qi upward to Tanzhong, Yindang, Daihui and so on. If the mind is guided downward from Middle Dantian to Qihai, Guanyuan, Huiyin, Yongquan and other acupoints, Qi can be induced to descend. Often observed in the clinic are phenomena such as raised blood pressure, shortened breath, dizziness and sensations of chest tightness while the mind is focused on the nose. When the mind is focused on Yongquan, blood pressure will drop, respiration gets deeper and comfortable sensations can be felt. Usually, the higher the position of focus is, the higher Qi will rise; likewise, the lower the position of focus, the lower Qi will descend. This illustrates that the mind and Qi arrive at the same place. So the Middle Dantian acupoint should be the center regardless of where else the mind is being focused.

For this reason, the navel region, also called Middle Dantian, used to described as the center of the human body or the middle ground of the spleen and pancreas. In addition to enhancing Middle Qi (digestive function) and harmonizing general Qi, clinical practice has proved that focusing the mind in this region, where the stomach, pancreas and spleen are located, can remarkably improve digestive system function, causing a series of favorable physiological changes in other parts of the body. So traditionally, focusing the mind at Middle Dantian is considered to be the method of laying foundation. On this basis, one can move the secondary focus elsewhere.

The regions of focus may be the Upper Dantian, Middle Dantian and Lower Dantian. Within the scope of Middle Dantian (inner navel), sometimes called Middle Trunk are Sheque (Front Dantian), Zhongwan (about 10 centimeters above the navel) and Qihai (about 3.5 centimeters below the navel), though Zhongwan is a little higher than the limit and Jianli a little lower. Patients with excessive Qi in the upper body and deficiency of Qi in the lower body should mainly focus the mind on the Lower Trunk. For people in normal health, Middle Qi is recommended and the Upper Trunk should not be used as a region of constant focus.

As to the opening and closing of the focused mind, opening

means Qi is guided by the mind to expand from the inner navel and creates the sensation of Qi overflowing the body. And closing means concentrating Qi from the extremities and superficial parts of the body which feels filled with Qi. Usually, the opening and closing methods should be conducted alternatively.

(II) Effects of Rising, Descending, Opening and Closing Movements of Respiration in Qigong Exercise

Respiration, or "Tu Na" in Chinese, is a specialty in Qigong exercise. The purpose of such training is to regulate the efficiency and rhythm of respiration mentally.

What does the training of respiration have to do with Qigong exercise? As we know, breathing is very important for vital activity. After the first breath, which takes place almost immediately after the fetus leaves the mother's womb, it continues to the end of life. So, what breathing is to the human body is what water is to fish. It means living. The body draws oxygen from the air and discards carbon dioxide. This process was described as "getting rid of the stale and taking in the fresh, and the program for respiration training is called the method of Tu (dispelling) and Na (absorbing). Breathing plays an important role in the metabolism of the human body. Physiological activities will be disturbed if the oxygen supply falls below the needs of the body's tissues. The nervous cells of the cerebral cortex are highly susceptible to lack of oxygen and will cease normal activity only 10 seconds after oxygen is suspended. If blood oxygen concentration falls below the limit, cell and tissue functions are disturbed. So proper respiration training can greatly improve the health and enhance working ability. Due to the tremendous attention paid to training respiration, Qigong experts throughout history have accumulated rich knowledge about respiratory methods.

All respiration training methods of Qigong have their own characteristics. Their common requirements include quieting the mind, evening respiration, letting Qi sink to (Middle) Dantian, inspiring through the nostrils, keeping respiration supple, slow, even and deep, and conducting abdominal respiration while naturally entering mental quiescence.

77

Besides enhancing the respiratory and digestive system functions and inducing mental quiescence, respiration training can play a role in the rising, descending, opening and closing movements of Qi flow. To be specific, inspiration corresponds to the rising and closing movements of Qi, and expiration guides the descending and opening movements.

Expiration guides Qi downward and expands it; inspiration closes and raises Qi. Clinical observations show that long expiration helps to reduce blood pressure by expanding blood vessels in the extremities and leading the blood downward; inspiration, causing the rising and closing movements of Qi, leads blood upward along the arteries and constricts the blood vessels in the extremities. Therefore, patients with symptoms of excess in the upper body and deficiency in the lower body should stress expiration and even normal practitioners should avoid overemphasizing inspiration and conduct respiration naturally at the learning stage of Qigong exercise.

The effects of Qigong respiration on Qi movement are not absolute but depend on many factors. That Qi follows mental direction is one example of how mental activity can influence the effects of Qi. When Qigong practice reaches a certain level, mental activity instead of inspiration can induce Qi descent and opening. This also applies to Qi rising and closing movements.

(III) Posture and Effects of the Rising, Descending, Opening and Closing Movements of Qi

Posture is also mentally directed during Qigong exercise. It demands a certain degree of muscle tension in keeping a certain posture. So posturing in Qigong exercise is basically the training of muscle tension while relaxing. In practice, the looseness or tensity of muscles and posture can influence body functions. Therefore, they selectively play a role in changing body functions including those of the viscera through the nervous systems as well as channels and collaterals. Each posture during Qigong exercise affects tension and so on. Therefore, the choice of posture depends on the practitioner's health and purpose.

Qigong postures can also be divided into four types, according to four types of Qi movement--rising, descending, opening and closing. Each type can be further divided into dynamic and quiescent postures.

The rising type features ascending body movement. Besides dynamic upward movement, the rising type also includes quiescent postures which assume higher positions. Rising postures guide Qi upward. Descending postures lead Qi downward. Opening movement features expansion from inside outwards as is characteristic of all dynamic postures. The quiescent postures usually appear to be wide-spread stance. Opening postures guide Qi outward. The closing type features inward, withdrawing movement and the quiescent postures assume a higher position. Such postures can concentrate Qi.

However, the effects of all these postures on Qi movement are not absolute. They have their limits and are restricted by respiration and mental activity.

Is it oversimplifying to divide Qigong postures into these four types? No. Each of the rising, descending, opening and closing types includes a variety of postures and movements. For example, the positions of the four types of postures can be further divided into upper, middle and lower, and directions can divide postures into four front types and four oblique types. Moreover, according to the arm movements, postures can be divided into Yin-facing, Yang-facing and half-Yin-and-half-Yang types. According to the rotating, bending and stretching movements of head, neck, trunk and the limbs, including both the ostensible and the real, postures are further classified. In practice, one should proceed from one type to another, from the simple to the complex, and practise a variety to achieve different effects.

Many postures combine the rising, descending, opening and closing movements. This subject merits further study and discussion. Here we will explain how these four types of postures work in coordination to make Qigong exercise an entity. These four types of postures not only contradict one another, but also interrelate, each being the precondition for the others' existence.

Without rising, there would be no descending; without opening, there would be no closing. They oppose, and yet supplement one another. All movements influence Qi flow.

In training, sometimes posture and Qi movement are in unity, but sometimes they may proceed in opposite directions. They mutually promote yet restrict one another at the same time. For example, as one raises the arms, Qi rises; if the trunk also rises, the rising power of Qi increases, a process of mutual promotion. But if the arms are raised while the trunk moves downward with sinking buttocks and bent knees, the upward movement contains a restraininh downward movement. Unrestricted upward movement of Qi can be avoided; on the contrary, if the downward movement is restrained by the upward movement, Qi will not descend below the allowed limit, implementing mutual restriction. Therefore, the rising and descending movements depend on each other for mutual restriction, as is also true of the principles on the opening and closing movements. How does one apply these principles to practice? It is my opinion that application should be done according to specific circumstances.

(IV) Coordinating Postures With Respiration and Mind Focusing

Focusing the mind, training respiration and postures are three major types of Qigong exercise methods. With the mind taking the lead, they mutually supplement and work together as components of Qigong exercise. However, different schools have different emphasis, some emphasizing mental training, some stress respiration, and others taking postures most seriously. Although each method has its unique function, it always includes all these three aspects. It is necessary to choose individual programs of Qigong exercise to suit the physiological condition of the practitioner.

The descending posture combined with expiration can guide Qi downwards. If the mind is focused in the lower trunk or if the mind guides Qi, Qi descent is much more powerful. When the rising posture is combined with inspiration, it vigorously promote the rise of Qi. Usually rising motion, including quiescent exercise with high-level postures, are not combined with mind focusing on the upper trunk in order not to overraise Qi or cause adverse results. The same is true of the opening and closing postures.

The rising posture is often combined with expiration to lead Qi downwards and avoid raising it too high. To restrain Qi rise, the mind is often focused on middle or lower trunk. Although rising and descending movements differ from opening and closing movements, they all merit attention to keep Qi under control and avoid excess. So, Qi movement is trained in accordance with the principle of restriction and avoiding excess.

Clinical experience also confirms the need to control and restrict Qi movement. Rising Qi often produces cases of excess in the upper part, and the descending movement leads to solidity in the lower body. From these points we understand that rise takes root in the descent, that Qi movement mustn't be forced, and that Qi should be allowed to return to its origin. Qi movement also includes opening and closing. As opening dissipates Qi and closing accumulates and stores Qi, too much opening may cause deficiency, and too much closing can solidify Qi and keep it from flowing. Opening does not mean forcing Qi outward by mind focusing, but letting it overflow of its own accord where inner Qi is plentiful. Therefore, guiding Qi back to its origin is often regarded as basic in Qigong practice.

IX. Illusion During Quiescent Exercise

Illusions refer to certain phenomena perceived by the practitioner during practice which reflect some impressions of the cerebral cortex but do not exist in reality. These illusions usually occur in the quiescent state, and are not morbid. Lacking knowledge of psychology and physiology, some practitioners are superstitious and mystical when trying to explain these illusions. This is an error which will impair the scientific development of Qigong.

These illusions are diverse and can be visual, auditory or olfactory. For example, a practitioner in the quiescent state may visualize himself/herself standing on the beach, or in a park with birds singing.

All functional activity of the human body is governed by the cerebral cortex through the nerves. This complex and extremely precise system consists of at least 4 million external nerves and about 1,400 million nerve cells. The eyes alone have about 1 million external nerves, and the ears about 10,000. Therefore, visual and auditory perceptions are particularly numerous.

Illusions are certainly not the best quiescent state, but illusions of beautiful scenery are beneficial to health. The illusion of a beautiful painting has a calming effect. But one should not let the mind follow illusions and lose the good effects of Qigong practice.

Some illusions may recall some unhappy or frightening personal experience. In this case, one must not continue practising the quiescent exercise.

Quiescent Qigong Exercises

Quiescent Qigong exercises include all the Qigong exercises without motion of the body and limbs, such as Relaxing Exercise (Fang Song Gong), Relaxing Quiescent Exercise (Song Jing Gong), Breathing Exercise (Tu Na Gong), and Standing Exercise (Zhan Zhuang Gong). Distinct from ordinary resting or sitting, quiescent Qigong exercise emphasizes quiescent Qi movement. It guides Qi flow, the body's physiological functions, with the cerebral cortex in special quietude, but fully conscious. This process features internal motion with external motionlessness as its prerequisite, or motion in a quiescent state. Its effects are achieved by certain posture, respiration methods and mind focusing. Under these circumstances, the body functions change from energy consuming to energy restoring, contributing to the body's ability to self-regulate, self-repair and self-regenerate.

Most quiescent Qigong exercises are practised to cure diseases and help the debilitated resume physical exercise. However, some kinds of quiescent Qigong exercise require great intensity.

The following are detailed instructions for carrying out several types of quiescent Qigong exercises.

I. Postures, Respiration and Mental Activity of Quiescent Qigong Exercise

Posture for quiescent exercise are numerous. They all maintain some muscle tension during general relaxation. The intensity of muscular tension affects the related parts of the body through nerve reflexes. Therefore, different postures produce different effects on the functional activity of different parts of the body. The exercise should be done with due consideration for the practitioner's condition. Usually the general principle is relaxation, naturalness and comfort vs. rigidity, stiffness and obsession with form. Unbuttoning collar buttons, loosening belts, urinating and defecating are necessary before exercise. It is better to wear comfortable, flat heeled exercise shoes.

(I) Postures

1. Standing Postures

(1) Natural Standing

Stand naturally with feet shoulder-width apart; flex the knees and turn them slightly inward with body weight distributed equally on both feet; slightly raise the heels and gently move the weight forward. Assume a slight "sitting position" with body weight centralized in the hips-lumbar area and feet standing firmly like a towering pine tree deeply rooted underground. Keep the upper part of the body upright; neither thrust the chest out nor hunch the back. Gently keep the stomach in, relax the lumbar vertebrae and slightly lower the shoulders. Let the arms hang at the sides with elbows flexed, turn the palms to face each other with fingers parted and slightly flexed as if holding a large balloon. Keep the head level, with eyes slightly opened and looking straight forward, gently close the mouth or barely open it with tongue tip gently touching the lower incisors, swallow the saliva when it increases.

Figs. 4 .   Fig .5.

84

(2) Ball-Pressing Standing Posture Keeping the natural standing posture described, move the hands in front of the lower abdomen, palms downward, with fingers parted and slightly flexed, allowing a fist's distance between the hands and imagine pressing a floating ball into water. The height of the hands can be adjusted upwards to between the umbilicus and tits. (Figs. 6 and 7.)

Fig. 6   Fig. 7

(3) Ball-holding Standing Posture Based on the natural standing posture, move the hands sideways to hold an imaginary tree trunk, with palms facing inward, fingers parted and slightly flexed as if holding a ball. The hands face each other separated by about one third of a meter. The height of the hands may be adjusted between the umbilicus and tits according to personal preference. Align the buttocks and heels. Compared with the natural standing posture, this posture requires greater muscle tension in the arms. (Figs. 8 and 9.)

2. Sitting Postures

These are exercises practised while sitting on a chair, stool, or hard bed. In these postures, the practitioner can put a soft cushion on the seat to avoid discomfort. Described below are some sitting postures.

(1) Simple Sitting Posture This is also called the ordinary sitting posture. It requires the practitioner to sit on a chair, stool, or

Fig. 8

Fig. 9

the edge of a hard bed. Sit solidly with knees flexed at about 100 degrees. To avoid discomfort, you can put a soft cushion on the seat, but do not sit on a soft chair with hard edges. Place the feet on the ground, parted parallel about the same width as the shoulders. Keep the head level and above the midline, let the shoulders hang, barely close the mouth with tongue tip gently touching the lower incisors, and swallow saliva when it is excessive. Keep the upper body erect and straight, and keep the whole body including the scalp as relaxed as possible. These points can be observed more easily if you keep this formula in

Fig. 10

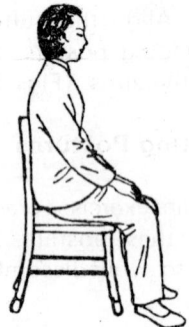

Fig 11

mind: Keep the upper body as erect as the trunk of a pine tree and sit like a desk clock. Slightly flex the elbows and drop the shoulders; gently place the hands on the ipsilateral thighs with palms facing downward (Figs. 10 and 11), or place the left hand between the lower abdomen and thighs and then place the right hand on the left hand, both palms facing upward, or vice versa (Figs. 12 and 13). Do not lean against the chair back unless in poor health. When practising, close or half-close the eyes, or leave them naturally open, the best method being half closing the eyes.

Fig. 12   Fig. 13

(2) Cross-legged Sitting Posture This can be subdivided into natural cross-legged sitting, single cross-legged sitting, and cross-legged back-leaning postures, which are described below.

Fig. 14   Fig. 15

(A) Natural Cross-legged Sitting Posture Sit firmly on a hard bed and cross the legs with the left on top or vice versa; place the feet under the middle part of each thigh. The posture of the upper part of the body, including the head, shoulders, chest, abdomen and back are the same as in the simple sitting posture. The palm of one hand loosely clasps the back of the other hand with thumbs crossed. (Figs. 14 and 15)

(B) Single Cross-legged Sitting Position Cross the legs with one foot placed on the other thigh. If the right leg is placed on the left, the left big toe points towards the right knee joint, or vice versa. Beginners may exchange legs to avoid numbness. Other requirements are the same as for the natural cross-legged sitting position. (Figs. 16 and 17.)

Fig. 16   Fig. 17

(C) Leaning Backwards Sitting Posture This exercise is usually practiced on a hard bed. Lean the back on a buttress of quilts or pillows; keep the body and legs at 120 to 140 degree angle. Lean the head against the support. Arrange the legs in the same way as for the natural cross-legged sitting posture (Fig. 18), or extend them straight until comfortable. This exercise can also be practised on a firm sofa. This posture is between the sitting and supine and takes more strength than the lying posture but less than the sitting posture. It is appropriate for one in poor health and provides a transition from the supine to the sitting postures by gradually increasing the strength requirements. (Figs. 18 and 19.)

Fig. 18

Fig. 19

3. Supine Postures The variations on this posture are numerous. The supine posture assumed with face up and by lying on the side are the most commonly used.

(1) Supine Posture Lie on the back face upward on a hard bed with a moderate-sized pillow under the head and shoulders. Stretch the arms out along the sides, relax the shoulders and elbows, and slightly flex the fingers or gently fold the hands (Fig 20), or fold the hands together with fingers crossed and put them on the lower abdomen (Fig. 21). This posture is helpful for focusing the mind, entering the quiescent state, and deepening abdominal respiration. The legs are naturally stretched out with feet touching each other or slightly parted. It is also correct to place one foot on the ankle of the other (Fig. 22). Exchange the foot positions during the exercise. Gently close the mouth and slightly close the eyes, looking forward a little above the tiptoes.

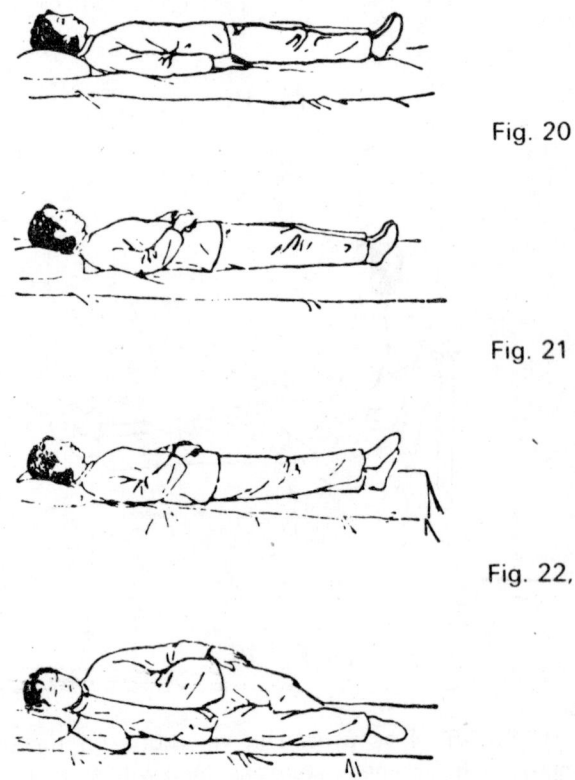

Fig. 20

Fig. 21

Fig. 22,

Fig. 23

(2) Lying on the Side Lie on either side of the body. Generally it is better to lie on the right side, reducing the pressure on the heart. For those with internal organ illness in the thoracic or abdominal cavity, lie on the healthy side. Lying on the right side, for example, keep the right shoulder underneath with head angled rightwards, and put a pillow under the head and the shoulder which is neither too high nor too low. Extend the right leg naturally and slightly, flex the left leg, and place the left foot behind the right leg and the left knee upon the right knee. The two legs can also be stretched out one on top of the other with knees flexed. The shoulder underneath is allowed to be slightly extended onto the pillow. Generally, put the right hand on the pillow in front of the eyes, palm up and leaving a fist's distance between the hand and face. The left hand is placed on the left hip. The mouth and eyes are arranged the same as in the supine posture, with eyes looking toward the feet (Fig. 23).

The three kinds of postures above are used often in Qigong exercise. The advantages of the standing position are: The flow of Qi can be easily regulated and promoted, and no facilities are needed. However, it may be tiring because of the relatively heavy weight bearing. So it is not suitable for those extremely ill or in poor health. Beginners can practise for 10 minutes or so, gradually lengthening the duration of exercise to 30 minutes in order to avoid fatigue. Exercise in the standing postures should be instituted during convalescence for building up the constitution, because Qigong can promote health and enhance strength. Exercise in the supine posture is comfortable, but is liable to inducing sleep. Lying down is suitable for those with serious diseases who are debilitated. It is also a sleep-inducing method. (Those in good health use the supine method 20 minutes every night as a supplement to dynamic exercise--Editor.)

(II) Respiration in Quiescent Qigong Exercise

Respiration is one of the three major components of Qigong exercise, especially for quiescent Qigong exercise. (In fact, some people have translated Qigong as Breathing Exercise, but that is oversimplifying--Editor.) In Qigong, respiration is defined as a breath-regulating method (Tu Na Xi Fa) or simply breathing method (Tu Na Fa).

There are many methods of respiration in Qigong exercise including inhaling and exhaling with the nose, inhaling with the nose and exhaling with the mouth, and inhaling and exhaling with the nose and mouth simultaneously. The process is; Breathe naturally, calm the mind, and conduct Qi down to Dantian; after entering cerebral quiescence, breathe supply, evenly and deeply. What are the advantages of the breathing exercise?

1. Inhaling and Exhaling With the Nose Advantages; (a) The nostril vibrissae can purify the air of the bigger dust particles. (b) The tunica mucosa nasi secretes sticky mucus to further cleanse the air of smaller dust particles and bacteria. (c) The numerous fine blood vessels in the nostrils warm the air. (d) This method helps stimulate many nerve endings in the tunica mucosa nasi. By nerve reflex action, many organs' functional activities will be affected, including the heart beat, blood pressure and respiratory muscle movement. Because Qigong respiration is gentle and rhythmic, this slight stimulation of the nerve endings produces beneficial effects on the organs. (e) Gentle expiration through the mouth helps the body to relax and Qi to travel downward. So, beginners who find it difficult to relax fully are advised to adopt this method. But with experience, breathing by the nose produces the same effects.

2. Natural Respiration Respiration in Qigong exercise should above all be natural. Therefore, it is inappropriate to inflict many requirements on beginners. If we restrict them with all the requirements at once, they will be overburdened and the attention may be diverted from the basic requirements about relaxation and quiescent. Since supple, soft, even and deep respiration is based on natural respiration, this basic breathing skill should be learned gradually. Therefore, breathing naturally is the key point in training Qigong respiration.

3. Conducting Qi to Dantian Here, Qi refers to deep respiration and the resultant Qi sensations. Dantian refers to the umbilicus or Guanyuan acupoint (3 inches below the umbilicus) Conducting Qi to Dantian refers to deep respiration during breathing exercise and mental direction of Qi down to Dantian in order to produce Qi sensations. The main effects of this exercise are: (a) induction of the quiescent state; (b) making natural abdominal respiration easy; (c) promoting Qi sensations in the Dantian area; (d) helping bring vitality to the lower body and flexibility to the upper body.

4. Soft, Supple, Even and Deep Respiration The main effects of this breathing skill are: (a) It helps to make abdominal respiration gentle and rhythmic, which gently and rhythmically stimulates the nerve endings in the tunic mucosa nasi and, by nerve reflex action, affects the related organ functions. (b) Deep but supple respiration helps the lungs to expand and contract fully, thoroughly changing the air. (c) Long-time practice can reduce the energy used in respiration, thus reducing the consumption of energy. (d) With abdominal respiration, the scope of diaphragm muscle movement is widened, which increases movement of the abdominal walls and diaphragm muscle, not only enhancing pulmonary ventilation but also gently and rhythmically massage the internal organs, regulating the functional activity of the vegetative nervous system and the cerebral cortex.

Some commonly used methods of respiration are described below.

1. Quiescent Breathing Method

This respiration is supple, even, and deep with cerebral cortex relatively quiet. It can be subdivided into the following methods.

(1) Natural Respiration Breathe as usual, but keep the whole body relaxed, get rid of distracting thoughts, and maintain inward peace. These requirements are made to help you breathe gently and slowly with mental direction and prepare you for acquiring other skills such as coordinating mental activity with the flow of Qi.

(2) Deep and Long Respiration On the basis of natural respiration, try to prolong and deepen the respiration. Gently close the mouth while inhaling with the tongue touching the hard palate, conduct Qi to Middle Dantian by mental direction, hold the breath for a second or two (do not force), and slowly exhale with the tongue relaxed and the mouth slightly open; release Dantian Qi out of the body through the mouth and again hold the breath a few seconds before inhaling. Repeat. Breath holding should never be forced.

(3) Respiration-counting Method Inhaling and exhaling once each constitute one count of respiration. There are many variations of this method. We present only one of them: Gently close the mouth and inhale with the nose or with both the nose and the mouth if the nostrils are blocked; count silently the times of respiration and conduct Qi down to the Middle Dantian. Hold the breath a few seconds after Qi arrives at Dantian, then inhale slowly with the mouth slightly open and silently recite the word "Hu" (exhale). To be simple, conduct Qi to Middle Dantian while inhaling and count the respiration, then relax the whole body with exhalation and silently say "Hu." For example, One--Hu--Two-- Hu and so on. Beginners may count 20 to 30 respirations, which take two to three minutes and then take short break. The times can be gradually increased to 100 respirations, which take about 10 minutes. If you breathe five times per minute, 50 counts are enough.

2. Abdominal Respiration

This is done by expanding and contracting the abdomen in response to inhalation and exhalation. It is beneficial to the physiological function of the internal organs of thoracic and abdominal regions, including the heart, lungs, liver, spleen, stomach and intestines. Such respiration acts as internal massage by increasing the diaphragm's up-and-down movement and abdominal wall's back-and-forth movement. It also benefits functions of the cerebral cortex through the nervous system reflex action. Abdominal respiration can be subdivided into direct respiration, retro-grade respiration, and the stop-go respiration which includes the inhale-exhale-stop method and the inhale-stop- exhale-stop method.

(1) Direct Respiration Inhale with the nose or both the

nose and the mouth, with the central part of the tongue touching the hard palate and the tongue tip touching the lower incisors; gently close the mouth and slowly conduct Qi to Middle Dantian. Hold the breath a few seconds and focus the mind at Middle Dantian. Expand the lower abdomen by inhaling, and then relax the tongue and slightly open the mouth while exhaling. Hold the breath a few seconds once again and focus the mind at Middle Dantian, contracting the lower abdomen. Repeat. Holding breath after inhaling and exhaling should be done naturally and do not force it. (Table 1.)

Table 1

Respiration	Inhaling	Pause	Exhaling	Pause
Tongue movement	touching hard palate	kept still	relaxed	kept still
Mind Focusing	di recting Qi to Middle Dantian	on Middle Dantian	natural	on Middle Dantian
Lower abdominal movement	ex panding slowly	pause	contracting slowly	pause

(2) Retrograde Respiration This is the opposite of direct respiration. It requires reverse abdominal movement. Inhale with the central part of tongue touching the hard palate and tongue tip touching the lower incisors; gently close the mouth and slowly conduct Qi to Middle Dantian. Contract the abdomen while inhaling, hold the breath a few seconds, focus the mind at Middle Dantian with tongue still touching the hard palate. Relax the tongue, slightly open the mouth and exhale through the nose and mouse while expanding the abdomen. Again hold the breath a few seconds, keeping the mind at Middle Dantian. Repeat the process. (Table 2.)

Table 2

Respiration	Inhaling	Pause	Exhaling	Pause
Tongue Movement	touching hard palate	without movement	relaxed	without movement
Mind Focusing	directing Qi to Middle Dantian	on Middle Dantian	natural breathing	on Middle Dantian
Lower Abdominal Movement	contracting slowly	pause	expanding slowly	pause

(3) Stop-go Respiration This combines conducting Qi by mental direction while silently reciting words and stopping the respiration. This method strengthens the abdominal respiration. It can be done in two ways.

The first way is also called the soft respiration method. Breathe with the nose or with both the nose and mouth; while inhaling, touch the hard palate with the tongue and silently recite the first word of a phrase such as "calm myself." Direct Qi to Middle Dantian and slowly expand the lower abdomen without exertion, then exhale slowly with tongue tip touching the lower incisors and silently recite the second word "myself" while slowly contracting the abdomen. While slowly contracting the abdomen, stop breathing a few seconds, keeping the tongue and abdomen motionless (Fig. 24). Repeat. The number of words recited may be increased gradually. (Table 3.)

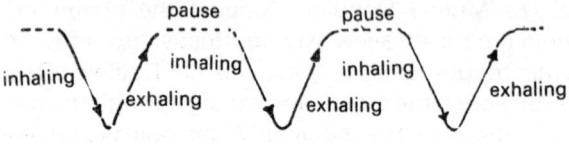

Fig. 24

The second method is sometimes called the hard respiration method. Breathe with the nose or inhale with the nose and exhale by mouth. Inhale with the tongue touching the hard palate and silently recite the first word of the command, "Sit silently by myself." Meanwhile, slowly conduct Qi to Middle Dantian while expanding the abdomen, hold the breath a few seconds without moving the tongue or the abdomen, and silently recite the second word of the command. Exhale slowly with tongue tip touching the lower incisors, silently recite the next word and gently contract the abdomen (Fig. 25). Repeat. The number of words can be gradually increased to eight. (Table 4.)

Table 3

Respiration	Inhaling	Exhaling	Pause
Tongue movement	touching hard palate	relaxed	without movement
Silently recite words	my-	self	calm
	my-	self	sit quiet
	my-	self	sit quiet, fit
	my-	self	sit quiet for fitness
lower abdominal movement	expanding slowly	contracting slowly	pause

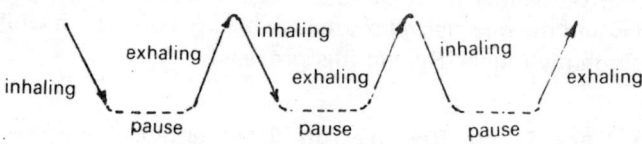

Fig. 25

Table 4

Respiration	Inhaling	Pause	Exhaling
Tongue Movement	touching hard palate	kept still	relaxed
Silently reciting the words	my-	self	calm
	my-	self sit	quiet
	my-	self sit quiet,	fit
	my-	self sit quiet for	fitness
Lower abdominal movement	expanding slowly	pause	contracting slowly

3. Mentally Controlled Respiration

The practitioner mentally guides Qi circulation and respiration in training Internal Qi and respiration. Three commonly used methods are detailed.

(1) Training Dantian Respiration This is also called the method of training congenital respiration. Focus the mind at Middle Dantian. When inhaling, concentrate on Qi being directed to Dantian and gathering in that area. As Qi gathers at Dantian and the abdomen contracts naturally with inhaling, pause for a while before exhaling slowly. Concentrate on Qi being exhaled and expanding outwardly from Dantian. As the abdomen naturally protrudes and the muscles relax while exhaling, pause for a while and then gently inhale. Repeat this process.

(2) Very Deep Respiration This requires very deep respiration. Although this method also combines deep respiration with mind focusing, it is different from other deep respiration training methods in requiring conducting Qi to the Yongquan acupoint during respiration. Of several different variations of this method, one is introduced. Mentally conduct Qi to Middle Dantian while inhaling, pause in quietude with breath held naturally and then exhale. While exhaling, mentally direct Qi from Middle Dantian past acupoints Qihai, Guanyuan and Huiyin along the legs to the Yongquan acupoint at the base of the balls of the feet. Pause in quietude to secure Qi there, holding the breath naturally before inhaling. When inhaling, mentally direct Qi from Yongquan back past the acupoints Chanagqiang and Mingmen to Middle Dantian. This exercise should be done gently, smoothly and slowly.

(3) Opening and Closing Method This is also called the body respiration method. It is based on the method of "training Dantian respiration." Two ways of practice are described. First, focus the mind at Middle Dantian, direct Qi/breath at Middle Dantian from all parts of the body, secure Qi/breath there, pause naturally for a few seconds, and then exhale. When exhaling, concentrate on Qi/breath spreading from Middle Dantian towards all parts of the body except the head, always keep the head cool and clear. When exhaling is finished, naturally pause for a while. After practice, respiration can bring the sensation of Qi permeating and being evenly distributed all over the body.

Focus the mind at Middle Dantian; while exhaling, concentrate on Qi breath being spread over all parts of the body except the head and direct all the pores of the entire body to open; then inhale and concentate on all the pores shutting with inhaling. Repeat, concentrating on the opening and closing of all of the body's pores with breathing. Qi movement sensations will be felt. This method is also called the pores' breathing method.

4. Respiration Conducted by Words

There are numerous methods of training respiration by silently reciting specific words. A major one is called the six- word formula, or the method of dispelling diseases and prolonging life. The phrase "breathing method" features coordinating six words with respiration in order to regulate the function of internal organs. According to ancient records, this method requires the words to be recited silently, though some variations call for audible recitation. The method we have used is clinically introduced. The author believes that these words may have acoustic ally with the corresponding body organs and tissues. The six words are: Xu, He, Si, Chui, Hu, and Xi. Different ancient documents have stated that these six words denote the five Yin visceral organs and the four seasons.

Records also indicate that this method was used throughout several dynasties and proved effective as a health care exercise. Some main variations of this method are presented here.

The Six Words and Five Yin Visceral Organs According to *Xiu Xi Guan Zuo Can Fan Yao* by Zhi Kai of the Sui dynasty, liver and gall bladder are combined with Xu exercise; the heart and small intestines with Si exercise; kidneys and urinary bladder with Hu exercise, and the Three Thirds (upper, middle, and lower) of the trunk and pericardium with Xi exercise. (Table 5.)

Table 5

The six words	Xu	He	Si	Chui	Hu	Xi
Viscera	liver	heart	lung	kidney	spleen	three thirds of trunk

The Six Words and Four Seasons According to *Xiu Ling Yao Zhi* by Leng Qian of the Ming dynasty, practising Xu exercise in spring is beneficial to the liver; He exercise in summer is beneficial to the lungs; Chui exercise, which can be practised in all seasons, can affect all the trunk's Three Thirds and harmonize Qi and blood; practising Hu exercise in all seasons helps vitalize the spleen and regulate spleen and stomach functions. (Table 6.)

Table 6

The six word	Xu	He	Si	Chui	Hu	Xi
The four seasons	spring	summer	autumn	winter	all seasons	dispelling heat

100

The Six Words and Movements In the Ming dynasty, the six words and movements of breathing exercises were studied and recorded in detail. We will describe how this method is used clinically today.

Xu is used with breathing exercises to harmonize liver Qi. Fold the arms at breast level with palms facing both feet upward with the force in the big toes; keep the eyes open and focus the mind on Middle Dantian. When folding the arms, softly memorize Xu in an inaudible, slightly vibrating voice. The same rule applies to the other words. Inhale and lower both hands to form a circle in front of the abdomen, the mind concentrated on relaxing. Pause for a while after inhaling and silently say Xu while exhaling. Repeat 30 times.

Use the word Si to harmonize lung Qi. Fold the arms in front of the forehead, palms forward, with force gathered in the palms. Relax the shoulders and focus the mind at Middle Dantian. When the arms rise in a circle, exhale and silently repeat the word Si. When the hands drop to breast level, concentrate on relaxing. Pause for a while after inhaling and silently say Si while exhaling. Repeat 30 times.

He harmonizes heart Qi. Cross the arms above the head, relax the elbows and shoulders, and focus the mind at Middle Dantian. When crossing the arms, say He while exhaling. When inhaling, lower both hands bilaterally to umbilicus level with the mind concentrated on relaxing. Pause for a while after inhaling and silently say He while exhaling. Repeat 30 times.

Chui harmonizes kidney Qi. Squat with hands pressed on the knees, relax the waist and elbows before exerting an outward force, and focus the mind at Middle Dantian or Rear Dantian (the Mingmen acupoint). When the elbows bow out, softly say Chui while exhaling. When inhaling, slightly draw in the waist with the mind concentrated on relaxing. Pause for a while after inhaling, silently say Chui while exhaling. Repeat 30 times.

Hu harmonizes spleen Qi. Sit (or stand or lie down) and clasp the hands (or place one hand on the back of the other), palms facing inward and pressed against the umbilicus (Front Dantian), focus the mind at Middle Dantian, exhale and naturally expand the abdomen by relaxing the muscles while silently saying Hu, rub the lips and swallow the saliva. When inhaling, contract the abdomen, thinking of relaxation. Pause for a while after inhaling, then say Hu silently while exhaling. Repeat 30 times.

Xi harmonizes Qi of the trunk's three segments. Sit (or stand or lie down) and flex the arms, letting the elbows slightly push out, and focus the mind at Middle Dantian. Silently say Xi while exhaling and relaxing the elbows and arms. Pause for a while after inhaling. Repeat 30 times.

Guidelines for the Six-Word Breathing Methods

(A)Six-word Practice Repeat the words silently while exhaling, then inhale naturally. Inhale with the nose and exhale with the mouth, or breathe with both the nose and mouth if the nostrils are impeded. One count of respiration includes inhalation and exhalation. Repeat the single-word practice 20 to 30 times; for the six-word practice, repeat each word seven times.

(B) Single-word Practice The practitioner can practise the single-word exercise according to different diseases. For example, patients with liver disease can mainly practise the word Xu. The word to be used can also be selected according to the four seasons: Xu can be practised in spring because Xu means liver and spring also associates with liver; Ha in summer because it associates with the heart and so does the heart; Si in autumn because Si associates with the lungs, and so does autumn; Chui in winter because it associates with the kidneys and so does winter. After practising the single-word exercise, either Hu or Xi, or the the method combining both words should be practised, even though the method was originally selected for an internal organ or season.

Because Hu is related to the spleen, the breathing method using Hu is helpful in regulating spleen and stomach function and beneficial to the other organs. Because Xi is related with the trunk's Three Thirds, the method using Xi helps recharge the body's Qi metabolism and regulate Internal Qi. Keep the mind tranquil throughout the exercise, regulate the respiration, conduct Qi to Middle Dantian and finish all the necessary preparations prior to exercise. Before the exercise ends, tap the teeth, rotate the tongue, swallow the saliva and conduct Qi to Middle Dantian to assume the closing posture.

(C) **The Order of the Six Words** The six words can be practised in one round of exercise. Their order is according to that of the Five Elements: Si belongs to metal in the lungs and metal produces water; Chui belongs to water in the kidneys and water produces wood; Xu belongs to wood in the liver and wood produces fire; Hu belongs to earth in the spleen and fire produces earth and Xi vitalizes the trunk's Three Thirds and regulates Qi.

(III) Mind Focusing in Quiescent Qigong Exercise

These methods feature focusing the mind at certain acupoints of the body or on certain objects in the surroundings. The mind can also be focused by thinking of some other things or words. It is essentially an approach to quiescence required by Qigong. Additional effects can also be achieved by the use of different mind-focusing methods. Therefore, mind-focusing methods should be selected according to individual physical condition or purpose. All methods of focusing the mind should be done naturally in order to achieve the desired effects and avoid stress.

Respiration and posture in Qigong exercise are all guided by mind activity. So, mind focusing plays a leading role in Qigong exercise.

Mental activity reflects messages from objective things. They therefore include messages in the brain. Under certain circumstances, mental activity can produce important effects on the health, aiding recovery from diseases and influencing physiological function. This has been proved through long-time practice. When a person runs, his heartbeat will quicken, usually to a frequency high enough to meet the physiological needs. However, a person who has just begun to learn running may experience accelerated heartbeat before the starting gun fires. A person who dreams of running a race may experience quickened heartbeat as in the actual running state or even be startled awake to find his heartbeat quickened, though his energy consumption remains at the lowest level--the state of sleep. These are illustrations of how the mind or consciousness can affect the body's physiological activity. Another example is that feedback psychological therapy has cured some diseases. This, too, illustrates how conscious mind activity can influence physiological and pathological activity. Many ancient Chinese fables, such as "quenching one's thirst by thinking of plums," and "mistaking the reflection of bow a in the cup for a snake," vividly demonstrate this point. Therefore, harmful mind activity can induce disease under certain circumstances. Mental training of Qigong helps normalize and strengthen physiological functions through mental direction.

1. Focusing the Mind at Certain Acupoints

Focusing the mind at certain acupoints brings about certain physiological changes and can cure﹒some diseases. Some commonly used methods are presented here.

(1) **Focusing the Mind at Dantian** Dantian is the traditional center of attention for ancient Qigong practitioners. Generally the term referred to the Lower, the Middle and the Upper Dantian points. Some practitioners included a fourth one, Rear Dantian, and others even included a fifth one, Front Dantian. All five Dantian points are to be described here. Each of these points refers to an acupoint along a channel or collateral. Upper Dantian is the Yintang acupoint between the eyebrows; Lower Dantian is the Guanyuan acupoint below the umbilicus which also serves as the midline; Front Dantian is the Qizhong acupoint on the umbilicus; Rear Dantian is the Mingmen acupoint at the waist level on the back midline, and Middle Dantian is located between the Front and Rear Dantian points where the Chong Channel travels through. (Figs. 27, 28 and 29.)

(A) **Upper Dantian** It is Yingtang located between the eyebrows (Fig. 26). According to Qigong specialists, Upper Dantian is where mental activities are based and where physical movement, breath regulation and mind-calming activities start. The guideline of "calming the mind and focusing it at the Qi point"

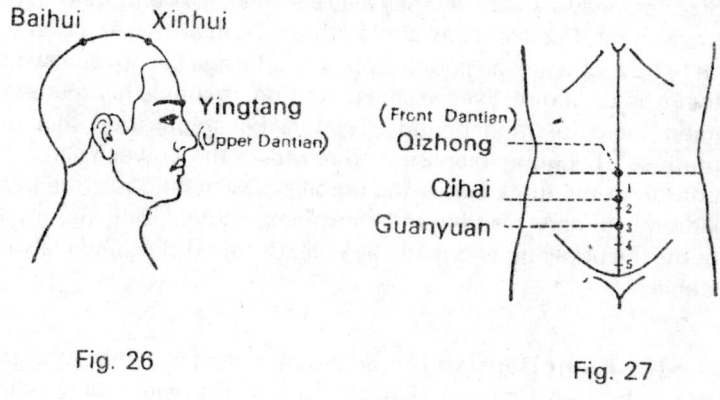

Fig. 26

Fig. 27

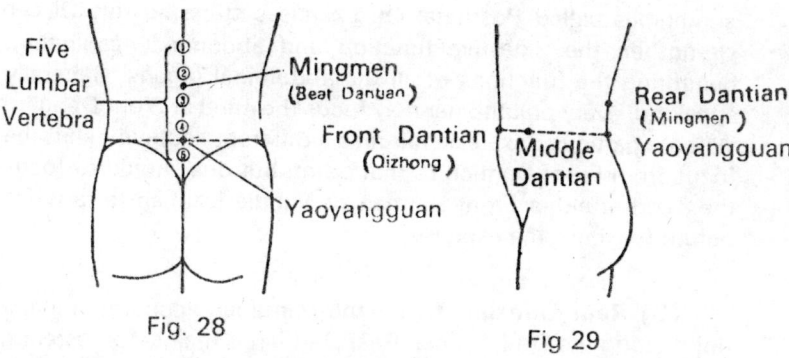

Fig. 28

Fig 29

refers to this very Upper Dantian acupoint. According to TCM theories of Yin/Yang and channels and collaterals, the Du Channel governs all Yang channels. And all Yang channels travel upward to end in the head and face. Focusing the mind at Upper Dantian can easily cause Qi to rush upward into the head. For this reason, those who have not acquired the basics of Qigong exercise or adopt incorrect methods may feel the head get heavy and tight if they focus on Upper Dantian.

Those who have passed middle age and do not keep up physical exercise are likely to suffer deficiency of Kidney (Original) Qi. In them, excessive Qi in the upper body with Qi deficiency in the lower body may occur. Lower limb weakness and dizziness may also occur. They may also feel dizzy and weak in the lower limbs. Focusing the mind at Upper Dantian makes it easy for Qi to flow upward, so people above middle age are not advised to focus on this point. Even skilled practitioners should not focus the mind there for long periods. It must be emphasized that the purpose of Qigong exercise is to reinforce the Lower Yuan--the portion of the trunk below the umbilicus which houses the liver, kidneys, urinary bladder and intestines. By vitalizing the lower body, the upper body is made flexible, the mind clear and walking stable.

(B) Front Dantian This acupoint is located at the umbilicus along the Ren Channel (Fig. 27). Front Dantian mainly trains abdominal respiration and gastric and spleen Qi, which is sometimes called Postnatal Qi. Exercises stressing this Qi can strengthen the digestive function and abdominal respiration, benefiting the functions of all the abdominal organs. Generally speaking, every practitioner may focus the mind at Front Dantian. When a particular exercise requires a different acupoint, shift the focus from Front Dantian to that point, but one should re-focus the mind at either Front Dantian or Middle Dantian for a while before finishing the exercise.

(C) Rear Dantian This is the Mingmen acupoint, a major point along the Du Channel. Rear Dantian is mainly for fostering the vital energy of Mingmen (Refer to the chapter on Qi transformation and Qigong exercise.--Editor), which is also called Congenital Qi. Throughout the dynasties, medical doctors and Qigong experts have paid special attention to the effects of Mingmen, which they regarded as the gate of life located on the most important of the 12 channels, the receiver of Congenital Qi and the source of changes benefiting growth. Focusing the mind at this point can reinforce kidney Yang, enrich the vital Qi of Mingmen and strengthen the body's Qi metabolism (transformation). Focusing on Mingmen is usually undertaken after one has mastered the basic skills of focusing at Front Dantian or Middle Dantian. After focusing at Dantian, Qi should be conducted to and fixed at Middle Dantian for a while before finishing the Qigong exercise.

(D) Middle Dantian This point is located behind the umbilicus and in front of the Yaoyangguan acupoint along the Chong Channel (Fig. 29). Focusing the mind here helps promote abdominal respiration, foster Internal Qi, cultivate Essential Qi, improve respiratory system function and blood circulation, and eliminate obstructions of the channels and collaterals. In addition, Middle Dantian dominates functions of the spleen and stomach. So focusing the mind here can strengthen their function, improving the appetite, and promoting digestion and absorption. Therefore, Middle Dantian is considered the basis of Qigong exercise.

(E) Lower Dantian This is the Guanyuan acupoint located about 10 centimeters below the umbilicus. It is an important point on the Ren Channel in the lower trunk and the reservoir of Original Qi. Focusing at this point enriches Yang Qi and strengthens the constitution. According to the Yin/Yang theory, the upper part of the body is Yang, and the lower part Yin. Yin and Yang always interact, but Yin is the basis of Yang. Therefore, Qi should be conducted downward during practice so that it returns to its source. Qigong specialists describe this method as "guiding fire to its source" because heart and kidneys complement and balance each other. The heart's fire and kidney's water mutually supplement; kidney Yin nurtures heart Yin and heart Yang nurtures kidney Yang, which is helpful in calming the mind. As long as kidney Qi coordinates with heart Qi, one is stable. When ending Qigong practice one should conduct Qi to Middle Dantian and focus the mind there for a while. Some people believe Lower Dantian is at the Huiyin acupoint midway between the anus and vagina or testes. But this book follows the theory identifying Lower Dantian with the Guanyuan acupoint.

(2) Methods of Focusing the Mind on Acupoints The practitioner can focus the mind on acupoints in other parts of the body by the same method as that for Dantian. On the channels alone, there are more than 360 acupoints, all acupoints of the body totaling more than 600 In addition, there are many new acupoints discovered since the Ming dynasty. After Dantian the most commonly used acupoints are Yongquan and Qihai.

(A) Qihai Acupoint Located about 5 centimeters below the umbilicus (Fig. 27), it is a major point along the Ren Channel. Some practitioners identify this point as Lower Dantian. Qihai is described as the Sea of Qi, which produces Original Qi and strengthens the constitution. Therefore, focusing at this point is helpful to abdominal respiration, training Internal Qi, reinforcing the lower trunk, promoting digestive function and strengthening the constitution. After focusing the mind at this point, one should conduct Qi to Middle Dantian just before finishing the Qigong exercise.

(B) Yongquan Acupoint This is a major point along the kidney channel (Fig. 30). Focusing on this point helps strengthen kidney Qi, conduct Qi to its origin smoothly, and reinforce the lower trunk. Because Yongquan's location is the lowest on the body, focusing the mind at this point can lead Qi to flow downward. Its benefits include preventing and treating excessiveness in the upper body and deficiency in the lower body and avoiding dizziness, irritability and weak lower limbs.

(3) Focusing the Mind on Channels and Collaterals The theory of channels and collaterals is one of the basic component of TCM. Many countries in the world have been studying the theory which states that there is a holistic system of channels and collaterals in the body. This system serves as channels for blood circulation and integrates the five Yin visceral organs, six Yang viscera and extremities into a holism. If the channels and collaterals are patent, blood circulation will be normal and no diseases can occur; if they are not patent, blood circulation will be obstructed and diseases may occur. Therefore, patency of the channels and collaterals figures prominently in the body's physiological and pathological state. According to TCM theories, the circulation of Qi and blood in the channels and collaterals relies on promotion of their Qi--physiological function. Essential Qi (Zhen Qi) is the motivating force of their Qi. Qigong exercise aims at the cultivation of Essential Qi dredging the channels and collaterals and harmonizing Qi and blood.

There are 12 cardinal channels in the system of channels and collaterals, each being related with one of the 12 internal organs-- heart, liver, lungs, spleen, kidneys, pericardium, bladder, stomach,

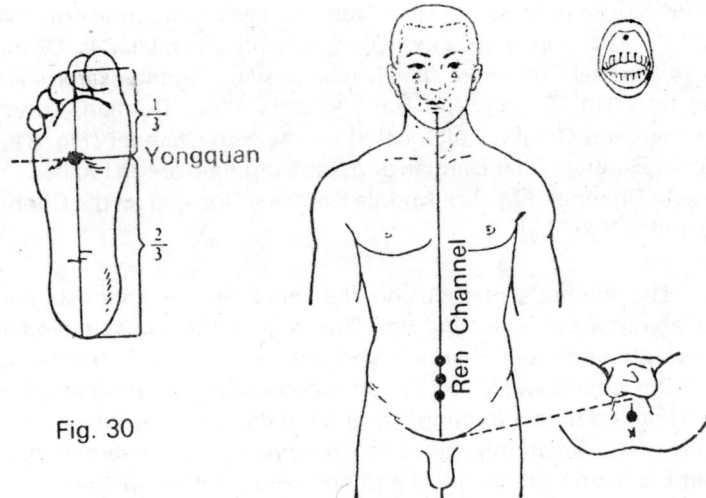

Yongquan

Fig. 30

Ren Channel

Fig. 31

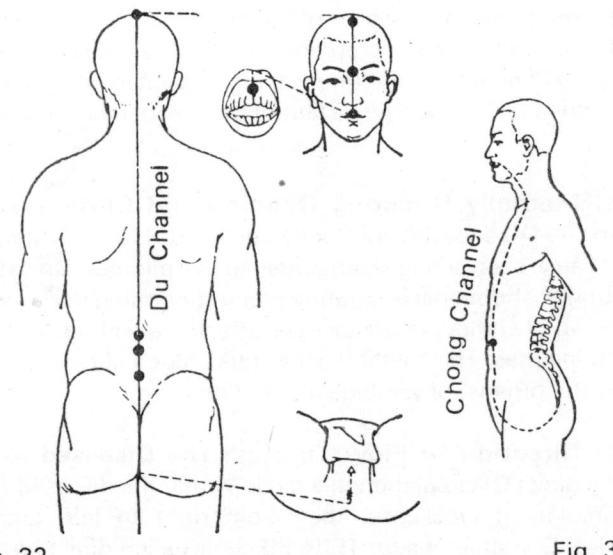

Du Channel

Chong Channel

Fig. 32

Fig. 33

large intestine, small intestine, urinary bladder, and the trunk (divided into three sections and regarded as one internal organ.-- Editor). There are eight extra channels and 15 collaterals. Of the extra channels, the most closely related with Qigong exercise are the Ren, Du, Chong, and Dai channels. Front Dantian, Lower Dantian and Qihai are all located on the Ren Channel (Fig. 31); Upper Dantian, Rear Dantian and Yaoyangguan are all located on the Du Channel (Fig. 32); Middle Dantian is located on the Chong Channel (Fig. 33).

The methods of focusing the mind on the channels and collaterals are dynamic in form. They require the focus of mind to move along certain channels and collaterals with Qi following. The Big Circuit and Small Circuit exercises fall into this category. The method for conducting Qi/breath to the heels described in the chapter on breathing methods exemplifies the combination of mind focusing on channels and collaterals with respiration.

(4) Focusing the Mind on Diseased Areas In this exercise, the mind is concentrated on a diseased area according to the basic mind-focusing requirements. Generally, these methods are not used in treating diseases of the head and chest, unless the patient has adequate comprehension of Qigong and is individually directed by a Qigong master. Presented here are three of the methods which should be taught by an experienced Qigong teacher.

(A) Mentally Directing Opening and Closing of Qi Flow in the Diseased Area Gently open and close Qi flow in the diseased area, each acting lasting three to five minutes. Do natural respiration or abdominal respiration while continuing the opening and closing of Qi flow in the disease-affected area for altogether 10 to 20 minutes. This method accelerates blood circulation and vitalizes the organs' physiological functions.

(B) Directing Qi Flow Through the Diseased Areas Mentally direct Qi circulation in a circle within the diseased area. First circulate it clockwise, then from right to left, counter clockwise. Continue this for 15 to 30 circles each direction. The entire process should last between five to 10 minutes. Before finishing the exercise, direct Qi to Middle Dantian and then practise abdominal respiration several times. This method produces effects similar to those of the proceeding exercise.

(C) Elevating Organs With Visceroptosis by Mental Direction and Qi By focusing the mind at the lower border of the diseased organ and mentally directing it to rise about 13 centimeters above the umbilicus. The organ with visceroptosis can be raised under the supervision of an experienced doctor.

2. Focusing Mentally on Objects in the Surroundings

This is another method of entering mental tranquillity. The objects on which the mind is focused can be fragrant flowers, verdant trees or grass, exquisite paintings, sculptures, green hills, twinkling stars, a river, the moon, or a clear blue sky. The mind is shifted to the chosen object only after one has calmed the mind, regulated respiration, conducted Qi to Dantian and eliminated distracting thoughts. The eyes, which can be half open, should look straight at the object. If sitting down, close the eyes after entering quiescence, but focus the mind at Dantian instead of an outside object. The object of focus should be at least one meter away. Generally, the line of vision should be on eye level, or a little bit higher or lower, in order to avoid elevating or depressing Qi/breath too much.

3. Focusing the Mind on Something

Thinking is a form of conscious activity. So focusing the mind by thinking of something is called the thinking method. As a Qigong method, it uses mental focus on remembrance of some thing or event which can induce quiescence. All things experienced leave an impression on the brain through the sense organs, such as the eyes, ears, nose, tongue, or skin. Recalling this, the practitioner re-animates the scenes preoccupying the cerebral quiescent state. Relaxing and comfortable experiences, such as a hot shower, and beautiful scenery like beaches, mountains, lakes and rivers, all can be recalled for this method.

4. Focusing the Mind on the Meaning of Words

This is also a thinking method. Imagine sensing the meaning of a word, which is beneficial to the health, in order to produce beneficial effects on the physiological activity of the human body. For example, relaxation, tranquillity, standing as a pine tree, sitting like a desk clock and walking through are words which can be considered and experienced imaginatively.

II. Common Methods of Quiescent Qigong Exercise

There are numerous methods of doing quiescent Qigong exercise. Each includes posture, respiration and mind focusing. To do the exercise correctly, the practitioner must skillfully coordinate these three steps appropriately for the individual constitution. For instance, a patient with hypertension can choose among sitting, standing and prone postures. Either natural or abdominal respiration may be used. The mind can be focused at Middle Dantian or Yongquan. A patient with indigestion can choose among the natural standing, sitting and prone postures, breathing methods and the points for mind focusing. Four basic methods are introduced here.

(I) Relaxing Exercise

This form of Quiescent Qigong Exercise is relatively easy to learn. Because both physical and mental relaxation are primary requirements in doing quiescent Qigong, Relaxing Exercise, which can be practised as a warm-up, is an essential form of quiescent Qigong exercise. It is often recommended to beginners as a preliminary method of Qigong exercise, though it can also be used to relieve fatigue, induce sleep, and treat hypertension, neurasthenia, bronchitis, bronchial asthma, toxemia of pregnancy, pelvic inflammation, heart paralysis, climacteric syndrome, etc.

1. Posture

This exercise can be done in all three postures. But the sitting posture is easier than the standing posture to master. The prone posture is mainly taken by people in poor health. When taking the selected posture, gently close the eyes, or keep them half open. If you find standing firm is difficult, open the eyes.

2. Respiration

Beginners should practise natural respiration first, and then proceed gradually to deep abdominal respiration.

3. Mental Activity

The practitioner should concentrate on muscle relaxation and the resultant sensations. The mental activity should also be directed to induce relaxation.

4. Exercise

The main points are the muscles and mental activity. To relax the muscles, one must relax the mind first. However, relaxation is not absolute. Since Relaxing Exercise requires maintaining a certain posture, some muscles are stressed a bit. Relaxation just means relatively less tension than usual. If the beginner fails to sense relaxation, the fists can be clenched and then relaxed slowly. Repeat this several times so the sensation of relaxation is understood.

Relaxation can be divided into four kinds:

(1) **Relaxing Part by Part** Divide the body into segments and relax from the head down. This method is also called the three- part relaxation method. First relax from the head to the shoulders, next from the shoulders to the hips including the arms, and finally from the hips to the toes. Relaxation can be fortified by coordination with respiration. Keep practising until the result is satisfactory. In the sitting posture, relax to the hips, concentrate on the idea of sitting like a desk clock, and then coordinate relaxation with respiration. In the standing posture, relax to the toes, concentrate on standing like a pine tree, and then coordinate relaxation with respiration.

(2) **Relaxing Line by Line** Divide the body up by several lines and then relax line by line. The three-line method, for example, refers to the head-sacral bone line along the spine as

Line 1, each of the two shoulder-hand lines is Line 2, and each of the two hip-foot lines is Line 3. Relax in that order and add respiration. Repeat until relaxation is satisfactory. The exercise should be done slowly and stably. Requirements for the sitting and standing postures are the same as those for the method of relaxing part by part.

(3) **Holistic Relaxation** Relax the body from head to feet. Relax to the buttocks in the sitting posture and follow the same guidelines as those for the method of relaxing part by part. During practice, imagine that it is drizzling or that your are taking a hot shower. Simultaneously, exhale and say the word "relax" silently. When you are totally relaxed, relax your mind and only partially concentrate on relaxation. This mental concentration is not suitable for patients with hypertension.

(4) **Relaxation of Certain Parts** This method is used to relax diseased viscera and is also called the selective relaxing method or partially relaxing method. It is a relatively difficult method of relaxation, which is used to train viscera relaxation and relaxation of the extremities. Relaxation here refers to intermittent relaxation which includes slight muscular movement in reaction to the movement resulting from the coordinated activities of the mind, muscles and respiration. After exhaling a long breath, the practitioner should combine inhaling with gentle contraction of the selected viscera. Relax and exhale again. Repeat the process gently. This method is not suitable for visceroptosis patients but is particularly effective in locally accelerating visceral blood circulation and relieving mental and physical fatigue.

(5) **Ending Exercise** Gradually focus the mind at and draw Qi from different parts to Middle Dantian, no matter where it is being focused, drawing Qi to this point. This is called returning Qi to its source. For beginners, place the palm of one hand in the umbilical region, and put the other hand on top of it. Press the hands clockwise around the navel for 20 to 30 circles, letting the orbit get bigger with the epigastrium and pubis as the upper and lower edges of the last circle. A moment later, press counterclockwise with the circle getting smaller and smaller and stop with hands at the navel. Rub the palms together, open the

eyes, and move all parts of the body, or do a set of exercise. This ending process is very important because it insures better effects of Qigong exercise. Therefore, it should not be done perfunctorily, and Qi should be stably returned to its source--the umbilicus. (Figs. 34 and 35.)

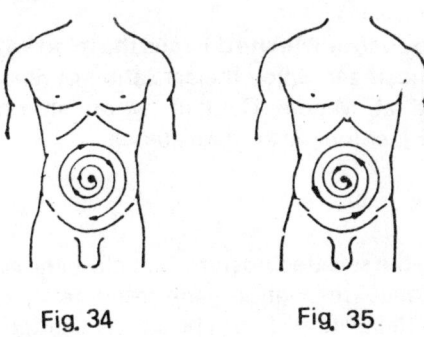

Fig. 34   Fig. 35

(II) Relaxing Quiescent Qigong Exercise

Relaxing Quiescent Qigong Exercise is an elementary part of Qigong. It should be practised in a relaxed and quiescent state, which aid in recovery of mental and physical strength. Therefore, it is considered a rudimentary course for all types of Qigong exercise. It is prescribed for hypertension, neurasthenia, gastric and duodenal ulcers, habitual constipation, gastrointestinal neurosis, vegetative neurosis, pulmonary tuberculosis, chronic bronchitis, bronchial asthma, chronic hepatitis, menopausal syndrome and chronic pelvic inflammation. It also provides painless labor and is often used to relieve mental and physical fatigue and as a sleep induction method.

1. Posture

Sitting, standing and prone postures are all satisfactory. However, relaxation is obtained easily in the sitting and standing postures, while the prone posture is recommended for those in poor health with chronic diseases. Half close the eyes or open them when practising in the standing or sitting postures, or open the eyes completely if it is hard to stand firm.

2. Respiration

Start with natural respiration, and gradually change to abdominal respiration.

3. Mind-focusing Method Focus the mind with any of the methods introduced and enjoy the sensation of relaxation. Then focus the mind at Middle Dantian or on an object in the surroundings or just look into the distance.

4. Exercise

After taking the selected posture, half close the eyes, calm the spirits and regulate respiration, and then relax to enter the quiescent state. Relaxation should be slowly carried out from the head down to Middle Dantian while exhaling, or from the head to Mingmen between the kidneys on the spine. The upper extremities are relaxed from scapula to elbow. Now inhale, and relax while inhaling again from Middle Dantian to the sacro- acetabular region (or from Mingmen to the sacro-acetabular region,) at the same time relaxing the upper extremities from the elbows to the hands. After inhaling, relax while exhaling once more from the sacro-acetabular region to the soles of feet. Relaxing the whole body, conduct Qi downward, just like the drizzle. (This method is inadvisable for those with hypertension. While exhaling, silently say Song (meaning relaxation) so as to induce relaxation physically and mentally. Relaxing the body requires cerebral cortex quiescence, and vice versa. When relaxing to the soles of the feet, focus the mind there, imagining yourself to be an old, deeply rooted tree. This is called the method of focusing the mind at Yongquan. The mind can also be focused at Middle Dantian or Mingmen. After focusing on Yongquan, the exercise of elevating and lowering Qi can be started. Lower Qi from Middle Dantian to Yongquan while exhaling, and hold the breath a while. While inhaling, conduct Qi upward from Yongquan to Middle Dantian through the coccygo-sacral region and Mingmen. This can be practised repeatedly, or alternately varied by focusing the mind at

Middle Dantian and breathing naturally.

5. Ending Exercise

Gradually focus on Middle Dantian, no matter where it was originally focused. Gather Qi from all parts of the body at Middle Dantian. This is called returning Qi to its source. For beginners, place the palm of one hand at the umbilicus region, and put the other on it, rub the abdomen clockwise around the umbilicus for 20 to 30 circles with the orbit becoming bigger and bigger. The epigastrium and pubis are the upper and lower edges of the last circle. One moment later, rub counterclockwise for 20 to 30 times with circle becoming smaller and smaller to stop the hands at the umbilicus. Rub the palms together, open the eyes, and move all parts of the body, or do setting-up exercises. This concluding process is very important, for it ensures better Qigong effects. It should not be done perfunctorily, and Qi should be stably returned to its source (umbilicus).

(III) Breathing Exercise of Qigong

This includes some special methods of abdominal respiration, such as direct respiration, retrograde respiration and stop-go respiration which can also be carried out in combination with focused mind activity. It markedly aids the functions of the respiratory and digestive systems and benefits the functions of other systems, especially in treating gastric and duodenal ulcers, dyspepsia, neurasthenia, pulmonary tuberculosis and gastroptosis, etc. It can also be used to build the constitution.

1. Posture

Simple sitting, cross-legged sitting, supine and sidewats lying postures are commonly used in this exercise.

2. Respiration

Clockwise and retrograde abdominal respiration are the best methods. Try to use the stop-go breathing method, which integrates mental direction of Qi by silently reciting words and using stop-go respiration. This can be subdivided into the inhale-exhale-stop method (also called soft respiration method) and inhale-stop-exhale method (also called hard respiration method.) The former is relatively soft and even, and is easily mastered. So it is suitable for beginners and those who are debilitated or ill. Patients in the recovery stage and healthy people prefer the latter form for building the constitution. But it may cause a sense of suffocation or abdominal distention if it is done improperly. Do not expand the abdominal region with exertion and avoid forced stop of breathing. Do it naturally and advance step by step.

The inhale-exhale-stop method needs training. Breathe with the nose, or with nose and mouth together. While inhaling, with the tip of tongue touching the hard palate, silently recite the first word, "calm" in the exemplary phrase "calm myself." Meanwhile, conduct Qi to Middle Dantian and slowly expand the lower abdomen without exertion. Now, exhale slowly with tongue tip touching the lower incisors, silently say the word "myself" in the previous phrase and contract the lower abdomen. Stop breathing without moving the tongue or abdomen. The process can be repeated and the number of the words may be gradually increased from two to nine.

The inhale-stop-exhale method also needs training. Breathe with the nose, or inhale with the nose and exhale with mouth. While inhaling, have the tongue touch the hard palate and read silently the first word "sit" in the phrase "sit silently by myself." Slowly conduct Qi to Middle Dantian and expand the lower abdomen. Then, hold the breath without any motion of the tongue or the abdomen and say to yourself the second word "silently" in the phrase. After that, exhale slowly with tongue tip touching the lower incisors and repeat silently the words "by myself" while gently contracting the lower abdomen. This process can be repeated. the number of words read can be gradually increased from four to nine.

(IV) Standing Qigong Exercise

Standing Qigong Exercise is practised in a variety of standing postures, which can be selected according to the individual's health. Generally, they are suitable for those in good health, o patients in the recovery stage. The exercise restores health and helps build the constitution. However, in order to avoid fatigue, the exercise should not last too long, especially for beginners. It is also contraindicated for those who are in very poor health or suffer from severe diseases. The advantage of Standing Qigong Exercise is that it can be done without any special facilities indoors or outdoors, and can be practised for a longer or shorter period of time at the practitioner's convenience. It is recommended for the treatment of hypertension, neurasthenia, chronic bronchitis and menopausal syndrome.

Standing Qigong posture can be divided into the resting postures, high-level postures, median-level postures and low-level postures. When the low body position is combined with a high position of hands, the weight sustained by the practitioner is heaviest. Therefore, the high-level postures are suitable for beginners, and the resting postures for those in poor health. This point will be made clear in the description of the three types of postures.

1. Basic Posture

This can be divided into the double-weighted basic posture and the single-weighted posture. In either posture, focus the mind either on something in the environment or at Middle Dantian. Use natural respiration or abdominal respiration.

(1) Double-weighted Basic Posture This refers to the feet bearing equal weight. Stand with the feet parallel and shoulder- width apart. Flex the knees and revolve them a bit inwards, and have the feet exert equal force just like a tree rooted in the ground. The upper body should be kept straight, with hips in a half sitting position. Keep the head level with the eyes gazing straight ahead. The chest is relaxed (not thrown out) and the abdomen slightly contracted. The neck and back incline a bit backwards. Lower the shoulders, hold the arms a little away from the body and hang downward naturally with flexed elbows slightly bowed out. (Figs. 4 and 5.)

(2) Single-weighted Basic Posture The feet are parted

obliquely at an 85-degree angle and the front foot slightly braced, with 30 percent of the weight on the front foot and 70 percent on the back foot. With the left foot in the back, the posture is a left-weighted one; if the right foot is in back, it is a right-weighted posture. The distance between the feet is about one foot to one foot and a half, whichever is more comfortable. The lower part of the body forms a slight lunge in a half sitting position (Figs. 36 and 37); the lunge is more apparent the farther the feet are separated, the greatest distance between them being two feet (Figs. 38 and 39). Revolve the knees a bit inwards while exerting an enclosing force, with the front foot taking 30 percent of the force and the back foot 70 percent. Stand like a tree deeply rooted in the ground. Requirements for the upper body are the same as those for the double-weighted basic posture.

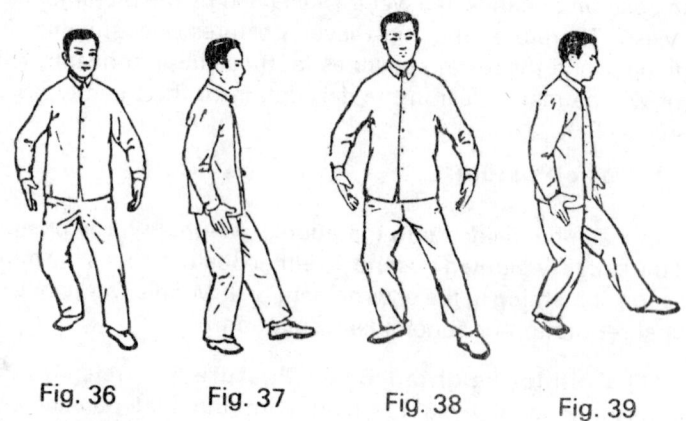

Fig. 36   Fig. 37   Fig. 38   Fig. 39

2. Resting Posture

This is the standing posture in which the body sustains the lightest weight. It is suitable for people with weak constitutions or those who need to relieve fatigue after practising standing Qigong exercise. It can also be practised if one is standing quietly for a rest. The body position is half a fist lower than the practitioner's height. The posture can be varied into several subtypes to suit the practitioner. The force required of the following postures increases gradually from the first to the last.

(1) Gently Leaning Resting Posture This can be based on either double-weighted or single-weighted postures. In the former, follow the basic guidelines for the double-weighted posture and stand beside a table, tree, or wall, gently rest the buttocks on the edge of the table or surface to lighten the body weight. Keep the upper body straight and comfortable; now put both hands into the trouser pocket hand back resting on the pocket edge to relieve the weight of the arm. This completes the posture. The hand positions can be varied in four different ways: resting the backs of the wrists on the ipsilateral hips (Fig. 40), hanging palms sideways beside the thighs (Fig. 41), palms facing down in front of the lower abdomen (Fig. 42), and palms facing up at waist level (Fig. 43). The muscle tension gradually increases with the posture changes. Respiration and mind-focusing methods are the same as for the basic posture.

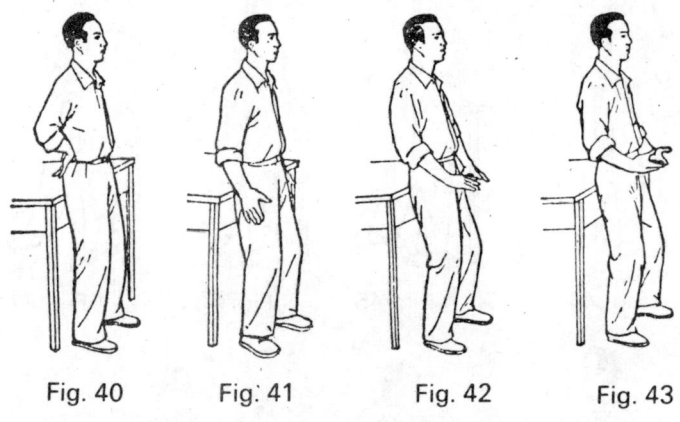

Fig. 40   Fig. 41   Fig. 42   Fig. 43

For the single-weighted posture, stand in the way described above. In the double-weighted posture with hands in the pockets, rotate the body leftwards with 70 percent of the body weight on the right side (Fig. 44); change to the left-weighted posture half way through the exercise, as is always done in single- weighted exercises. Other single-weighted postures are: gently leaning resting posture weighted right with wrists on the hips (Fig. 45); gently leaning resting posture weighted right with palms facing thighs (Fig. 46); gently leaning resting posture weighted right with palms facing down (Fig. 47), and gently leaning resting posture weighted right with palms facing up (Fig. 48).

(2) Resting Posture With Hands Supporting This can be done with either double weight or single weight. In the double weight, stand in the standard double-weighted posture; place both hands on the back of a chair, banister, or the edge of a table, with the body leaning forward 15 to 20 degrees and the hands about 20 degrees above stomach level; relax the chest and abdomen while half sitting, the eyes looking forward and downwards (Fig. 49). To do the single-weighted exercise, place the body weight 70 percent on the back foot. In the right-weighted exercise, move the right foot one or two feet backwards,

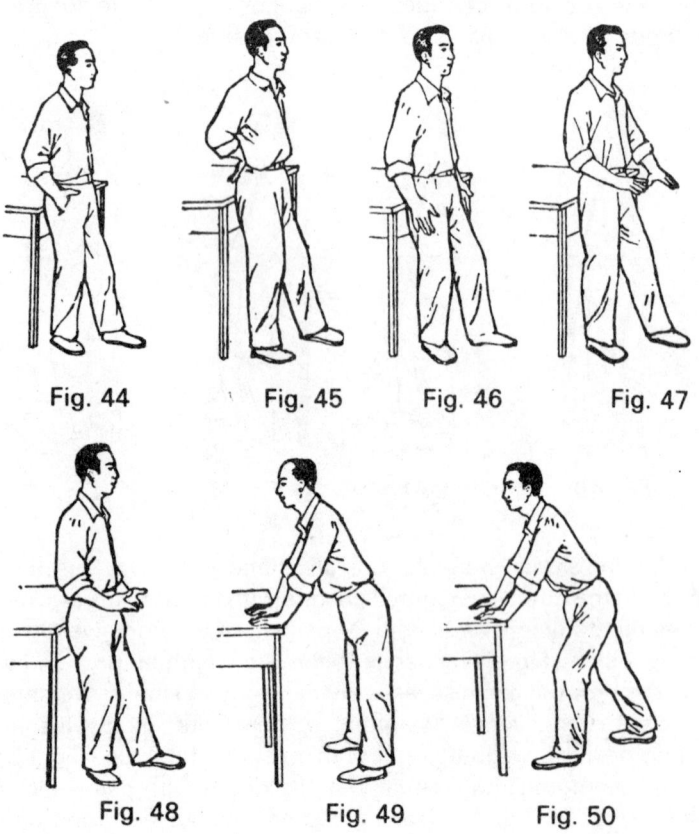

Fig. 44   Fig. 45   Fig. 46   Fig. 47

Fig. 48   Fig. 49   Fig. 50

flex the front leg, keep the back leg straight with the trunk slightly leaning forward, and relax the chest and abdomen with buttocks inclining backwards and eyes looking forward and down (Fig. 50). Alternate the right-weighted with the left-weighted posture. Respiration and mind focusing in this posture are the same as in the basic posture.

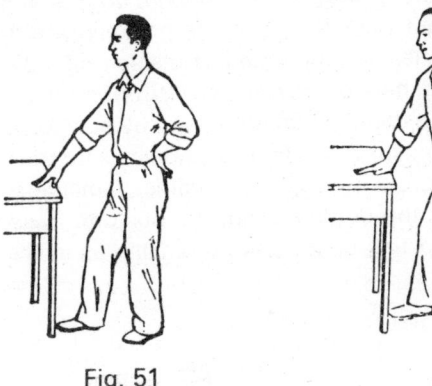

Fig. 51   Fig. 52

(3) Resting Posture With one Hand Supporting This is a single-weighted posture. In the left-weighted posture, place the right foot in front and the left foot in back, about one foot apart, rest the right hand on the edge of a table or the back of a chair with the forearm bent or straight, place the back of the left wrist on the ipsilateral hip, slightly rotate the head and trunk leftwards to shift the body weight onto the left side while eyes look straight forward or forward and down, and slightly flex the knees to form a small lunge in a half sitting position with body weight on the left foot. The front foot takes 30 percent of the weight and the back foot 70 percent, or leave 40 percent on the front foot and 60 percent on the back foot. The mind should be concentrated on "I want to walk, but have stopped here" or "I want to stop, but am walking" or "I can neither stop nor walk." The right shoulder and elbow should not be overloaded with the weight of the upper body. Keep the upper body straight (Fig. 51), or stoop slightly (Fig. 52). For a variation, place the front foot one fist forward and raise the toes with the heel as pivot; move the toes leftwards and then

123

rightwards, or tap the foot for movement. The respiration and mind-focusing methods used are the same as in the basic posture. Repeat and alternate the left-weighted with the right-weighted posture.

(4) **Resting Posture With Hands Pocketed** This can be practised either double weighted or single weighted. In the double-weighted posture, stand in the standard double-weighted basic posture, and put both hands in the pockets of either the jacket or the trousers, leaving the thumbs outside (Fig. 53). Since this posture requires neither leaning nor support, the weight bearing is increased in comparison with the previous postures. In the single-weighted posture, follow the guidelines for the single-weighted basic posture with upper extremities remaining in the same position as for the double-weighted posture. Respiration and mind focusing in this posture are the same as in the basic posture (Fig. 54).

Fig. 53   Fig. 54

(5) **Back-supported Resting Posture** This can be practised in both the double-weighted and single-weighted postures. In the double-weighted basic posture, use both hands to support the lumber region with palms facing outward, finger pointing downward and the dorsal sides of the hands placed against the rear of the crista iliaca, relax the shoulder joints leaving the armpits naturally open, and slightly droop the elbows (Fig.

55). For this exercise in the single-weighted posture, take the single-weighted basic posture. In the right-weighted posture, turn the trunk slightly leftwards with 70 percent of the body weight on the right foot and hands resting on the buttocks on either side of the spine (Fig. 56). When completing the right-weighted posture, shift to the left-weighted posture. Other requirements are the same as for the basic posture.

Fig. 55   Fig. 56

3. High-level Postures

These are the most basic of all the common postures. They can be used to treat diseases and for prophylaxis. The body position of high-level postures is half a fist lower than the resting postures, or one fist lower than one's height. The lower the position, the heavier is the weight sustained by the practitioner. High-level postures require greater muscle tensity than the resting postures. Seven variations are presented here.

(1) Drooping Posture This is suitable for either double-weighted or single-weighted posture. In the double-weighted posture, stand in the basic double-weighted posture, slightly flex the knees which should not protrude beyond the tips, half sit and slightly contract the abdomen with weight centered at the hips, keep the buttocks aligned with the heels, keep the upper body upright, relax the shoulders with armpits naturally open, flex the

elbows following the guideline "the arms in semicircles and semi-empty at the armpits," and slightly bow out the elbows with palms facing the body and rotating inwards (Fig. 57).

Besides the mentioned effects, this posture is mainly used to train elbow force. With increased force in the upper extremities, muscle tension in other parts of the body increases. In addition to the mind-focusing and respiration requirements of the basic posture, mental activity in this exercise is mainly concentrated on the sensation induced by drooping arms while elbowing and sensations of Qi/breath movement throughout the body. The mental activity should be spaced out with relaxation, to avoid fatigue. For the single-weighted posture, take the basic single-weighted posture. In the right-weighted posture, shift 70 percent of the body weight onto the right foot. Requirements for the upper extremities are the same as in the double-weighted drooping-while-elbowing posture, but the force exerted by the arms should be changed in response to changes of the body position (Fig. 58). Alternate the left-weighted posture with the right-weighted posture during exercise.

(2) Palms Down Posture The feet can be in either double-weighted or single-weighted stance. For the double-weighted posture, stand in the double-weighted basic posture, gently raise both hands palms downward to umbilicus level with about one

Fig. 57   Fig. 58

fist's space between the thumbs and navel, keep the fingers parted and slightly flexed, leave about three fists' space between the opposing finger tips, and slightly bow the forearm out while both hands press downwards. (Figs. 59 and 60 .)

Apart from the common effects, this posture is employed to train the pressing force of both arms. The mind-focusing method and respiration in this posture follow the requirements for the basic posture. In addition, the mind should concentrate on the sensations induced by the downward-pressing action and sensations caused by the Qi/breath movement throughout the body. The mental activity in this posture can be divided into the light and heavy types. The light activity is concentrating on pressing a ball floating in the water and the heavy is increasing the downward pressure which can intermittently be exerted for relaxation in order to avoid fatigue. For the single-weighted posture, stand in the basic posture. Requirements for the upper extremities are the same as in the double-weighted downward-pressing posture, except that the left arm is moved slightly forward and the right arm backward, both arms exerting force which changes with the force of the whole body (Fig. 61). Alternate the left-weighted with the right-weighted posture.

(3) Lifting and Embracing Posture The feet can be in

Fig. 59   Fig. 60

Fig. 61   Fig. 62   Fig. 63

either the double-weighted or single-weighted stance. In the double- weighted posture, take the basic posture, gently raise both hands in front of the lower abdomen with palms facing obliquely upward, leaving a distance of two fists between the hands and abdomen, and slightly part and flex the fingers with their tips facing one another at a distance of about three fists (Figs. 62 and 63). Besides the common effects, this exercise is employed mainly to train the lifting and embracing force of the hands and arms. In addition to the requirements for the basic posture, respiration and mental activity in this posture are mainly concentrated on the sensations induced by lifting and embracing as well as sensations caused by the Qi breath movement throughout the body. The lifting and embracing activities of the mind in this posture are divided into light and heavy types. The light activity is concentrating on embracing a balloon, and the heavy, which is intermittently interrupted by relaxation in order to avoid fatigue, is adding to the weight lifted according to the practitioner's constitution. In the single-weighted posture, requirements for the upper body are the same as for the double-weighted posture, except that the left arm is moved slightly forward and the right arm backward, both arms exerting a force which changes with the force of the whole body (Fig. 64). Alternate the left-weighted with the right-weighted posture during exercise.

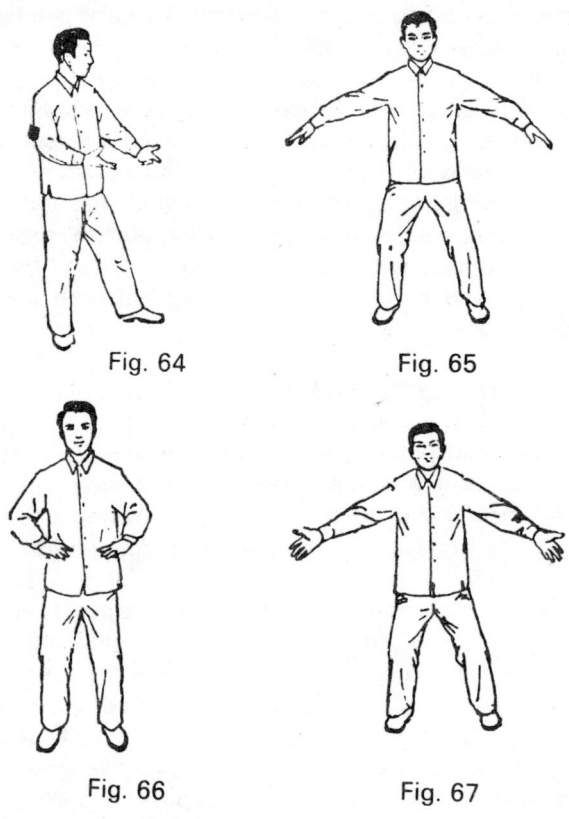

Fig. 64   Fig. 65

Fig. 66   Fig. 67

(4) Water-cleaving Posture The feet can be in either double- weighted or single-weighted stance. In the double-weighted posture, stand in the basic posture, raise both arms bilateral, straighten the arms with fingers of both hands leveling with the pubic bone or umbilicus (the higher the hand position, the heavier is the weight sustained by the upper extremities as well as the weight sustained by the whole body), and turn the palms to face either downward or upward (Figs. 65, 66, and 67).

Besides the common effects, this posture is employed mainly to train the upper extremity extensors when the hands press downward, and the musculus radialis when the hands face forward. In addition to requirements for the basic posture and respiration, mental activity in this posture are mainly concentrated on the sensations induced by the bilateral lifting action and sensations caused by the Qi/breath movement throughout the body. The mental activity should be interspersed with relaxation in order to avoid fatigue. For the single-weighted posture, take the basic posture. Requirements for the upper extremities are the same as for the double-weighted water- cleaving posture, except that the arms exert a force which changes with the force of the whole body. Repeat and alternate the left-weighted with the right-weighted posture.

(5) Embracing Posture The feet can be in either double-weighted or single-weighted stance. Stand in the standard double- weighted posture, extend the forearms in front of the chest at breast level with palms facing inward and fingers parted and slightly flexed and, while imagining embracing a ball or tree trunk, keep the hands two fists apart (Figs. 68 and 69).

Besides the common effects, this exercise is mainly employed to train the arms' embracing force. Respiration and mind focusing in this posture call for concentration on the sensations induced by the embracing action as well as sensations caused by the Qi/breath movement throughout the body. The mental activity should be interspersed with relaxation in order to avoid fatigue. For the single-weighted posture, take the basic posture, place the arms according to the requirements for the double-weighted embracing posture, except that one arm moves slightly forward and the other slightly backward, both arms' force and position changing with those of the whole body (Fog. 70). Repeat and alternate the left-weighted with the right-weighted posture during exercise.

(6) Forward-pushing Posture The feet can be in either double-weighted or single-weighted stance. Take the double-weighted basic posture, place the forearms in front of the chest at breast level with palms facing out and downwards and fingers parted and slightly flexed, keep the hands two fists apart, and bow out the elbows to make a circle or the arms while pushing forward with the wrists and palms (Figs. 71 and 72).

Fig. 68 Fig. 69 Fig. 70

Fig. 71 Fig. 72 Fig. 73

Besides the common effects, this posture is mainly employed to train the pushing force of the arms and wrists. Concentrate on experiencing the sensations induced by the pushing action and sensations caused by the Qi/breath movement throughout the body. The mental activity should be interspersed with relaxation in order to avoid fatigue. During intermission, perform the embracing exercise. For the single-weighted posture, take the basic posture, and place the arms as in the double-weighted pushing posture, except that the left arm moves slightly forward and the right one backward, both arms changing with the position and force of the whole body (Fig. 73). Repeat and alternate the left-weighted posture with the right-weighted.

(7) Wrists-drooping Posture The feet can be in either double-weighted or single-weighted stance. Stand in the double-weighted basic posture, extend the arms straight forward in front of the chest at breast level with elbows slightly flexed, droop the wrists palm downward and slightly turning inward with the naturally parted fingers pointing to the ground, and keep the wrists shoulder-width apart.

Besides the common effects, this posture is mainly used to strengthen the arms' lateral muscles (Figs. 74 and 75). In addition to the requirements for the basic posture, respiration and mind focusing in this posture should concentrate on experiencing the sensations induced by the wrists-drooping action and sensations caused by the Qi breath movement throughout the body. During exercise, mental activities should be interspersed with relaxation to avoid fatigue. During intermission, practise the wrist-pushing movement. For the single-weighted posture, take the standard posture following the requirements for the double- weighted wrists-drooping posture, rotate the arms leftwards in correspondence to changes of the body position, and meanwhile move the left hand slightly forward and the right hand backward, while the force exerted by both wrists and the position of both shoulders change with relative changes in the whole body (Fig. 76).

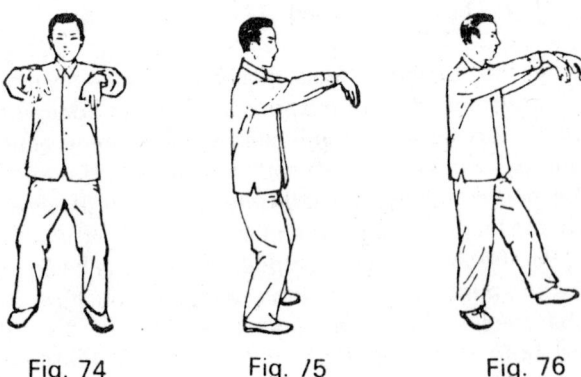

Fig. 74   Fig. /5   Fig. 76

4. Median-level Postures

In terms of body position, median-level postures are one fist lower than high-level postures and about two fists lower than the practitioner's height. So the muscle tensity in these postures is greater than in high-level postures. Requirements for the double-weighted median-level postures are the same as those for the double-weighted high-level postures, except that the position is lowered to the required height. Single-weighted median-level postures can be divided into seven varieties according to the purposes and requirements of the exercise.

(1) Press-down-to-push Posture This is a single-weighted posture. In the right-weighted posture, stand in the basic posture with the left foot in front and the right foot one step behind, slightly rotate the body leftwards with the weight on the right foot, align the buttocks with the right heel, raise both arms to a level between the breasts and shoulders, thrust out the downward-facing palms with fingers parted into a triangle and exerting a force like a tiger's paw, forming the press-down-to-push-forward movement, and then place the left hand in front of the left chest and the right hand in front of the right chest, the two hands separated by a distance of about two fists with one further forward than the other. Now gently thrust out the arms while rotating the elbows slightly inward, keep the upper body upright and tilted forward, and place the right hip slightly backwards to form an opposing yet complementing force to the arms' press-down-to-push-forward movement with arm position and force changing with changes in the Qi/breath movement throughout the body. Mental activity in this posture should be interspersed with relaxation in order to avoid fatigue. During intermission, do not think about the exercise. The intensity of the pressing and pushing movement depends on the practitioner's constitution (Figs. 77 and 78).

(2) Lifting and Embracing Posture This is a single-weighted posture. For the right-weighted exercise, stand in the basic posture with feet obliquely parted at an 85-degree angle, the left foot in the front and the right foot one step behind. Slightly rotate the body leftwards with body weight on the right foot, and

Fig. 77   Fig. 78

align the right buttock and the right heel. Then raise both arms and
stretch them in front of the chest at shoulder level with palms
facing each other at a distance of two fists and pushing out with a
triangular force. Keep the fingers slightly parted and flexed and
exert a force as a tiger does with its paw. Flex the elbows and lift
and embrace with the arms. Keep the upper body upright and tilted
slightly forwards. Keep the right hip a little behind to form an
opposing yet complementary force to the arms. Besides the
requirements for the basic posture, mental activity should be
concentrated on experiencing the sensations induced by lifting
and embracing and by changes in Qi/breath circulation throughout
the body. The mental activity should be interspersed with
relaxation in order to avoid fatigue. During the relaxation
snatches, do not think about the exercise. The force put into lifting
and embracing depends on the individual's constitution. Change
to the left-weighted posture after the right-weighted and repeat
(Figs. 79 and 80).

(3) **Lifting and Forward-pushing Posture** This is a
single- weighted posture. In the right-weighted exercise, stand in
the basic posture with feet obliquely parted at 85 degrees, the left
foot in front and the right one step behind, slightly rotate the body
leftwards and put 70 percent of the body weight on the right foot,
align the right buttock with the right heel, and extend both arms
forward to a level between the shoulders and breasts, with palms

134

Fig. 79   Fig. 80

obliquely facing inwards and up as if lifting a heavy object. Slightly flex the fingers, keep the hands two fists' distance apart, and have them exert force as a tiger does with its paws. Slightly flex the elbows as if to embrace something; while the hands lift, keep the body upright and forward; keep the right hip slightly behind to form an opposing yet complementary force to the hands. Besides the requirements for the basic posture, the mental activity should be concentrated on experiencing the sensations induced by lifting and pushing forward and by the changes in Qi/breath circulation in the whole body. The mental activity should be interspersed with relaxation in order to avoid fatigue. During the relaxation snatches, do not think about the exercise. The force put into lifting to push forward should be gauged to the individual's constitution. Change to the left-weighted posture after this side and repeat (Figs. 81 and 82).

(4) Horizontal Posture With Forward-pushing Palms
This is a single-weighted posture. In the right-weighted exercise, stand in the basic posture with the feet parted at an 85-degree angle, the left foot in the front and the right foot one step behind. Slightly rotate the body leftwards with 70 percent weight on the right foot. Align the right buttock and the right heel. Extend both arms at breast level, flex the elbows with palms facing obliquely inward and downwards and thrusting with a triangular force, while the parted and slightly flexed fingers exert force as a tiger

Fig. 81   Fig 82

does with its claws. The hands being two fists' distance apart, try to twist the wrists outwards horizontally with palms facing obliquely inwards and down. Keep the upper body upright and tilted forward. The right hip is kept slightly behind to form an opposing yet complementary force to the hands. Besides the requirements for the basic posture, mental activity should be concentrated on experiencing the sensations induced by the exercise and by the changes in Qi/breath circulation throughout the body. The mental activity should be interspersed with relaxation in order to avoid fatigue. During the snatches of relaxation forget the exercise. The force used in the arms should be gauged to the individual's constitution. Alternate the left-weighted posture with the right-weighted and repeat (Figs. 83 and 84).

(5) Embracing Posture With Twisting Hands This is a single- weighted posture. In the right-weighted exercise, stand in the basic posture with feet parted at an 85-degree angle, the left foot in the front and the right foot one step behind. Slightly rotate the body leftwards with 70 percent of the body weight on the right foot. Align the right hip with the right heel. Extend both arms to breast level, the left hand in the front with elbow flexed. Thrust the left hand outwards palm down and exert a triangular pulling force with the fingers. Slightly flex the fingers to exert a force as a tiger

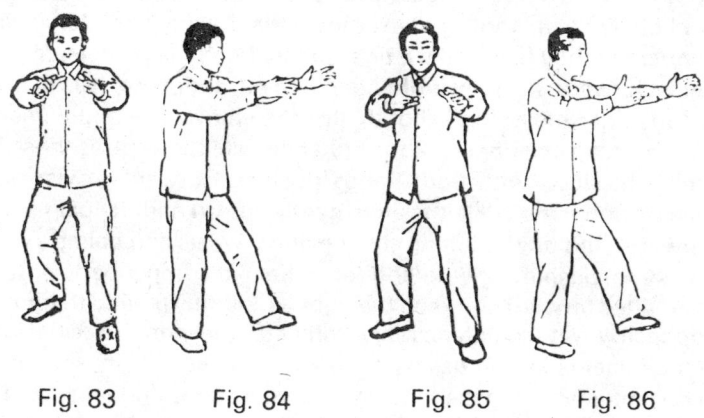

Fig. 83   Fig. 84   Fig. 85   Fig. 86

does with its claws while the wrist pushes out. Keep the right hand slightly behind, about two fists in front of the right breast. Requirements for the right hand and its fingers are the same as those for the left hand, except the palm faces obliquely inwards and upwards and exerts a pulling force in the opposite direction to the left hand. Keep the body upright and tilted forward, with the right hip slightly behind the left one to form an opposing yet complementary force to the hands. Besides the requirements for the basic posture, mental activity should be concentrated on experiencing the pulling force in the hands and the changes in Qi/breath circulation throughout the body. The mental activity should be interspersed with relaxation, and the twisting and embracing movements practised alternately in order to avoid fatigue. During the snatches of relaxation, forget the exercise. Intensity of the twisting and embracing actions should be gauged to the individual's constitution. Alternate the left-weighted posture with the right-weighted and repeat (Figs. 85 and 86).

(6) Twisting and Pushing Posture With Hands Pulling

This is a single-weighted posture. For the right-weighted exercise, stand in the standard posture with feet obliquely parted at an 85-degree angle, the left foot in the front and the right foot one step behind. Slightly rotate the body leftwards with 70 percent of the weight on the right foot. Align the right hip and right heel. Extend both arms forwards at breast level, the left palm facing inwards and obliquely downwards and exerting a triangular pulling force with fingers slightly flexed like a tiger's paw. Push the left forearm and wrist forward. Keep the right hand behind, about two fists in front of the right breast, and slightly flex the elbow. The requirements for the palm and fingers of the right hand are the same as those for the left. Now, with both hands pushing outwards, twist both hands outwards while the arms gently spread and the palms turn inwards and down, letting the the arms, wrists and palms exert a twisting, pushing and pulling force. Keep the upper body upright and tilted forward and keep the right hip slightly behind to form an opposing yet complementary force to the arms. Besides the requirements for the basic posture, the mental activity should be concentrated on experiencing the sensations induced by the pulling movement and by the Qi/breath movement throughout the body. The mental activity should be interspersed with relaxation in order to avoid fatigue (Figs. 87 and 88). During the snatches of relaxation, do not think about the exercise. Intensity of hand movement depends on the individual's constitution. Alternate the left-weighted posture with the right-weighted.

(7) Lifting and Downward-pressing Posture This is a single- weighted posture. For the right-weighted exercise, stand in the basic posture with feet obliquely parted at an 85-degree angle, the left foot in the front and the right foot one step behind. Slightly rotate the body leftwards with 70 percent of the body weight on the right foot. Align the right arm with the right heel. Extend both arms forward with the left arm at shoulder level and the right palm at the waist, abdomen or hip. Slightly flex the left arm, the palm facing obliquely downwards. Exert a triangular pulling force with the left palm and, with the parted fingers, exert a force as a tiger does with its claws, while the wrist and palm thrust upwards. The other requirements for the right hand are the same as those for the left, except that its palm exerts downward pressure and backward force. This completes the lifting and downward-pressing posture (Fig. 89). Keep the right palm facing downwards and at any of the three levels. Described above is the high level; in the median position, the back hand is about one fist and a half in front of the abdomen and the the elbow thrusts backwards and out at an 45-degree angle (Fig. 90); in the lower position, the back

Fig. 87   Fig. 88

Fig. 89   Fig. 90   Fig. 91

hand is about one fist to the side of the ipsilateral hip and the
elbow thrusts backwards for about 45 degrees while the palm
presses downwards with the torso upright and tilted forward. (Fig.
91) Keep the right hip slightly behind the left hip to form an
opposing yet complementary force to the hands. Besides the
requirements for the basic posture, activity should be
concentrated on experiencing the sensations induced by the
pulling movement and by the Qi/breath movement throughout the
body. Mental activity should be interspersed with relaxation in
order to avoid fatigue. During the snatches of relaxation, do not
think about the exercise. Intensity of the movements should be
controlled according to the individual's constitution. Alternate the
left- weighted posture with the right-weighted and repeat.

5. Lower-level Postures

The body position in lower-level postures is one fist lower than that of the median-level postures and about three fists lower than one's height. They are the lowest in body position of all the standing postures and require the practitioner to sustain the heaviest weight. They are mainly for training stamina and building up the constitution. It is not advisable to practice these postures for long periods. These postures can be divided into two kinds, riding a horse and tiger exercises.

(1) Riding a Horse This is also called the crouching posture, horseback squatting posture, or the horse gait posture. All these postures demand double-weighted bearing. Described below are seven variations.

(A) Riding Posture With Drooping Arms Stand naturally and move the left foot parallelly leftwards about seven fists' distance, or 70 centimeters. Squat with the legs bent at an angle between 60 and 70 degrees, but never more than 90 degrees. Keep the torso upright and tilted forward. Relax the chest and contract the abdomen. Drop the shoulders and extend the arms sideways with elbows flexed, palms facing the body and fingers pointing down. Gently close the mouth and teeth, keep the head erect, and concentrate on riding a galloping horse. To avoid fatigue, relax the mind ir snatches during the exercise by letting it blank out and thinking of nothing. The knees clutch the horse's back and the feet press the spurs. Sit firmly in saddle, keep the upper body integral with the lower body. The requirements for the arms are the same as those for the high- level double-weighted drooping and elbowing posture. (Figs. 92 and 93.)

(B) Riding Posture With Hands Pressing Downward The requirements for the head, body and lower extremities are the same as those for the previous posture. The requirements for the arms are the same as those for the double-weighted downward-pressing posture (Figs. 94 and 95).

(C) Riding Posture With Arms Lifting and Embracing The head, body and lower extremities follow the same

Fig. 92   Fig 93.

Fig. 94   Fig. 95

requirements as those for the riding posture with drooping arms; the arms follow the same requirements as those for the high-level double- weighted lifting and embracing posture (Figs. 96 and 97).

   (D) Riding Posture With Water-cleaving Hands The head, body and lower extremities follow the same requirements as those for the riding posture with drooping arms; the upper extremities follow the same requirements as those for the high-level double- weighted water-cleaving posture (Fig. 98).

Fig. 96   Fig. 97

(E) Riding Posture With Embracing Arms The head, body and lower extremities follow the same requirements as those for the riding posture with drooping arms; and the requirements for the arms are the same as those for embracing a tree (Figs. 99 and 100).

Fig. 98   Fig. 99   Fig. 100

(F) Riding Posture With Forward-pushing Hands The head, body and lower extremities follow the same requirements as those for the riding posture with drooping arms; the arms follow the same requirements as those for the high-level double-weighted forward- pushing posture (Figs. 101 and 102).

Fig. 101   Fig. 102

(G) Riding Posture With Drooping Wrists The head, body and lower extremities follow the same requirements as those for the riding posture with drooping arms; the arms follow the same requirements as those for the high-level double-weighted wrist- drooping posture (Figs. 103 and 104).

Fig. 103   Fig. 104

(2) Tiger-subduing Postures This is the lower-level position in standing postures practised at the same height as the horse- riding postures. Being the single-weighted postures, the weight sustained in this exercise is greater than in the horse-riding posture. So the duration of this exercise should not be longer than that of the horse-riding postures. All the tiger-subduing postures are single-weighted. Some commonly used postures are described here.

(A) Downward-pressing Tiger-subduing Posture Stand at attention with heels closed and toes parted at an 85-degree angle. Flex the left knee and turn it slightly inwards with the left buttock lining up with the left heel and the left knee about one fist beyond the tiptoe. Slightly flex right knee and keep the right foot flat on the ground with 70 or 80 percent of the body weight on the left foot. Slightly rotate the body rightwards. Keep the the left hip a little backwards and the upper body slightly forwards. Relax the chest and contract the abdomen with shoulders turned slightly forward and armpits naturally open. Gently close the mouth and teeth with eyes looking straight forward. Raise the left hand to level with the left hip, leaving one fist's distance to the hip. Flex and bow out the left elbow with palm facing downward and exert a triangular force, the fingers parted and pressing down like a tiger claw. Move the right hand forward about two fists and a half to the right hip with the palm lining up with a point about one fist beyond the right knee and the middle finger parallel to the corresponding foot. The fingers and palm of the right foot follow the same requirements as those for the other hand. The body position and spirit are suggestive of the action to subdue a tiger. While no slackness is allowed, the force exerted should not be too strong (Figs. 105 and 106). The exercise should be interspersed with relaxation in order to avoid fatigue. The same guideline applies to the following postures.

(B) Tiger-subduing Posture With Drooping and Supporting Arms The head, body and lower extremities follow the same requirements as those for the tiger-subduing posture; the arms follow the same requirements as those for the high-level single-weighted posture with drooping arms (Figs. 107 and 108).

Fig. 105　　　　　　Fig. 106

Fig. 107　　　　　　Fig.108

(C) Tiger-subduing Posture With Lifting and Embracing Arms The head, body and lower extremities follow the same requirements as those for the tiger-subduing posture; the arms follow the same requirements as those for the high-level single-weighted posture with lifting and embracing arms (Figs. 109 and 110).

(D) Tiger-subduing Posture With Water-cleaving Hands The head, body and lower extremities follow the same requirements as those for the tiger-subduing posture; the arms follow the same requirements as those for the high-level single-weighted posture with water-cleaving hands (Figs. 111 and 112).

Fig. 109   Fig. 110

Fig. 111   Fig. 112

(E) Tiger-subduing Posture With Embracing Arms The head, body and lower extremities follow the same requirements as those for the tiger-subduing posture; the arms follow the requirements as those for the high-level single-weighted posture with embracing arms (Figs. 113 and 114).

(F) Tiger-subduing Posture With Forward-pushing Hands The head, body and lower extremities follow the same requirements as those for the tiger-subduing posture; the arms follow the same requirements as those for the high-level single-weighted posture with forward-pushing hands (Figs. 115 and 116).

Fig. 113   Fig. 114

Fig. 115   Fig. 116   Fig. 117

(G) Tiger-subduing Posture With Drooping Wrists
The head, body and lower extremities follow the same requirements as those for the tiger-subduing posture; the arms follow the same requirements as those for the high-level single-weighted posture with drooping wrists (Figs. 117 and 118).

Fig. 118   Fig. 119   Fig. 120

Fig. 121   Fig. 122

(H) Press-down-to-push-forward Tiger-subduing Posture The lower body follows the same requirements as those for the tiger- subduing posture; the head, upper body and arms follow the same requirements as those for the median-level press-down-to-push- forward posture (Figs. 119 and 120).

(I) Lifting, Embracing and Forward-pushing Tiger-subduing Posture The lower body follows the same requirements as those for the tiger-subduing posture; the head, upper body and arms follow the same requirements as those for the median-level lifting and embracing forward-pushing posture (Figs. 121 and 122).

(J) Lifting and Forward-pushing Tiger-subduing Posture The lower body follows the same requirements as those for the tiger- subduing posture; the head, upper body and arms follow the same requirements as those for the median-level lifting and forward- pushing posture (Figs. 123 and 124).

Fig. 123   Fig. 124

(K) Tiger-subduing Posture With Horizontal Palms Pushing Forward The lower body follows the same requirements as those for the tiger-subduing posture; the head, upper body and arms follow the same requirements as those for the median-level posture with horizontal palms pushing forward (Figs. 125 and 126).

Fig. 125   Fig. 126

(L) Tiger-subduing Posture With Embracing and Twisting Hands The lower body follows the same requirements as those for the tiger-subduing posture; the head, upper body and arms follow the same requirements as those for the median-level embracing posture with twisting hands (Fig. 126).

(M) Tiger-subduing Posture With Twisting and Pulling Hands the lower body follows the same requirements as those for the tiger-subduing posture; the head, upper body and arms follow the same requirements as those for the median-level twisting and pulling posture (Fig. 127).

(N) Lifting and Downward-pressing Tiger-subduing Posture The lower body follows the same requirements as those for the tiger- subduing posture; the head, upper body and arms follow the same requirements as those for the median-level lifting and downward- pressing posture (Figs. 128 and 129).

Fig. 127   Fig. 128   Fig. 129

Dynamic Qigong Exercises

Dynamic Qigong Exercise has a myriad of varieties. Examples are the Prophylactic Exercise (Bao Jian Gong), Eight Elegant Movements (Ba Duan Jin), Tendon-training Exercise (Yi Jin Jing), *Taiji* (Shadow Boxing) and Frolics of Five Animals (Wu Qin Xi).

Some dynamic Qigong exercises are used for treating diseases, and some for building the physical constitution. Dynamic Qigong exercise is different from other physical exercises in many ways. It is done in relative inward peace achieved through certain postures, methods of respiration and mind focusing. Its requirements feature calming the spirit, regulating Qi, combining dynamic and quiescent states, coordinating the internal and external parts of the body, integrating relaxation and tension, and stressing both gentleness and firmness. It is an exercise in a state of outward motion and inward peace, or in a dynamic state with a quiescent state as its prerequisite.

I. Postures, Respiration and Mind-focusing Methods of Dynamic Qigong Exercise

The postures of dynamic Qigong exercise can be divided into the standing, walking, sitting, and prone categories. The standing and walking postures are most commonly adopted, while the sitting and prone positions are suitable for those who are feeble or patients confined to bed. The dynamic exercises differ from one another. Some are complicated and need great strength, and others are simple and need less effort. The choice depends on the individual's health and the purpose of exercise.

Natural breathing is the main method of respiration which

gradually changes to deep abdominal respiration.

To focus the mind, four points must be taken into consideration: motion with inward peace as its prerequisite; focusing the mind at Middle Dantian; focusing the mind on certain gestures of dynamic exercise such as shooting an arrow and, lastly, imagination including imitating actions of animals such as the tiger or bear while performing "Frolics of Five Animals."

II. Eight Elegant Movements of Internal Exercise

(I) Eight Elegant Movements of Internal Exercise in Sitting Postures

This is a prophylactic exercise taken in bed before sleep at night or before getting up in the morning.

1. Calming the Mind and Sitting Quietly

Sit with legs crossed; keep the head level and look straight forward with eyes half closed; straighten the back and relax the body; relax the shoulders with armpits open; relax the chest and contract the abdomen; place one hand on the other, palms up in front of the lower abdomen; gently close the mouth with the tongue placed naturally inside, and breathe evenly. Eliminate all distractions to calm the spirit and use the mind to guide Qi downwards to Middle Dantian. In three to five minutes, a warm sensation may occur in the lumbar and abdominal regions as well as the four extremities. Keep the mind focused at Middle Dantian throughout the exercise. This is essential for practising the Eight Elegant Movements of Internal Qigong Exercise. If time permits, practice may be prolonged for a few extra minutes (Fig. 130).

2. Holding Kunlun With Both Hands

Kunlun refers to the external occipital protuberance. The Naohu acupuncture point is located in its center; and the Yuzhen acupoints are located on each side of Kunlun. They are punctured in cases of headache, vertigo, eye pain, myopia, and pain in the nape and occiput. Gently click the upper and lower teeth against each other 20 to 30 times, and swallow the saliva when it increases; cross the fingers of both hands, slowly move the hands to the back of the head and cradle the occiput with them; push the head forward with both hands while the head is pushed backwards, forming a counteracting force. This pushed oppositional force exerts certain effects on the acupoints. The force can be pulsed and coordinated with respiration. Push the head forward and resist this while inhaling, and relax both forces while exhaling. Repeat this process more than 10 times (Fig. 131).

3. Tapping Yuzhen With the Fingers

The left and right Yuzhen are conventional acupoints. After the first set of exercise, remove the crossed hands from the back of the head and cover the ears with the palms, the heels just covering the front ear edges; put the index finger on the ipsilateral Yuzhen point; now place each index finger on top of the ipsilateral middle finger; snap the index fingers off the middle fingers to tap the ipsilateral Yuzhen points 10 times (Fig. 132).

Fig. 130   Fig. 131   Fig. 132

4. Rotating the Head

Rotate the head from side to side bilaterally, which stimulates the left and right Tianzhu acupoints. In ancient times, this was called shaking Tianzhu by rotating the head. Tianzhu are punctured with a needle for treating ophthalmopathy, otopathy, pharyngopathy, laryngopathy, neurasthenia, and pain in the head and nape. Continuing from the above exercise, relax and slowly lower both hands; place the hands one on top of the other, palms above the thighs in front of the lower abdomen. Tilt the head downwards keeping the nape muscle a bit tense; rotate the head from side to side bilaterally 20 times with the force generated from the base of the head; then click the upper and lower teeth against one another, coil the tongue while rinsing the mouth by expanding and contracting it, and swallow the increased saliva (Fig. 133).

5. Massaging the Shenshu Acupoints

The Shenshu points are located on both sides of the spine between the second and third lumbar vertebrae. These acupoints are used clinically for treating diseases of the urogenital system, menopathy, leukorrhagia, neurosis, and pain in the lumbar region and legs. Massaging the Shenshu points may vitalize kidney Qi. Continuing from the above exercise, sit upright after breathing deeply several times; conduct Qi to Dantian; then hold the breath for a few seconds for the umbilical area and the abdomen to grow warm. Rub the two hands until they feel hot, and massage the Shenshu points with the palms 20 times. Focusing the mind on the massage may produce a warm sensation in the lumbar and abdominal regions (Fig. 134).

6. Hand Circular Exercise

In this exercise, the extended hands, palms down, trace a circular orbit as if turning a wheel. An old saying describes the process as winding a windlass with both hands over extended legs. Move the hands from the lumbar to the subcostal region; extend the legs straight forward, side by side; rest the heels on the bed; keep the ten fingers parted and slightly flexed at the joints; move the hands upwards and then downwards along a circular orbit several times as if turning a wheel. Repeat the movement several times in the opposite direction. This exercise has proved to be very effective in treating lumbago and leg pain and extending the muscles of the lumbar region and the flexors of the lower extremities (Fig. 135).

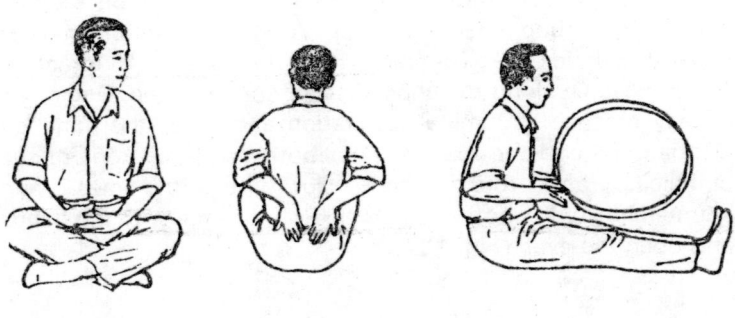

Fig. 133   Fig. 134   Fig. 135

7. Pulling and Pressing the Toes

This exercise trains a wide range of muscles in the lumbar, thoracic, and abdominal regions as well as the four extremities. Continuing from the above exercise, cross the fingers of both hands with palms facing downward as the hands rotate downwards; then raise the crossed hands past the chest with palms facing upward, and extend them upward above the head; after a few seconds, turn the crossed hands, letting the palms face downward and cover the top of the head; stretch the head upwards while pressing downwards with the crossed hands; after a few seconds, relax the crossed hands and bend the upper body to hold the feet with the hands and press the left and right foot's Yongquan points; keep the knees straight. This move should be repeated several times (Fig. 136).

8. Conducting Qi Along the Ren and Du Channels

The Ren Channel travels along the spine on the ventral side of the body, and the Du Channel on the dorsal side. They are connected and are the major arteries for all channels and collaterals of the body, the former being Yin and the latter Yang. Regulating the two aids in balancing Yin and Yang. Qi travels from Dantian down the Ren Channel, up the Du Channel and back down Ren. This is also called the Small Circuit (Xiao Zhou Tian).

155

Sit upright with closed eyes; regulate respiration and calm the mind; exclude distracting thoughts and concentrate on Dantian and practise abdominal respiration. A warm sensation may be experienced in the Dantian area after constant practice. Conducting Qi along the channels can not be forced. Beginners usually practise abdominal respiration and focus the mind on Dantian. To end the exercise, put both hands in front of the umbilicus, and rotate them clockwise 20 times, and counterclockwise another 20 times. Rub the face with the hands and open the eyes (Fig. 137).

Fig. 136   Fig. 137

(II) Eight Elegant Movements of Internal Qigong Exercise in the Standing Posture

1. Supporting Heaven With the Hands

This is a popular exercise. It yields better results if the requirements for dynamic Qigong exercise are followed properly.

Stand naturally with feet parallel and divided by a shoulder width. Slightly flex the knees, lower the shoulders, flex the elbow and let the hands hang at the sides of the body. Relax the chest and contract the abdomen, relax the spine, and keep the head straight with eyes looking forward. Calm the mind and regulate respiration. Inhale with the nose and exhale with the mouth, and mentally conduct Qi to Dantian. Keep the fingers pointing forwards with palms facing down. Move both hands upwards before turning the palms to face upward and crossing them in front of the lower abdomen; then turn the crossed hands palm downwards and move them anteriorly upward until above the head. This process is traditionally called supporting heaven with the hands. After a while, relax the crossed hands, lower them laterally, and put them in front of the lower abdomen. This can be done about 10 times (Figs. 138 and 139).

Fig. 138   Fig. 139

2. Drawing a Bow to Shoot Vultures

With parallel feet, stand naturally; move the left foot a step to the left, and flex the knees to take a half sitting posture; rotate the knees inwards slightly, with both feet pressing the ground and hips set back as if sitting on a horse; gently clench the hands and lower them beside the hips about one fist's distance away; then raise the fists breast high; flex the right elbow joint and extend the right arm horizontally to the right until it is 16 centimeters from the breast, as if holding a bow (bow hand). Extend the thumb and index finger of the left hand, as if it were the arrow hand holding an arrow, and draw this hand further left; meanwhile turn the head leftwards with eyes looking the direction of the "target" which lines up with the left index finger. After a few seconds, straighten the knees, lower both hands along a circular orbit and withdraw the left foot to its original position. That completes the left-side posture. Change to the right-sided exercise. Alternate sides about 10 times (Figs. 140 and 141).

Fig. 140   Fig. 141

3. Raising one Hand to Regulate the Spleen and Stomach

Stand naturally and press both palms downwards. Extend the hands forward with palms up and place the hands in front of the lower abdomen. Rotate the hands inwards to turn the palms down; raise the left hand very slowly, until it is above the left top of the head, palm facing up. Move the right hand until it is beside the right hip; open the fingers and rotate the right hand outwards and, palm pressing downward, place it lateral to the right hip at a distance of two fists, forming a counteracting force with the left hand. After a few seconds, rotate and lower the left hand while rotating the right hand until both hands face each other in front of the lower abdomen, as in the beginning posture. This is the left-side posture. Change to the right- sided posture. Practise this with alternate hands raised 10 times (Figs. 142 and 143).

4. Looking Backwards to Mend the Body

Stand naturally with the feet shoulder-width apart; slightly flex the knees and put the body weight equally on both feet, thinking of a deeply rooted tree. Let both hands hang down comfortably at the sides with elbows slightly flexed. Extend the hands outwards along a circular orbit while turning them palms up, letting the two middle fingers almost touch in front of the the lower abdomen. Slowly turn the palms to face down while exhaling. Turn the head left and move the hands outward along a circular orbit to place them beside the hips. Stare at the right foot as if looking at the acupoint on the sole of the foot. After a few seconds, inhale and face forward and move the hands back in front of the lower abdomen with palms up. This is the left-side posture. To begin the right-side posture, exhale while turning the head right, as though looking at the sole of the left foot. Alternate the two postures about 10 times (Figs. 144 and 145).

Fig. 142

Fig. 143

Fig. 144

Fig. 145

5. Shaking the Head and Wagging the Tail to Dispel Heart Fire

Stand naturally, and move the left foot one step to the left. Lower the body to form the horse-riding posture as in drawing a bow to shoot vultures, and imagine a weight on the hips. Relax the chest and contract the abdomen, lower the shoulders and flex the elbows, mentally guiding Qi to Dantian. Tilt the torso forward with eyes looking straight ahead, and grasp the legs with the hands a little above the knees; stand firm as a deeply rooted tree trunk, and focus the mind at the Yongquan points. Keeping the spine straight as a tree trunk, tilt the torso; align the head with the left knee, with the right shoulder leading; flex the left elbow and straighten the right arm, fix the eyes on the right toes. Move the torso so as to let the left shoulder lead; flex the right elbow and straighten the left elbow aligning the head head with the right knee; weigh down the buttocks to form a counteracting force to the left shoulder. Fix the eyes on the tip of the left foot. Repeat these, alternating sides about 10 times (Figs. 146 and 147).

Fig. 146   Fig. 147

6. Touching the Feet to Strengthen the Kidney and Waist

Stand naturally and move the left foot to keep the feet shoulder-width apart; slightly flex the knees and keep the palms down; straighten the spine and look straight ahead; move the hands backwards, then return them to the sides and raise them along a circular orbit over the head with palms facing upward and fingers pointing backward. Exert a lifting force with the palms. After a few seconds, straighten the knees and bend the upper body at the waist to touch the feet with both hands; keep the hands on the feet for a moment before straightening the body and withdrawing the left foot to stand at attention. This completes the left-sided posture and the right-sided posture is done the same way by a side step with the right foot. Repeat these alternately about 10 times (Figs. 148 and 149).

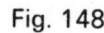

Fig. 148

Fig. 149

7. Clenching the Fists and Stretching the Arms for Strength

Stand naturally and move the left foot one step leftwards to squat in the posture of drawing a bow to shoot vultures; weigh down the hips and relax the chest and contract the abdomen; drop the shoulders and elbows, and conduct Qi to Dantian. Very gently clench the fists and raise them parallel to the lower margins of the chest, leaving two fists' distance between the two fists which are thumb sides up; bend the elbow and place the forearms in front of the chest to form a semi-circle, leaving three fists' distance between the fists and the chest midline; push forward the left fist powerfully with eyes following it to look at the target; in the meantime draw the right fist down to waist level, fingers down to form a counter force between the two arms. After a pause, withdraw both fists to the starting position in front of the chest. Open the hands and raise them over the head before lowering them bilaterally to the hips; withdraw the left foot and stand erect at attention. This is the left-side posture. Move the right foot one step to the right to begin the right-side posture. Alternating sides, repeat the exercise about 10 times (Figs. 150 and 151).

Fig. 150   Fig. 151

8. Shaking the Back to Cure Diseases

Stand at attention with knees and heels closely together, the toes of the feet forming a 90-degree angle. Keep the head erect and the eyes looking straight forward; focus the mind at Dantian. Let the arms hang at the sides of the body with elbows slightly flexed outwards; keep the fingers of each hand straight and pointing forward. Raise both heels, press the hands downwards and exhale. Relax the whole body and lower the heels to the ground. Now suddenly shake the body, and relax both hands. Repeat this process about 10 times (Figs. 152 and 153).

Ending Exercise: Stand at attention and focus the mind at Middle Dantian for a while, then breathe naturally 10 times.

162

Fig. 152   Fig. 153

III. Thirteen Prophylactic Exercises

The Thirteen Prophylactic Exercises form one method of combining dynamic movements with a quiescent state, and internal training with external training. These exercises can be taken in either sitting or standing postures. The practitioner can go through all 13 sets of exercises, or select three to five of them per session. During the selective practice, each movement can be repeated several times. The practitioner can also start practice with the beginning exercise and finish with the ending exercise. Each practice session should last at least five to 10 minutes.

1. Calming the Spirit and Regulating Respiration (Beginning Exercise)

< Posture > Stand naturally with feet shoulder-width apart, knees flexed; let both arms hang naturally exerting a slightly outward force; relax the waist and spine, and drop the shoulders with armpits open. Slightly flex the elbows with hands pressing down, palms facing down and fingers slightly curved. Half close the eyes and look straight ahead. For the sitting exercise, use the simple sitting or the cross-legged sitting postures. This posture can be practised two to three times.

< Respiration > Breathe naturally; mentally direct Qi to Middle

163

Dantian or Yongquan. Respiration can be combined with movements. Exhale while relaxing and inhale while focusing the mind.

< Mind Focusing >   Focus the mind at Middle Dantian or the Yongquan acupoints. Or, focus the mind by a device suitable to the individual's constitution. For instance, the practitioner can recite the words "Relax and Quiet Down" to enter quiescence.

< Effects >   This exercise induces one to enter the quiescent state.

2. Clicking the Teeth and Rotating the Tongue

< Posture > Remaining in the previous posture, click the teeth 10 times, rotate the tongue 10 times, repeatedly rinse the mouth by expanding and contracting it, and swallow the increased saliva (Figs. 154 and 155).

< Respiration > Breathe naturally and conduct Qi to Dantian.

< Mind Focusing >   Pay attention to the tongue only.

< Effects > This exercise helps strengthen the teeth, produces saliva, invigorates spleen and stomach function and helps digestion.

3 Rubbing the Hands and Face

Continuing in the previous posture, put both hands in front of the umbilicus, gently rub the palms 20 to 30 times and, after feeling a warm sensation, gently close the eyes. Place both hands on the face and gently rub it 10 times as if washing it; then open the eyes (Figs. 156 and 157).

< Respiration > Breathe naturally and mentally direct Qi to Middle Dantian or Yongquan. When rubbing the hands, pay the most attention to the palms (the Laogong acupoints) and the finger tips (the Shixuan acupoints); do not concentrate on the rubbing action when rubbing the face so as to avoid moving Qi upwards.

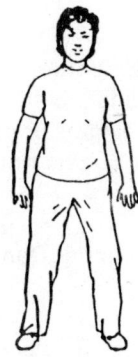

Fig. 154

Fig. 155

Fig. 156

Fig. 157

< Effects > This exercise regulates Qi and the heart and lung channel. It also strengthens resistance against colds.

4. Tapping the Yuzhen Acupoints

< Posture > Continuing from the previous exercise, cover both ears with the heels of the palms, the elbows at shoulder level and the index fingers facing each other on the Yuzhen acupoints. Place

the index fingers on the ipsilateral middle fingers, snap the index fingers off the middle fingers to tap the Yuzhen acupoints 10 times (Figs. 158 and 159).

< Respiration > Breathe naturally and mentally direct Qi to Middle Dantian. The respiration may coordinate with the tapping of Yuzhen; when inhaling, place the index fingers on the Yuzhen acupoints; when exhaling, snap the index fingers onto Yuzhen. Repeat this process rhythmically.

< Mind Focusing > Focus the mind on either Dantian or the Yongquan acupoints.

< Effects > This exercise regulates bladder Qi, clears the mind and sharpens the ears.

5. Gliding to the Fengchi Acupoints

< Posture > Continuing from the previous exercise, massage from Yuzhen to the Fengchi acupoints with the index fingers, middle fingers and ring fingers. Repeat the process 10 times (Figs. 160 and 161).

< Respiration > Breathe naturally and mentally direct Qi to Middle Dantian.

< Mind Focusing > Focus the mind at Middle Dantian and coordinate mental activity with the massage.

< Effects> This exercise regulates the channels and collaterals, vitalizes brain, improves sleep, clears the eyes and sharpens the ears.

6. Massaging the Shenshu Acupoints

< Posture > Continuing the previous exercise, massage with the palms 10 times from the Fengchi acupoints down past the shoulders to the Shenshu points at the waist, putting the most force in the wrist. Continue massaging all the way down to the sacral bone before repeating (Figs. 162 and 163).

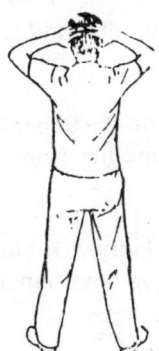

Fig. 158

Fig. 159

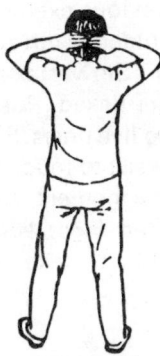

Fig. 160

Fig. 161

Fig 162

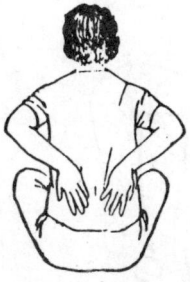

Fig 163

< Respiration >   Breathe naturally, or conduct abdominal respiration.

< Mind Focusing > Focus the mind on the Shenshu, Mingmen (Rear Dantian), or Middle Dantian acupoints. Coordinate mental activity with massage.

< Effects >   This exercise invigorates kidney Qi, strengthens the abdomen, nurtures the liver and kidneys, and benefits the brain and heart.

7. Stretching Exercise

< Posture > Continuing from the previous exercise, withdraw the left foot and move the right foot shoulder-width apart. (For the sitting posture, stretch the legs forward.) Slowly raise both hands with palms facing upwards and fingers flexed. Push the palms upwards in the lifting movement three to five times. Straighten the knees and bend the upper body at the waist to touch the feet with the hands, rest the hands on the feet for a moment, stand straight, and resume the beginning posture (see Figs. 164 and 165). Practitioners with hypertension should not take the standing posture.

< Respiration >   Breathe naturally.

< Mind Focusing >   Focus the mind on the Dantian or Yongquan acupoints.

Fig. 164   Fig. 165

< Effects > This exercise invigorates the liver and kidneys, vitalizes Essential Qi, and relaxes the tendons and bones.

8. Vertical Double Circles

< Posture >Continuing from the previous exercise, withdraw the right foot, and move the left foot half a step to the left. (For the sitting posture, cross both legs.) Let the arms hang palm downwards, raise the hands gradually to ear level; extend the hands forward and then down along a circular orbit as if turning a windlass; flex the knees and tilt the body forward and downwards while moving the hands. Straighten the legs a bit and keep the knees flexed. Repeat the exercise several times (Figs. 166 and 167).

< Respiration > Breathe naturally. Or coordinate the respiration and movements. Lower the hands while exhaling and mentally direct Qi to the Yongquan acupoints. Raise the hands while inhaling and focus the mind on Middle Dantian.

< Mind Focusing > Focus the mind on Middle Dantian. All attention should be concentrated on the sensations of the moving Qi/breath.

9. Horizontal Circles

< Posture > Continuing from the previous exercise, withdraw the left foot and move the right foot half a step to the right. Let both arms hang down naturally with palms facing downward; raise the hands to breast level before they are extended to draw two identical horizontal circles in front of the chest. Resume the beginning posture. For the standing postures, flex the knees and tilt the torso forward as the hands move forwards at the midline; when the hands part, move the body slightly upward, and then resume the beginning posture. Repeat about 10 times before resuming the natural standing posture (Figs. 168 and 169).

< Respiration > Breathe naturally, or coordinate the respiration with movements. When the hands spread out, exhale and spread Qi outward from Middle Dantian; when the hands finish the circles near the chest, inhale and gather Qi at Middle Dantian. The

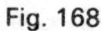
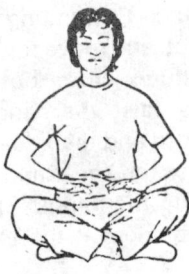

Fig. 168   Fig. 169

method of combining respiration with movements makes the
movement smoother, slower and stronger.

< Mind Focusing > Focus the mind at Middle Dantian. All
attention should be concentrated on the circular movements and
sensations induced by the spreading and gathering movement of
Qi/breath and felt throughout the body.

< Effects > This exercise regulates Qi/breath.

10. Lateral Circles

< Posture > Continuing from the previous exercise, withdraw
the right foot, and move the left foot half a step to the left. Let the
arms hang down naturally with palms facing downward and
fingers pointing forwards. Move both hands toward the midline in
an arc until level with the Qihai acupoint in the abdomen; raise the
hands past the chest to head level. Extend the arms sideways and
lower them gradually, each forming a circle. Slightly stretch the
legs while raising the hands and bend the legs slightly while
lowering the hands with the torso also moving slightly
downwards. Repeat several times (Figs. 170 and 171).

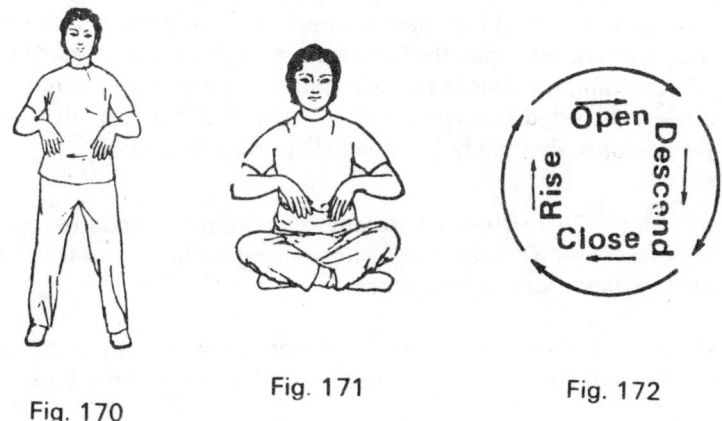

Fig. 171

Fig. 170

Fig. 172

Exercises 8, 9 and 10 can be practised as one set of three parts (Fig. 172).

< Respiration >   Breathe naturally, or coordinate respiration with the movements. Part the hands and move them downwards while exhaling and, inhale as the hands come together and move upward.

< Mind Focusing > Focus the mind on Middle Dantian and on the circles.

< Effects > This exercise regulates the opening, closing, rising and falling of Qi.

11. Drawing a Bow on Both Sides
< Posture > Continuing from the previous exercise, withdraw the left foot and move the right foot one step to the right. Let the arms hang down with palms facing down and elbows slightly flexed. Extend both hands outwards each drawing a small circle and stop at Qihai level about two fists in front of the lower abdomen; raise the hands to chest level and make fists; draw the right elbow as if drawing the bow string. Extend the left hand leftwards from the body, as if holding the bow, while the eyes look

171

the target direction beyond the index finger of the left hand. Bend the knees to form a horse-riding posture. After a pause, bring the hands back in front of the chest, move them upwards to part them drawing an arc, and open the fists; then let the hands fall gradually while standing up. This is the left- sided posture of the exercise. Do the right-sided posture in the same way and repeat left and right postures alternately 10 times (Figs. 173 and 174).

< Respiration > Breathe naturally, or coordinate respiration and the bow-drawing movements. When raising the hands, inhale and when lowering the hands, exhale.

< Mind Focusing >   Mentally direct the gathering of Qi at Middle Dantian and pay attention to the drawing of the bow.

< Effects >   This exercise improves respiratory function, regulates lung Qi, and strengthens the lumbar region and the extremities.

12. Crane Spreading its Wings

< Posture > Continuing from the previous exercise, withdraw the right foot and move the left foot half a step to the left. With arms hanging down naturally and wrists crossed in front of the Guanyuan acupoint, remain in this preparatory posture for a moment. Raise both arms bilaterally until the hands are at shoulder level, flex the elbows with wrists and fingers forming arcs; after a pause, lower the arms bilaterally and cross the wrists in front of the Guanyuan acupoint again. Simultaneously, draw back the left foot, bending the legs a little. To do the right-sided exercise, move the right foot half a step to the right. Repeat the exercise alternating sides several times (Figs 175 and 176.).

< Respiration > Breathe naturally, or coordinate respiration and movements: Inhale while raising the arms and exhale while lowering the arms.

< Mind Focusing > Focus the mind on Middle Dantian or the Yongquan acupoints, or coordinate respiration and mind activity. Concentrate on Middle Dantian while inhaling and on Yongquan

Fig. 173

Fig. 174

Fig. 175

Fig. 176

while exhaling. Also pay attention to the movement of the hands.

< Effects > This exercise stimulates the up-and-down movements, increases vitality, and strengthens the muscles of the chest and arms.

13. Mentally Conducting Qi to Dantian to Conclude These Exercises

< Posture > This posture is the same as the beginning posture. Following the previous exercise, bring the hands together and rub them gently several times. Then place both hands against the

umbilicus with the right palm against the back of the left hand; massage with both hands from the umbilicus clockwise to the left, from inside to outside, progressing from small circles to bigger circles 20 to 30 times, never going above the heart for the biggest circle, or lower than the pubic bone. After a pause, massage counterclockwise, from the heart to the right, from outside to inside, from big circles to small circles 20 to 30 times before stopping at the umbilicus. Lower both hands and return to the natural standing posture (Figs. 177 and 178).

< Respiration > Breathe naturally and mentally conduct Qi to Middle Dantian.

< Mind Focusing > Focus on Middle Dantian; coordinate Qi movement and hand movements, silently counting the number of circles and bringing the mind back to the ordinary state at the end.

< Effects > This movement reinforces spleen function, regulates respiration and vitalizes Original Qi.

Fig. 177

Fig. 178

IV. Fifteen Formulas of Taiji Exercise (Shadow Boxing)

1. Regulating Respiration and Calming the Mind

Stand naturally; move the left foot half a step to the left; flex the knee joints turning them inwards a little, and weigh down the

174

hips. Straighten the spine, relax the chest and contract the abdomen. Relax the shoulders with open armpits, and slightly flex the elbow; press the hands down palms downwards, as if pressing a floating ball in the water. Keep the head level with eyes looking straight ahead, and focus the mind within the body. Gently close the mouth with the tongue placed naturally; inhale through the nose and exhale through the mouth, or inhale and exhale through both the nose and the mouth. Calm the mind and regulate respiration while mentally directing Qi to Middle Dantian. Extend the hands forward and outward to draw an arc; turn the palms up and place them in front of the lower abdomen with middle fingers touching each other. After a while, raise the hands to breast level while inhaling; turn the palms to face down; lower the hands to the front of the lower abdomen while exhaling, and again turn the palms to face upward (Figs. 179 and 180). Repeat the breathing exercise as directed four times-- counting eight, silently recite the odd numbers while inhaling; raise the hands and recite the even numbers while exhaling and lowering the hands, then place the hands in front of the lower abdomen.

2. Holding the Moon

Continuing in the same posture, raise the hands along a curve to head level with palms facing inward and then up; slightly extend the head upwards with eyes looking past the hands which extend laterally to the shoulders at a distance of one fist; after a pause, turn the hands inwards as if holding the moon; then slowly lower the hands past the chest to the front of the lower abdomen (Figs. 181 and 182). Repeat this process four times. Each time includes two actions--count one while raising the hands and count two while lowering them. If this is combined with respiration, raise the hands while inhaling and lower them with exhaling. The mind is focused at Middle Dantian. This method can be applied in all the following exercises. Slightly raise the body when the hands rise and lower it when the hands move downward, moving the whole body.

3. Holding Balls at the Sides

Continuing in the same posture, draw in the left foot heel

toward the inner side of the right foot; place the body weight on the right foot and move the left foot half a step to the left front. Raise the left hand palm upward obliquely to the front of the left

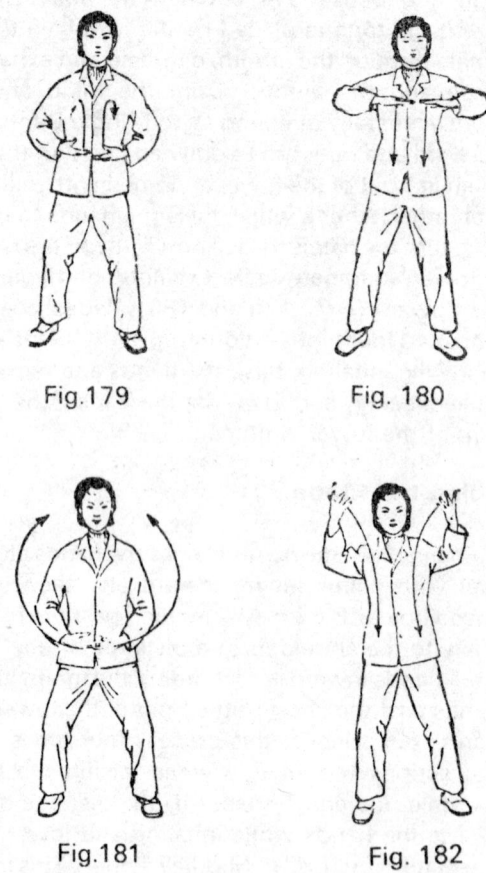

Fig.179   Fig. 180

Fig.181   Fig. 182

shoulder as if holding a ball and turn the right palm to face down and move it back in an arc a little beyond the right hip. Shift the body to form a small lunge. This completes the first movement (Fig. 183). After a short pause, turn both palms over simultaneously with the right palm facing down and the left palm facing up; move the right palm upward in an arc to the front of the right shoulder and push back with the left palm a little beyond the left hip. Move the body's center of gravity backward to form a big lunge with the right heel aligned with the right hip. This completes the second movement. Practise the two movements twice each, making it a four-movement series. While withdrawing the hands to end the fourth movement, turn the left toes inward and shift the weight onto the left foot. Draw in the right foot heel to the inner arch of the left foot and then take half a step to the right front with the right hand in the front and the left hand in back; simultaneously turn both palms over. Extend the left hand forward along a curve to the front of the ipsilateral shoulder, and press the right hand downward until just forward and below the ipsilateral hip and shift the body weight forward to form a small lunge, completing the fifth movement. After a short pause, simultaneously turn both palms over and extend the right hand forward and upward beyond the ipsilateral shoulder and press the left hand downwards, stopping palm side up in front of the ipsilateral hip. Shift to form a small lunge in the sitting position, completing the sixth movement. Alternate the left-sided with the right-sided exercise and repeat to make a series of eight movements. The difference is in the low palm, which faces down in one set and up in another (Figs. 183 and 184).

Fig. 183   Fig. 184

4. Pushing a Mountain With Both Hands

Continuing in the previous posture, turn the right foot inward and draw in the left foot heel to the inner side of the right foot which bears most of the body weight. At the same time, move both hands, placing them palms down in front of the lower abdomen. Move the left foot one step to the left front while pushing both hands forward up to chest level. With palms facing forward and fingers slightly parted, exert a triangular force as if to push a mountain. Keep the torso erect; shift the body's center of gravity forward; keep the left knee slightly flexed and lined up with the toes of the left foot. Tilt the torso forwards a bit with eyes looking between the hands in the distance. This is the left-sided mountain-pushing movement, or the first movement (Fig. 185). After a pause, simultaneously turn both palms towards the chest with elbows about one fist's distance from the body; move the body's center of gravity backward with the right buttock in line with the right heel, forming a big lunge in the sitting position. This is the second movement (Fig. 186). Practise these two movements twice each to make a series of four movements. While withdrawing the hands to end the fourth movement, turn the left foot toes inward to bear the body weight while drawing the right foot heel to the left foot's inner side before moving it one step to the right front. Extend both hands to form a right-sided lunge, completing the right-sided mountain- pushing movement, the fifth movement. Now, rotate the hands to let the palms facing inwards while moving the body weight backward to form a big lunge in the sitting position. This completes the sixth movement. Alternate the left side with the right and practise the last two movements four times each to make a series of eight movements.

5. Circling With Both Hands

Continuing from the end of the seventh movement above, spread the left palm and move it leftwards while pressing the right hand downwards; turn the right foot inward and the left foot outward each for 30 degrees to assume a horse-riding posture; simultaneously part the hands with the inward-facing left palm rotating leftwards to draw an arc while the eyes follow it and and the head turns in the same direction; spread out the right palm, turn the eyes onto it and move the right hand in an arc, while the head follows the movement and the body rotates. This completes the exercise on both sides. Continue this exercise by repeating the movements eight times. (Figs. 187 and 188.)

Fig. 185   Fig. 186

Fig. 187   Fig. 188

6. A Roc Spreading its Wings

Continuing the eighth movement of the last exercise, shift the body's center of gravity onto the right foot and draw the left foot heel to the inner side of the right foot, forming a T gait. Move the left hand forward up in a curve to the same level as the right hand; lower both hands bilaterally and cross them in front of the lower abdomen; move the left foot half a step to the left front forming a right weighted small lunge in the sitting position. Raise both hands bilaterally to head level; hold the fingers together in extension; slightly flex the wrists, elbows and shoulders. Each arm forms a curve and exerts force like a roc spreading its wings (the first movement is thus completed). Let the body rise with its upper part erect and eyes looking straight forward (Fig. 189). After a short pause, bilaterally lower the arms and cross them in front of the lower abdomen while the body sinks a little. This completes the second movement (Fig. 190). Practise these movements twice each. On finishing, turn the left foot inward and draw the right foot heel to the inner side side of the left foot; move the right foot half a step to the right front while the body's center of gravity moves onto the left foot to form a small lunge in the sitting position. Continue with the wing-spreading movement twice.

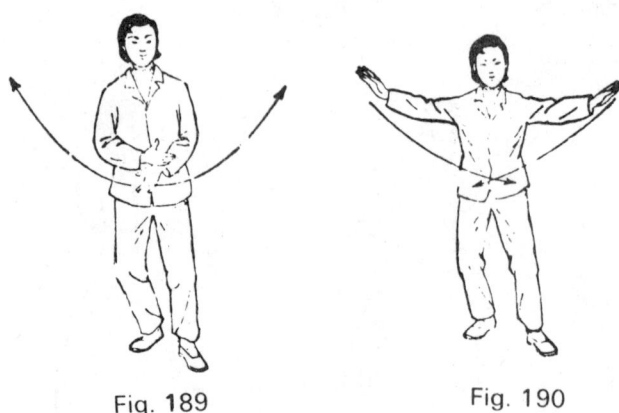

Fig. 189   Fig. 190

7. A Red Dragon Spreading its Claws

Continuing the eighth movement of the last exercise, turn the right foot inward and draw the left foot heel to the inner side of the right foot while shifting the body's center of gravity onto the right foot, forming a T-shaped gait. Move the left foot half a step to the left front, forming a small lunge in the sitting position, while turning the palms face up. Extend the left hand towards the left front of the left shoulder with fingers parted, elbow flexed and palm up at shoulder level. Extend the right hand backwards past the right hip with fingers slightly parted, elbow flexed and palm face up, as if the hand intends to reach forward, but has stopped behind the right ear. This is the first movement. After a short pause, extend the right hand, palm down, to the left front, and stop at chest level while the body rotates leftwards a little. While turning the right palm up, stretch the left hand backward drawing an arc past the left hip with fingers slightly parted, palm up and elbow flexed into an acute angle, as if the hand tends to stretch out to the left front but has stopped short behind the ear. This is the second movement. Repeat the two movements. Then, turn the left foot inward and draw the right foot to the inner side of the left foot while moving the body weight onto the left foot; move the right foot half a step to the right front; reach the right hand forward and the left hand backward, completing the fifth movement. After a short pause, reach the left hand forward to the right, palm up at chest level while rotating the body rightwards a little; move the right hand outward and then backward along a curve from beside the right hip, palm up, fingers parted and elbow flexed into an acute angle. Turn the left palm up while the right hand tends to stretch out but stops behind the right ear. This completes the sixth movement. Repeat the fifth and sixth movements to make four movements, or eight movements including the left-right alternation. In order to proceed to the next movement, the left hand should be stretched out and the right hand placed behind the right ear at the end of the eighth movement. (Figs. 191 and 192.)

8. Ducking a Floating Ball

Continuing from the eighth movement of the last exercise, turn the toes of the right foot inward 15 degrees and those of the left foot outward also for 15 degrees to form a shoulder- width stance. Press the right hand downward from behind the right ear to the front of the right shoulder while turning the left hand palm down and bring the hands together. Press both hands downward in a U shape in front of the right shoulder. Without stop, raise the hands in the other side of the U as if the ball has come to the surface in front of the chest. This completes the first movement.

Press the hands downwards again and draw them up at the right front of the chest to complete the second movement. When pressing the hands downward from the right front of the chest, move the upper body leftwards and rightwards correspondingly with the knee flexion and bob the whole body. Repeat eight times. (Figs. 193 and 194.)

Fig. 191   Fig. 192

Fig. 193   Fig. 194

9. Left- and Right-sided Ball Play

Continuing from the eighth movement of the previous exercise, draw an arc in front of the right hip as the hands press downwards from the left side of the chest; shift the body's center of gravity to the right foot and draw the left foot to the inner side of the other foot forming a T-shaped gait; move the left foot one step to the left front with the lower abdomen contracted, hips weighed down, and palms facing down; extend the hands forward to the left as if pressing a ball. Lower the hands to hip level and at the inner side of the left leg, move the body weight forward to form a lunge with the left knee and toes in alignment. This is the first movement. Extend both hands backwards along an outward curve nearly to the right hip while moving the body weight backwards; relax the chest and contract the abdomen and form a big lunge in the sitting position with the right hip and heel in alignment and eyes looking forward to the left. This completes the second movement. Repeat both movements to make a total of four movements. Now turn the left foot inward to bear the body weight; draw the right foot nearly to the inner side of the other foot forming a pseudo T gait; move the right foot one step to the right front; turn the palms face downwards and extend them forward to the right while moving the body's center of gravity forward to form a right-sided lunge. This is the fifth movement. Extend both hands toward the left and stop them a little way in front of the left hip while moving the body weight backwards; contract the lower abdomen and to form a big lunge in sitting position with the left hip and heel in alignment and eyes looking forward to the right. This completes the sixth movement. Repeat the last two movements. Combine all these movements into an exercise of eight movements including the left- right alternations. (Figs. 195 and 196.)

10. A Peacock Opening its Tail

Continuing from the eighth movement of the last exercise, join the hands palm to palm in front of the lower abdomen. This is a single-weighted exercise. Turn the toes of the right foot inward; draw the left foot to the inner side of the right foot; shift the body's center of gravity to the right foot to form a pseudo T gait; move the left foot one step to the left front. Extend the hands forward and upward to breast level while shifting the center of gravity to the left foot forming a lunge; part the hands, opening the arms sideways, the shoulders, elbows and wrists flexed; the eyes looking straight ahead, be sure the elbows are at breast level, and the hands at shoulder level about one fist's distance from the chest. This is the first movement. Return the hands to the midline; then let them drop downwards in front of the lower abdomen while moving the body weight backwards onto the left foot to form a big lunge in sitting position with the right buttock and heel in alignment. This completes the second movement. Repeat both movements. Turn the toes of the left foot inward to bear the body weight; draw the right foot to the inner side of the left foot to form a pseudo T gait and move the right foot one step to the right front. Extend the hands in front of the chest before parting them to open the arms. Move the body weight forward to form a lunge, completing the fifth movement. Finally, bring the hands to the midline and then lower them so they are in front of the lower abdomen while moving the body weight backward to form a big lunge in the sitting position, with the left hip and heel in alignment. This is the sixth movement. Repeat the last two movements. Combine all the movements making it an exercise of eight movements. (Figs. 197 and 198.)

Fig. 195   Fig. 196

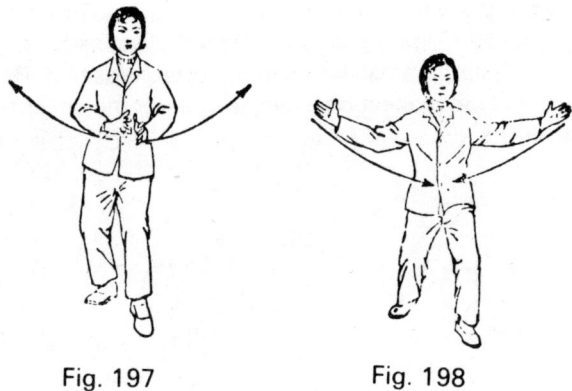

Fig. 197   Fig. 198

11. A White Crane Spreading its Wings

Continuing the eighth movement of the last exercise, join the hands palm to palm in front of the lower abdomen and form a big lunge in the sitting position. Turn the toes of the right foot inward and draw the left foot heel to the inner side of the other foot to form a pseudo T gait while shifting the body's center of gravity to the right foot; move the left foot half a step to the left front forming a small lunge in the sitting position. The hands are in front of the lower abdomen. Raise the left hand, elbow flexed, palm facing forward, fingers slightly bent and parted; bow the elbow while the wrist twists outward on the same level as the head. Simultaneously, push the right hand backwards and lower it until one fist's distance behind the right hip, palm facing backwards and fingers pointing downwards with the force at the elbow. Slightly turn the head and body leftwards to integrate and balance all the forces of the body. This completes the first movement. After a short pause, lower the left hand along a curve at the body midline until it is behind the left hip; as the right hand is behind the right hip, raise the hand along a curve to the body midline and stop when the wrist is lateral to the head. Slightly turn the head and body rightwards, completing the second movement. While lowering the upper hand, raising the lower hand and joining them in front of the lower abdomen for a moment, gather all forces of the trunk and extremities back at Middle Dantian. Repeat both movements. Now turn the toes of the left foot inward to bear the body weight; draw the right foot to the inner side of the left foot, forming a pseudo T gait, and move the right foot half a step to the right front, forming a small lunge in the sitting position. Repeat all the movements to make it an exercise of eight movements. (Figs. 199 and 200.)

Fig. 199   Fig. 200

12. A Wild Horse Parting its Mane

Continuing from the eighth movement of the last exercise, turn the toes of the right foot inward to bear the body weight; draw the left foot heel to the inner side of the right foot and, move it one step to the left, forming a horse-riding stance in the half sitting position. Lower the right hand along a curve past the chest to press downward above the right knee's outer side, fingers slightly flexed and parted and palm exerting a triangular pushing force; outwardly raise the left hand along a curve from the outer back of the left hip past the chest to push outward above the left shoulder's outer edge, elbow pushing outward and palm facing inward. Slightly turn the head and trunk leftwards with eyes looking at the lower front of the right knee. The hands exert a counteracting force. This is the first movement. When the hands meet in front of the chest, the falling hand should be outside of the rising hand. Keep the right hand moving counter clockwise and the left clockwise. Now lower the left hand along a curve past the chest to press downward above the left knee's outer side while outwardly raising the right hand along a curve from the outer side of the right hip past the chest to push outward above the right shoulder's outer edge. Slightly turn the head and trunk leftwards, eyes looking at the lower front of the left knee. This is the second movement. Repeat the movements to make it an exercise of eight movements. (Figs. 201 and 202.)

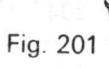

Fig. 201   Fig. 202

13. Circling the Moon

Continuing from the eighth movement of the previous exercise, shift the body's center of gravity onto the right foot; withdraw the left foot heel to the inner side of the right foot, forming a pseudo T gait and move the left foot half a step to the left to form a shoulder-width stance. Lower the right hand while raising the left to let them face each other in front of the lower abdomen. Raise both hands above the head from in front of the chest; after a short pause, separate and lower them sideways palms facing downwards and elbows bowing out. Simultaneously, tilt the upper body, stretch out both hands and connect them in front of the feet with arms flexed into a circle while keeping the

187

knees straight. This is the first movement as well as the first circle. After a pause, straighten the spine, relax the chest and contract the abdomen, and raise the crossed hands over the head. Keep the head level with eyes looking straight ahead. This is the second movement as well as the second circle. Repeat the movements to make it an exercise of eight movements. (Figs. 203 and 204.)

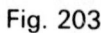

Fig. 203   Fig. 204

14. Standing and Squatting With Straight Arms

Continuing from the eighth movement of the last exercise, place the body's center of gravity on the right foot; draw in the left foot to the inner side of the right foot to connect the heels and separate the toes for 60 degrees. Keep the wrists crossed in front of the lower abdomen. Then, laterally elevate the arms to shoulder level extending them from the sides, palms facing downwards with finger tips slightly upturned. This is the first movement (Fig. 205). After a short pause, squat with the knees held closely together and heels slightly off the ground, the upper body remaining in the original posture. This is the second movement (Fig. 206). Now, stand up with the upper body remaining in the same posture and let the heels touch down to complete the third movement. After another short pause, lower the arms to cross them in front of the lower abdomen, completing the fourth movement. These four movements make up one cycle. Practise this practised four times to complete an exercise of 16 movements.

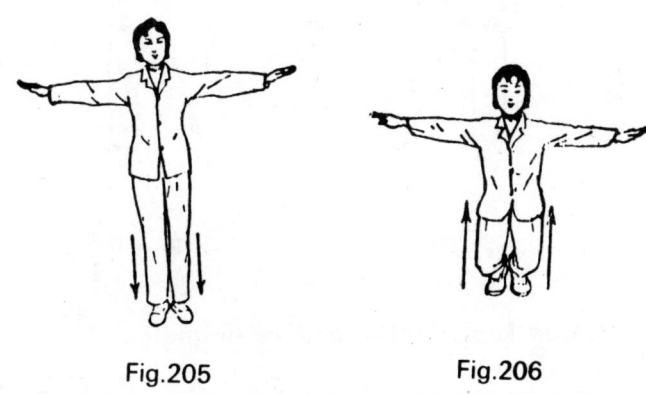

Fig.205   Fig.206

15. Elephant Exercises its Waist

After finishing the previous exercise, shift the body's center of gravity to the right foot and take a half step step to the left, the feet standing shoulder-width apart. Straighten the spine; relax the chest and contract the lower abdomen; calm the spirit and focus the mind at Middle Dantian. Now place the opened hand backs against the waist beside the Mingmen acupoint. Straighten the legs with toes grasping the ground like a deeply rooted tree. Making the waist an axis, slowly rotate the body counter clockwise, leading the movement of whole trunk and the center of gravity which shifts between both feet. The first movement is completed when the body rotates leftwards 180 degrees. The second movement is 180 degrees rightwards. Do this four times in each direction for a total of eight movements. Finally stand firm with the body upright and gathering Qi at Middle Dantian. (Figs. 207 and 208.)

Fig.207   Fig. 208

V. Hua Tuo's Frolics of Five Animals

(I) My Experience With the Frolics

Towards the end of the Eastern Han dynasty (A.D. 25-220), the renowned medical scientist Hua Tuo created a set of exercises called "Wuqinxi"--five movements mimicking tiger, deer, bear, monkey and birds and coordinating the body's movements. They have been widely applied for health care and building up the constitution.

Many schools were formed and became popular for their unique approaches to the Frolics of Five Animals during ensuing dynasties. I started to learn the frolics in 1958 from Hu Yaozhen, an elderly TCM doctor. In 1961, I learned the "Twelve Postures of Mt. Ermei, Thirteen Taiji Postures of Mt. Wudang, Tiger Footwork and Tiangang (the Big Dipper) Qigong Massage. And in 1962, I learned standing postures from Qigong master Wang Xiangzhai. During practice, I tried to combine the features of these exercises with Shaolin Boxing, which I had practised as a teenager. In addition, I tried to combine some key points of *Taiji* with the Frolics of Five Animals from famed schools including those represented by Gao Shiguo, author of *Wuqinxi,* Wang Liting, who wrote the book *Illustrated Wuqinxi,* and the ancient document of Essence of Chifeng. Much credit for my research and systematization should be attributed to the numerous books on physical training and TCM health preservation by modern authors.

These systematized Wuqinxi exercises which I present consist of the basic postures, basic skills and free practice. These exercises also include a method called Wuqin guidance. Practice can start from either of the basic skills or postures. Each basic exercise consists of five movements, and the five frolics total 25 movements. The practitioner can select from one to all five movements for each exercise session. Usually one set is sufficient for one session. The intensity of exercise is adjusted to the individual. Generally, the crane and bear movements are suitable for the physically weak people; the bear movements are suitable for the aged and the crane movements for women. Adolescents are advised to practise the crane and monkey frolics.

Features of the Frolics of Five Animals introduced include the combination of internal and external movements, and dynamic and quiescent states, mutual assistance between softness and toughness, integration of mental and physical activity, and the unity of mind, posture, Qi and force. Every movement of these exercises is rather simple and easy to learn, though combining the internal with the external and the dynamic with the quiescent may need long-time practice. In order to grasp the key points of these frolics, I paid many visits to the zoo studying as well as imitating the characteristics of the five animals' movement. From my own experience and practice, I created a Seven-word Guideline and a Twenty-eight-word Formula to help beginners understand and remember the key points.

(II) Development of the Frolics of Five Animals

These exercises, which are based on the habits and movements of tiger, deer, bear, monkey or birds, require imitation of the five animals' movement. Describing the state of my mind during exercise, I often tell practitioners to move as if playing with waves and currents while the mind soars over the sea.

The Frolics of Five Animals originated in ancient times. *Zhuang Zi,* a Taoist book more than 20 centuries old, describes the exercise as inhaling the fresh and exhaling the stale. Moving like a bear and stretching like a bird to achieve longevity. A contemporary book of his times,*Huainan Zi,* carries a description of six animals' movements. Hua Tuo, who lived in the later Eastern Han dynasty and is regarded as the most outstanding doctor of ancient China, created the Frolics of Five Animals. He was not only good at surgery, herbal medicine and acupuncture, but also famous for his knowledge of prophylacxis. His theory stressing the importance of exercise contains a saying cherished by many people today: "As a door hinge never gets worm-riddled, exercise improves digestion, helps to assimilate and regulate Qi, promote blood circulation, dispel diseases, and activate the limbs to offer you the joy of longevity." Hua Tuo's disciple Wu Pu was said to have had acute senses even in his 90s. Hua Tuo's creative work significantly influenced the later development of prophylactic physical exercises.

The Frolics of Five Animals are also mentioned in other books such as *Yimen Guangdu* and *Essentials of Internal and External Exercises With Illustrations.* Although the descriptions are quite brief, changes in the methods are shown. The exercise is not only employed to cure diseases, keep fit, strengthen the constitution and massage acupoints by using Qi, but is also applied in martial arts. According to *Quan Jing* (The Book of Martial Arts), dragon boxing trains the mind; tiger boxing the bones; leopard boxing strength; snake boxing Qi, and crane boxing essence. Xing Yi (Formal and Suggestive) boxing was further developed into the 12 animals' movements. The Frolics of Five Animals provide a basis for the development of a variety of martial arts. In this sense, Qigong massage of acupoints and martial arts can be regarded as the offspring of the Frolics of Five Animals.

Today, there are numerous schools of the Frolics of Five Animals, each with its own special characteristics. Generally, some exercises stress imitative movements, others emphasize the training of Qi; some stress softness, and others strength. Some are used for treatment and fitness and others for combat. Most important of all, however, the exercises are effective in training Qi or essence. Because these exercises combine external motion with internal quietude, both the posture and Qi, internal and external movement, and the dynamic and quiescent states, they all merit equal emphasis. While implementing the external movements, the practitioner should keep the mind focused, to maintain quietude within motion and combine toughness with softness.

(III) Key Points of the Frolics

In addition to the key points of Qigong exercise, the Frolics of Five Animals require attention to the following points.

1. Integration of Form and Mind

The Frolics of Five Animals not only mimic an animal's movements, but also its bearing. Examples are the impressive strength of the tiger, the alertness and resourcefulness of the monkey, the lightness of the crane, the relaxation of the deer's limber movement, and the stable and honest bearing of the bear. Only in this way can practice reach the organic wholeness of the body and mind.

2. Flexible and Circular Movement

Circular movement indicates that all movements in the frolics exercises are carried out in the form of arcs, spirals, wave or spin. The circular movement, which is always complete and coherent, may not be obvious in some postures, but actually underlies all mind activity and the use of subtle forces. Flexibility suggests that each movement should follow its own requirements and, to avoid stiffness, should also be flexible and adaptable to other movements.

3. Slow and Fast Movement

The exercise includes fast movement and slow movement. Slow movement is like spinning silk, and fast movement like a frightened snake. The beginner is advised to stress slow movement, because in this way it is easier to sense the spirit, Qi, and the force. Start training fast movement on the basis of slow movement. To practise the whole exercise, a combination and alternation of fast and slow movement is required.

4. Heaviness, Stability and Subtlety

Heaviness and stability require the movement to be full of energy. Subtlety means that the movements for using and training strength should not be too obvious. All the three qualities are required in learning how to use force in the exercises.

5. Softness and Toughness

The training of strength in the Frolics of Five Animals aims at toughness as well as softness. Training toughness is to overpower softness and training softness is to overcome toughness. Neither toughness nor softness is perfect, each containing the opposite. Therefore, practice should lead to the state of softness coordinated into toughness and toughness into softness. Softness and toughness should interchange naturally during exercise, as force is exerted when necessary. Beginners, however, will not easily sense this subtlety.

6. Order of the Frolics

Generally it is advisable to practise one or two animal frolics in one session. Beginners can practise the frolics in the order of bear, crane, deer, tiger, and monkey. The bear's movement is slow and stable, and the crane's light and stretchy; both animals' movements require much strength. Movements of the deer, the tiger and the monkey are much more powerful and difficult to imitate. Having mastered all the frolics, the practitioner can practise the whole series in the order of bear, deer, tiger, monkey and crane. The reason is, Qi circulation is most stable in the bear posture, from which intensity and difficulty of the exercise can gradually increase. Qi is best regulated in the crane posture as the intensity decreases before the exercise comes to a natural stop.

7. Coordination of Movements With Respiration

Natural respiration is used in practising the Frolics of Five

Animals. Beginners are advised to forget breathing in order to get it to be natural. In other words, beginners are not supposed to combine respiration with movements until they have mastered the movements.

8. Three-way Stability

The practitioner must maintain stability when taking a step, walking and completing the exercise.

9. Preparation

Do not take the exercises when hungry, too full, tired, unhappy or over-excited. Defecate and urinate before practice if necessary. Loosen collar buttons and the waistband. The time for practice can be either in the morning or evening. The environment can be outdoors or a well ventilated room. After sweating, take care not to catch cold.

10. Conscientiousness

The Frolics of Five Animals require the coordination of motion and quietude and should be practiced conscientiously. Otherwise, it may be impossible to gain quietude within motion or seek motion through quiescence.

11. Perseverance in Practice

The Frolics of Five Animals are a kind of dynamic Qigong exercise which is effective in curing and preventing diseases and strengthening the physical constitution. But the effects show only after continued practice. The practitioner should not only continue the exercise but alto take it seriously.

(IV) Basic Movements

1. Bear Frolic

< Key points > Awkward looking but clear in mind,
It walks with lightness inside heavy steps.

Gathering Qi at Middle Dantian,
It shakes and rampages with force in the shoulders.

The bear looks awkward and clumsy, soft as if without bones. Its temperament is stable, simple, and honest, and it walks with heavy steps. However, flexibility and steadiness are hidden within the heavy steps. Do not mimic the heavy, simple and honest bearing of the bear only, but also try to show the flexibility and steadiness during the exercise. Shaking and rocking are features of a bear's movements, so exert forces with the upper arms (including the shoulders, elbows, hands, hips, knees and feet). Conduct Qi to Middle Dantian, so as to accelerate deep abdominal respiration and form Dantian Qi. Persistent practice will help strengthen the constitution as well as functions of the spleen and stomach. (Fig. 209.)

Beginning Exercise Stand naturally; take a half step leftwards with the left foot so the feet are shoulder-width apart; slightly flex the knees while the feet exert equal forces; relax the elbows and shoulders with arms slightly flexed, fingers parted and slightly flexed as if pressing two floating balls in the water. Keep the head straight with eyes looking straight ahead. Straighten the spine, and relax the chest and contract the abdomen. Calm the mind and regulate respiration; exclude disturbing thoughts and mentally direct Qi to Dantian. Gently close the mouth, inhale with the nose and exhale with mouth, or breathe with both the nose and the mouth. Now extend the hands outwards along a curve and upward to breast level while inhaling. After a short pause, turn the palms face downwards and without stopping, turn the palms to face upward, and lower them to the lower abdomen while exhaling. Take another short pause. (Figs. 210 to 214.) Practise this exercise for five times or more. This is the beginning exercise for all the other frolics, too.

(1) Bear Footwork Continuing from the beginning exercise, slightly stretch the head forward, with neck and back exerting a light backward force; draw in the left foot, toes touching the ground and heel off the ground to the inner side of the right foot while inhaling. Shift the weight to the right foot and, at the same time, slightly lower and rotate the body leftwards. Clench the hands very gently with elbows slightly flexed, fists tending backward, and forearms slightly exerting an outward force from the upper wrists. Take a half step forward with the left foot while imagining wading against a current and challenging a resisting force. Then, withdraw the right foot toe touching the ground and heel off ground to the inner side of the left foot; shift the body weight onto the left foot while rotating the body rightwards. This is the left-sided movement. (Figs. 215 to 218.) Take one step forward with the right foot to do the exercise in the opposite direction. Practise the movements alternating left and right exercises.

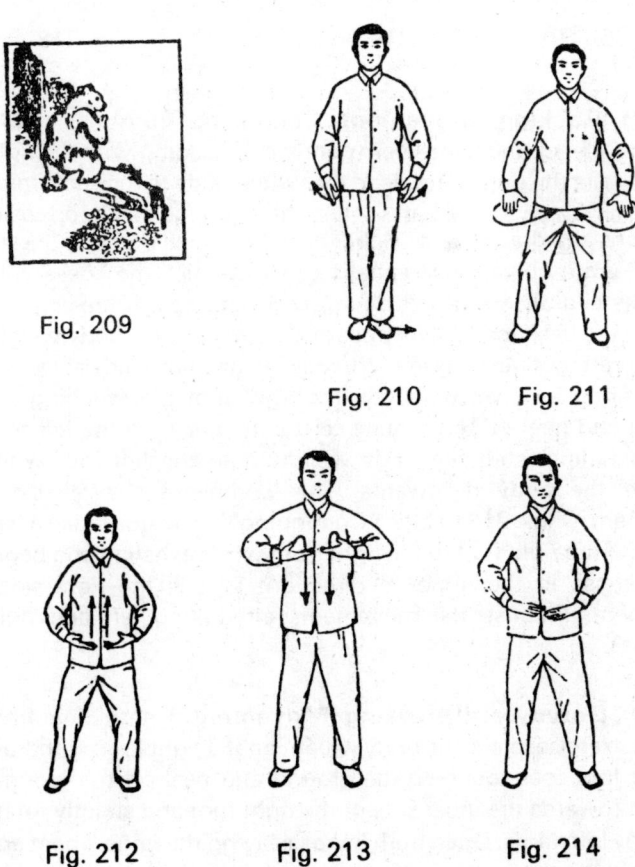

Fig. 209

Fig. 210

Fig. 211

Fig. 212

Fig. 213

Fig. 214

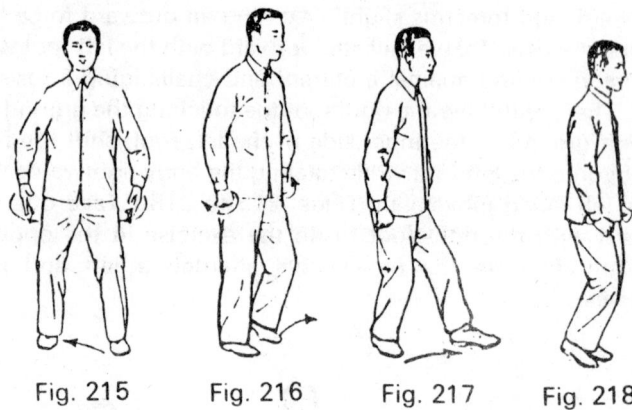

Fig. 215   Fig. 216   Fig. 217   Fig. 218

(2) Rocking Movement Continuing from the above exercise, clench the hands very gently and, leading with the right shoulder, let the upper arms lead the whole body to rock and spiral downward three to five times while the forearms pull in opposite directions and draw an arc. Move the left foot half a step to the left front along a curve while exhaling. Slightly flex the knees with buttocks slightly weighted down; rock and spiral three to five times in the described way. Pause and then place the body weight on the right foot; turn the left foot toes inward, with the heel as the pivot; along a curve, withdraw the right foot toe touching the ground and heel off the ground to the inner side of the left foot while inhaling; shift the body weight onto the left foot while rotating the body rightwards. This completes the left-sided movement. (Figs. 219 to 222.) Continuing this posture, take a half step with the right foot to the right front while exhaling and begin the exercise in the opposite direction. This is the right-sided movement. Practise the movements alternating left and right exercises.

(3) Downward-pressing Movement Continuing from the last exercise, place the body weight on the right foot; withdraw the left foot toes touching the ground and heel off the ground; move it towards the inner side of the right foot and slightly rotate the body leftwards. Open both hands, leaving the fingers bent and parted; move the hands in circles three to five times and open the palms completely. In the meantime, drop the shoulders a little, hold the forearms out from the body; press the hands downward and, while moving the hands outward along a curve, slowly spiral the arms downwards three to five times, with the force and arc larger than the previous time and a lower body position. Now move the left foot half a step to the left front while exhaling. Slightly flex the knees with buttocks slightly weighted down and continue the rocking movement three to five times. After a short pause, withdraw the right foot toes touching the ground and heel off the ground toward the inner side of the left foot; place the body weight on the left foot while rotating the body rightwards. This completes the left-sided posture. (Figs. 223 to 226.)

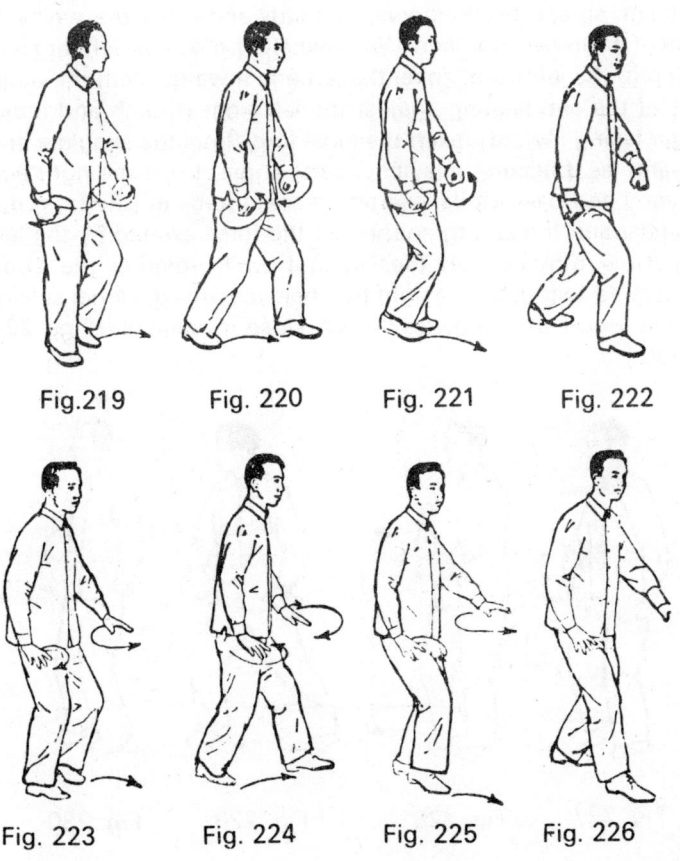

Fig.219   Fig. 220   Fig. 221   Fig. 222

Fig. 223   Fig. 224   Fig. 225   Fig. 226

Continuing from the last exercise, turn the left foot toes inward, and take a half step with the right foot to the right while exhaling. Follow the requirements for the previous exercise to complete the right-sided exercise. Practise the movements alternating left and right exercises.

(4) Leaning Movement Continuing from the previous exercise, move both **hands** out to draw an arc; gently clench the hands and, following the requirements for the rocking movements, rock the arms three to five times in slow motion. Now, elbows outwards, part the thumbs and index fingers and face them inwards, rotating the whole body slightly downwards. Pause a moment, spread both elbows outwards and cross the wrists in front of the lower abdomen. While exhaling, move the left foot half a step to the left front; spiral the left arm inwards, with the outer side of the arm leaning against the left front (thumb and index finger facing inward); exert the most force from the shoulder and forearm, as if leaning heavily against a tree. Twist the right arm outward and backwards, exerting a spiral force mostly from the shoulder and forearm to counteract the force exerted by the left arm. Now turn the left toes inward while rotating the body rightwards; withdraw the right foot heel towards the inner side of the left foot. This completes the left-sided movement. (Figs. 227 to 230.)

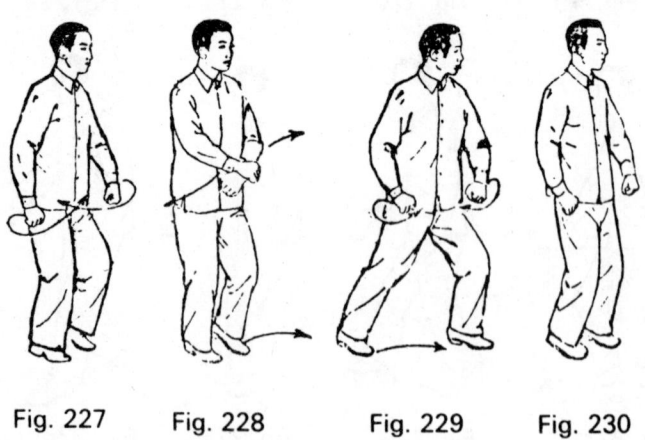

Fig. 227   Fig. 228   Fig. 229   Fig. 230

Continuing from the left-sided exercise, rock both arms three to five times; then cross the wrists in front of the lower abdomen; take a half step with the right foot towards the right front and do the 'right-sided movement. Practise the exercise alternating left and right exercises.

(5) Forward-pressing Movement

Continuing from the leaning exercise, place the body weight on the right foot; withdraw the left foot, toes touching the ground and heel off the ground towards the inner side of the right foot while slightly rotating the body leftwards. Hands still gently clenched, slowly rock the arms three to five times according to requirements for the rocking movements. Without stopping, bring both arms to shoulder level, then stretch them outwards with fists breast-width apart. Place the left fist in front of the right fist with palm sides facing inwards. Bend the arms into bows with elbows drooping and wrists turned slightly inward to exert an outwards force. Pause a moment; take a step with the left foot to the left front with expiration; in the meantime, press both arms forward with a spiral force and elbow outward, while contracting the abdomen and pressing the back backward with a force exerted from the spine to counteract the arms' movement. Now withdraw the right foot heel to the inner side of the left foot while inhaling and rocking the arms in slow motion. Afterwards, turn the left foot toes inward while slightly rotating the body rightwards, lower the fists along a curve to the sides of the hips and shift the body weight onto the left foot. This completes the left-sided movement. (Figs. 231 to 235.)

Continuing from the above movement, rock the arms three to five times; move the right foot one step to the right front while inhaling and finish this right-sided exercise as directed. Practise the movements alternating left and right exercises.

After learning all these basic movements, practise them in a series from the first through the fifth and then in reverse order. The same rule also applies to all the following frolics.

Ending Exercise Resume the beginning posture and

regulate the respiration five times. The ending exercises for the other frolics are the same.

Fig. 231   Fig. 232   Fig. 233   Fig. 234   Fig. 235

2. Crane Frolic

< Key points > Slim and graceful
The crane stands like a pine tree.
High above a layer of clouds,
It flies as if playing with them.
Now displaying its wings, now standing on one leg,
Qi travels gently up, down and around.

The Crane flies so well that its flight is described as playing with clouds and the moon. It stands as tranquil as a pine tree. During practice, one should try to be as natural and free as if flying with a crane in the sky. Or, in fixed postures, imitate the tranquillity and lightness of the bird's bearing. Displaying the wings, alighting and standing on one leg are major characteristics of a crane's movements. To avoid stagnation of Qi, mind activity in this exercise should be conducted softly, gently, slowly and delicately. (Fig. 236.)

(1) Crane Footwork After finishing the Beginning Exercise, draw in the left foot, toes touching the ground, to the inner side of

202

the right foot while rotating the body leftwards and moving the body weight onto the right foot. While inhaling, move the left foot half a step to the left front, toes touching the ground and foot back and shank fully stretched out. Straighten the other leg, imagining standing in the flowing water and trying to feel the force of the current against the shanks while spreading the hands outwards with elbows flexed, palms facing forwards, and fingers parted and flexed. Extend the chest while looking straight forwards. Pause a moment; while exhaling, relax the elbows and withdraw the arms, palms facing inwards; withdraw the right foot, toes touching the ground, to the inner side of the left foot, slightly flex the knees, turn the left foot toes inward while rotating the body rightwards, and shift the body weight onto the left foot. This is the left-sided movement. (Figs. 237 to 240.)

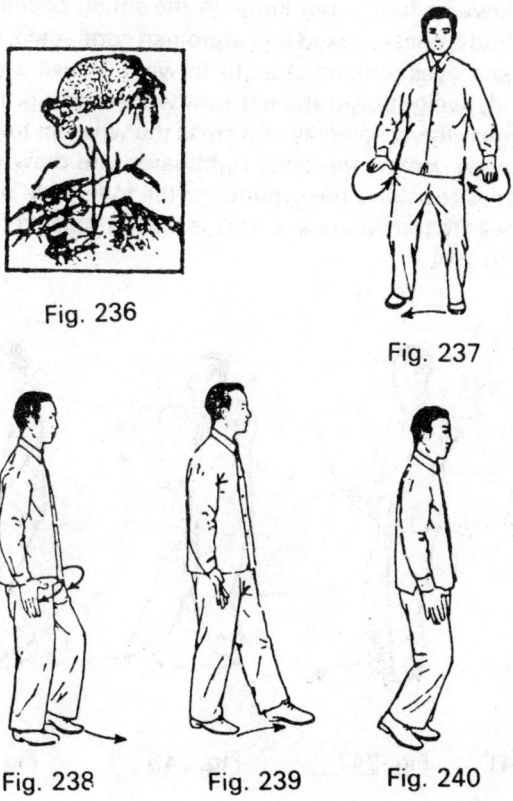

Fig. 236

Fig. 237

Fig. 238   Fig. 239   Fig. 240

Continuing from the left-sided movement, move the right foot half a step to the right front while inhaling and do the exercise as described. Repeat the exercise alternating left and right exercises.

(2) Displaying the Wings Continuing from the previous stance, stand naturally, raise and move both hands to cross the wrists in front of the lower abdomen; flex the knees and shift the body weight onto the right foot. Inhaling, open the arms sideways raising the hands to head level. Elbows, wrists and fingers slightly flexed, wriggle the fingers and make wavy movements with the rising arms, just like a crane displaying its wings. While raising the arms, move the left foot one step to the left front, toes touching the ground; flex the right knee, foot flat on the ground and buttocks weighted down to form a big lunge in the sitting position. Fully extend the body, chest relaxed and abdomen contracted, the back held erect and eyes looking straight forward. Pause a moment; shift the body weight onto the left foot while moving the body; lower the arms slowly, laterally and cross the wrists in front of the lower abdomen. Rotate the body rightwards and draw back the right foot, toes touching the ground, to the inner side of the left foot. The toes are turned inward. This is the left-sided movement. (Figs. 241 to 244.)

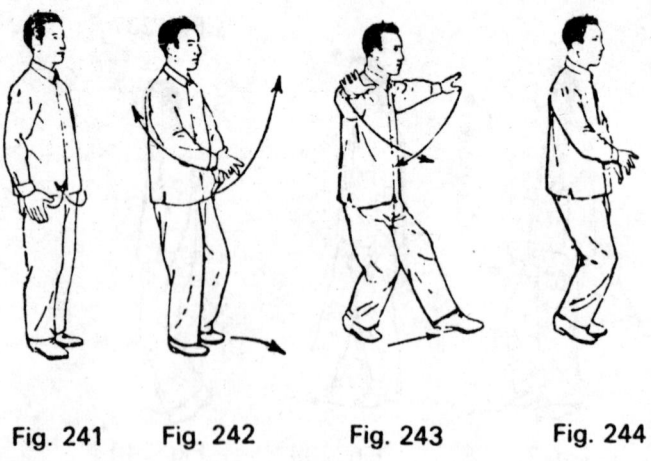

Fig. 241   Fig. 242   Fig. 243   Fig. 244

Continuing from the left-sided movement, move the right foot one step to the right front while inhaling and complete the right-sided movement as described. Repeat, alternating left and right exercises.

(3) **Standing Posture** Continuing from the right-sided movement, withdraw the left foot to the inner side of the right foot and cross the wrists in front of the lower abdomen. Raise the arms sideways while inhaling to head level, the elbows, wrists and fingers flexed. While raising the arms, bend and lift the left knee with toes facing downward and shank and foot back fully stretched; slightly bend the right knee and straighten the spine with eyes looking straight ahead. This posture resembles that of a standing crane. Pause a moment; lower the left foot to land in the left front of the right foot and place the body weight on the left foot. Draw in the right foot, toes touching the ground, to the inner side of the left foot; slowly lower both arms and cross the wrists in front of the lower abdomen. Turn the left foot toes inwards while rotating the body rightwards. This is the left-sided posture. (Figs. 245 to 248.)

Continuing in the left-sided posture, withdraw the right foot to the inner side of the right foot; lift the right knee in front of the lower abdomen while inhaling, and do the other movements as described. Repeat the exercises alternating left and right exercises.

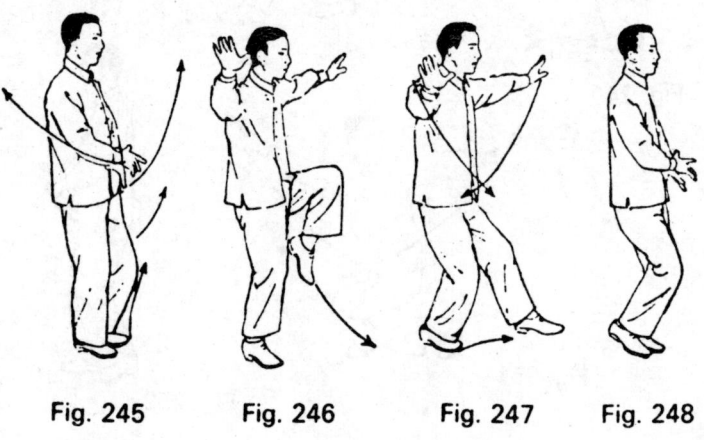

Fig. 245   Fig. 246   Fig. 247   Fig. 248

(4) Alighting Movement Continuing in the same posture, place the body's center of gravity on the left foot; let the arms hang down at the sides; move the right foot half a step in front of the left foot, both toes turned outwards, the feet about one foot apart; cross the hands and slowly raise them sideways until they are eyebrow level. Crouch down so both knees are bent as far as they will go, alighting, and bring the hands down to cross in front of the abdomen. Pause for a moment, the head turned and eyes looking backwards. Rotate the body rightwards. Afterwards, rotate body on tiptoes to face forward, stand up while spreading the arms, after standing, lower both arms slowly to cross them in front of the lower abdomen; rotate the body to resume its original position while withdrawing the left foot to the inner side of the right foot which now bears the body weight. This is the right-sided movement. (Figs. 249 to 252.)

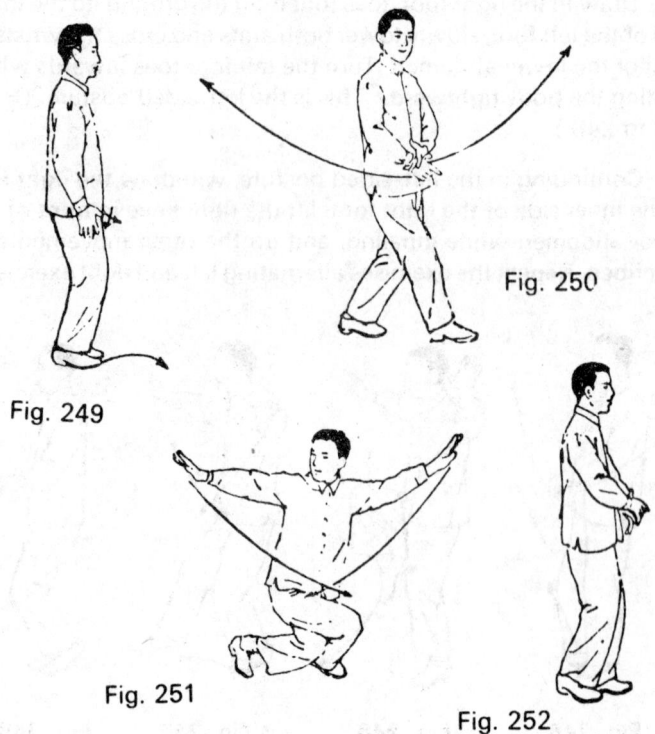

Fig. 250

Fig. 249

Fig. 251

Fig. 252

Continuing from the right-sided movement, move the left foot half a step to the front of the right foot and complete the left- sided movement as described, reversing left and right. Repeat, alternating right and left exercises.

(5) Flying Movements Continuing from the alighting movement, place the body weight on the left foot; withdraw the right foot, toes touching the ground, to the inner side of the left foot. Lower both arms and and hold them slightly out; move the right foot half a step to the front of the left foot with toes turned outwards while crossing both hands in front of the abdomen, and rotate the waist rightwards with eyes looking rightwards and to the back. Simultaneously, raise both arms sideways until the left hand is shoulder level and the right hand hip level; flex the right knee and shift the body weight onto the right foot and lift the left foot backwards, tilting the body forward like a flying bird. Elderly people can balance the hind leg on the ground, according to their physical condition. After a pause, slowly lower the arms to the front of the lower abdomen. Bring the left foot, toes touching the ground, to the inner side of the right foot which bears the body weight. This is the right-sided movement. (Figs. 253 to 257.)

Continuing from the previous posture with body weight on the right foot, bring the left foot forward and take a step to the left front for the left-sided movement as described. Repeat and alternate left and right exercises.

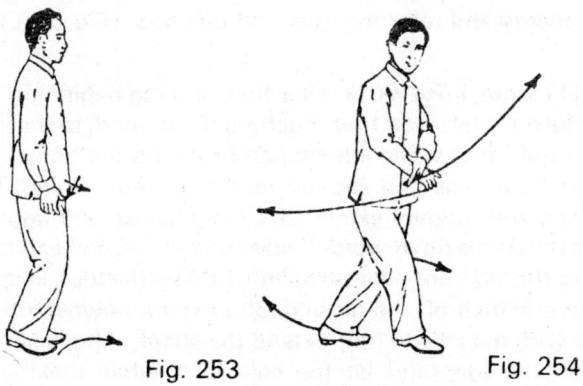

Fig. 253   Fig. 254

| Fig. 255 | Fig. 256 | Fig. 257 |

3. Deer Movements

< Key points > Relax the body and limbs and be in high spirit,

Beware of rigidity and reluctance in movement,

Jump, lean forward and look backwards at times,

Conduct Qi to the tail to train the tendons.

The deer movements are very relaxing. To achieve this effect, one should first of all relax the mind and avoid being nervous. Focus the mind on the Weilu acupoint located at the lower end of the Du Channel and, after practice, try to feel the sensation of Qi traveling along the dredged Du Channel. Continued practice can stimulate and smooth blood circulation as well as invigorate the vital energy and relax muscles and tendons. (Fig. 258.)

(1) Deer Footwork After finishing the beginning exercise, withdraw the left foot, toes touching the ground, to the inner side of the right foot while inhaling and rotating the body leftwards. Lower both arms and slightly hold them out; stretch the arms forward with fingers extended close against one another, and press the palms downward. Pause for a while, and extend the left foot to the left front while exhaling; turn up the toes, keep the sole about one inch off the ground, and exert a downward-pedaling force with the sole to fully extend the shank. After a short pause, stretch the toes and let the sole land while looking straight forward, as if walking in mud. Shift the body weight onto the left foot and withdraw the right foot, toes touching the ground, to the inner side of the left foot while inhaling; turn the left foot toes inward, rotating the body slightly rightwards, and relax the hands letting fingers point down. This is the left-sided movement. (Figs. 259 to 263.)

Continuing in the left-sided posture, withdraw the right foot to the inner side of the left foot and, while exhaling, stretch the right foot forward and complete the right-sided movement as described, substituting left for right. Repeat and alternate left and right exercises.

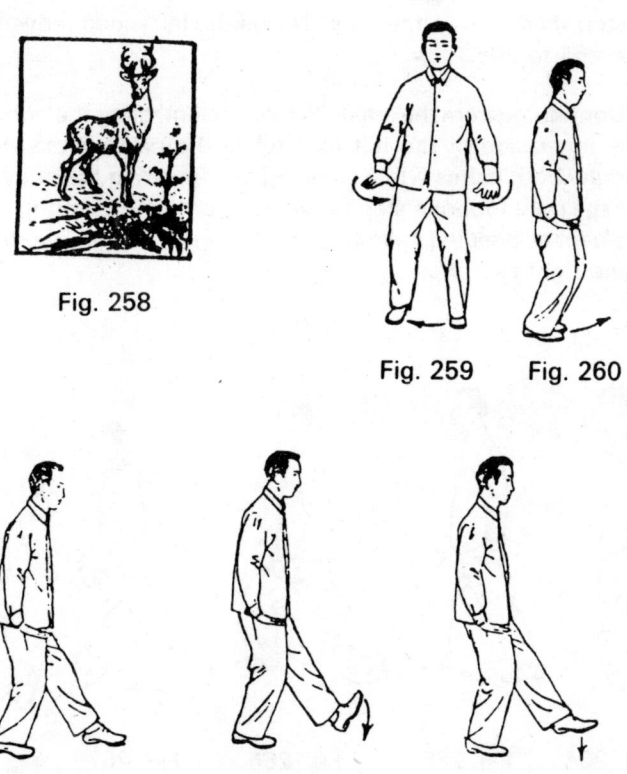

Fig. 258

Fig. 259   Fig. 260

Fig. 261   Fig. 262   Fig. 263

(2) Body-straightening Movements Continuing from the previous exercise, withdraw the left foot to the inner side of the right foot; flex the knees while inhaling and lowering the body a bit; press both hands down, fingers extended and palms down, and slightly flex the arms and elbows outwards. After a short pause, move the left foot one step to the left front forming a lunge; move the hands first backward and then, along an outward curve, to stop beside the hips, arms still tending outwards. Tilt the upper body forwards and look straight forward; keep the neck and spine erect with a slight stiffness and align the left knee and right tiptoe. Bring the right foot forwards, toes touching the ground, to the inner side of the left foot, and turn the left foot toes inward while rotating the body slightly rightwards to place the body weight on the left foot. Push the hands forward and outward to draw arcs and stop them beside the hips. This is the left-sided movement. (Figs. 264 to 268.)

Continuing from the left-sided movement, bring the right foot to the inner side of the left foot while the palms press down, withdraw both hands while exhaling and lowering the body, and move the right foot one step forward to complete the right- sided movement as directed, changing left for right. Repeat, alternating left and right exercises.

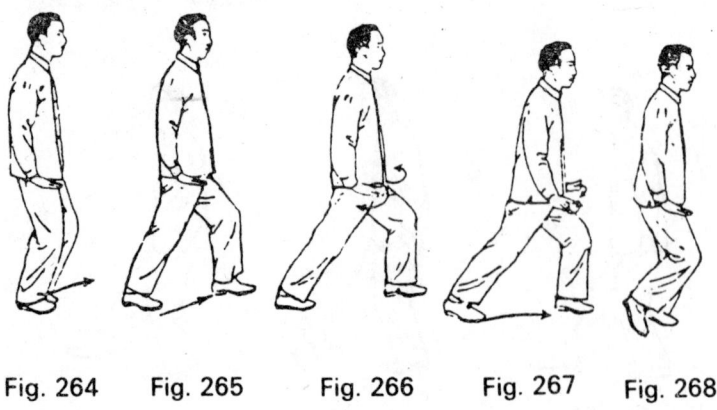

Fig. 264   Fig. 265   Fig. 266   Fig. 267   Fig. 268

(3) Forward Exploration Continuing from the above exercise, with body weight on the right foot, bring the left foot to the inner side of the right foot while pressing the palms downwards. While exhaling, turn the fingers of both hands backwards and have the left foot take one step to the left front to form a lunge. Raise both hands to armpit level before extending them forward in a lunge. With arms at shoulder level, fully extend the elbows, wrists and hands with palms facing downward, wrists turned inward, eyes looking straight forward, with spine and neck erect. Now draw in the right foot, toes touching the ground, to the inner side of the left foot while inhaling and rotate the body rightwards, arms slightly elbowing outward and hands pressing downward. Withdraw the hands to the armpits and drop them to the hip; place the body weight on the left foot. This completes the left-sided movement. (Figs. 269 to 272.)

Continuing in the previous posture, with body weight on the left foot, bring the right foot up to the inner side of the left foot with palms pressing down. While exhaling, hold both hands back and lower the body; advance the right foot one step to the right front and complete the right-sided movement as directed, changing the right-sided movement for the left-sided. Repeat, alternating left and right exercises.

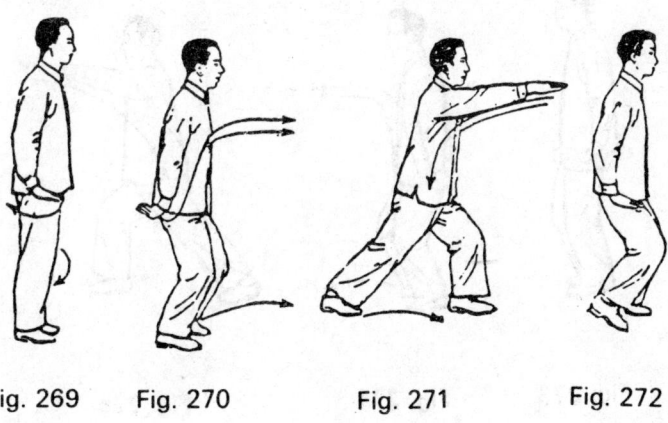

Fig. 269   Fig. 270   Fig. 271   Fig. 272

(4) Backward-looking Movements Continuing from the previous exercise with body weight on the right foot; bring the left foot to the inner side of the right foot and lower both arms exerting an elbowing force. Keep the extended fingers close together and press the palms downward. Now trace circles with hands pressing down. While exhaling, place the left foot one step to the left front to form a lunge while drawing both hands backwards and turning the fingers backwards, raise the hands to the armpits, extend the hands forward, straightening the elbows, wrists and fingers with palms facing downward. The wrists are turned inward, and the arms level with the shoulders, the eyes looking straight forward. Inhale while withdrawing the right hand to the side of the right ribs, flexing its fourth and fifth fingers with the wrist turned outward, and rotate the head rightwards and backwards with eyes looking straight ahead. Focus the mind on the Weilu acupoint. Pause a while before rotating the head and extending the right hand forward to parallel the left hand, fingers extended, now withdraw both hands from to the armpits and drop them to the hips, palms still extended. Bring the right foot, toes touching the ground, to the inner side of the left foot and turn the left foot toes inward, and rotate the body rightwards, shifting the body weight onto the left foot for the left-sided movement. (Figs. 273 to 278.)

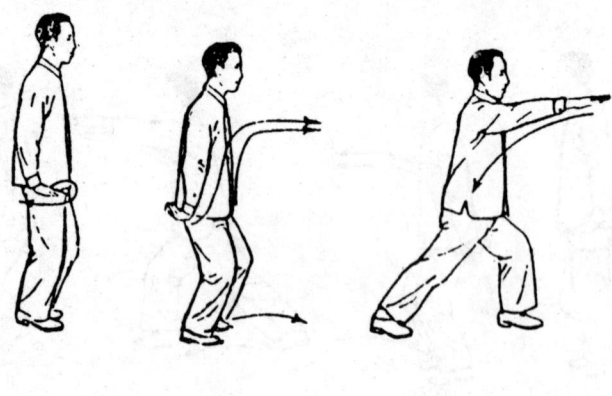

Fig. 273   Fig. 274   Fig. 275

Fig. 276   Fig. 277   Fig. 278

Continuing with weight on the left foot, move the right foot one step to the right front while exhaling. Bring the hands up to the armpits and extend them forward, and continue with the exercises as described, exchanging left for right. Repeat, alternating left and right exercises.

(5) Leaping Movement Continuing with weight on the right foot, draw the left foot to the inner side of the right foot with arms hanging down and elbows flexed and fingers extended straight ahead and palms pressing downwards. Hold the knees close against each other flexed while lowering the body, move the fingers so that they point backwards. After a pause, leap with the left foot in the front and the right foot following closely behind, the right foot kept on tiptoe. When making the jump, keep both hands at the hips, raise them to the armpits and extend them forwards so that they are level with the shoulders. Elbows, wrists and fingers are fully extended, palms facing down, wrists turned inward and eyes looking straight ahead. Inhale and withdraw both hands to the armpits, then lower them to the hips, palms pressing downwards, elbows outwards and the body rising to resume its position of flex-kneed standing. The weight is on the left foot. Turn the left toes inwards and rotate the body rightwards a little. This is the left-sided movement. (Figs. 279 to 282.)

Continuing with body weight on the left foot, exhale while making a leap forward with the right foot leading. Repeat, alternating left and right exercises.

213

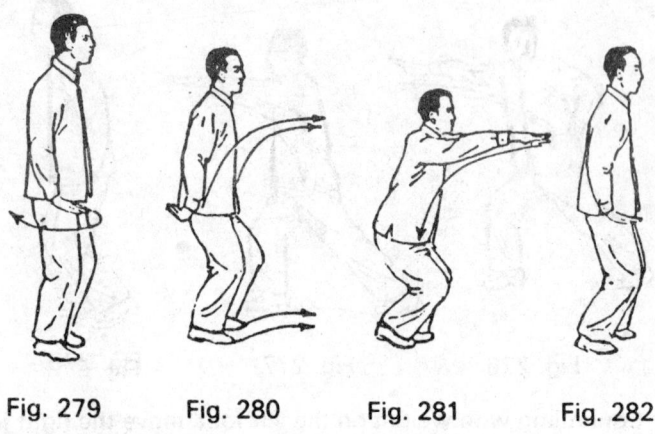

Fig. 279   Fig. 280   Fig. 281   Fig. 282

4. Tiger Frolic

< Key points > Looking majestic, the tiger is the king of beasts.

Its toughness shields inward pliability Protected by its outward strength.

Violent as a hurricane and quiet as the moon,

Tiger leaps, preys and combats, displaying its mighty strength.

To imitate a tiger's movements, the practitioner should keep in mind that the animal shows its spirit in the eyes and power in the claws, and that nothing can stop the ferocious animal prowling in the mountains. The movements should contain tremendous forces. The actions should not only suggest a hurricane, but also contain the quietude of the moon, so as to achieve the combination of motion with quietude and the interaction between toughness and pliability. Preying and combating make up the main actions in the tiger exercise. Persistent practice can increase the essences, strengthen the waist and kidneys, and reinfoce the bones and tendons. (Fig. 283.)

(1) Tiger Footwork After finishing the beginning exercise, draw in the left foot by lifting it one centimeter off the ground (beginners can keep the toes on the ground) to the inner side of

the right foot while inhaling; turn the right toes inward and rotate the body leftwards. Simultaneously, exert force with both hands as a tiger does with its claws and reach the hands forward along a curve before lifting them bilaterally to hip level with arms slightly flexed and elbowing outward and buttocks weighted down a little. Keep the upper body erect, relax the chest and contract the abdomen, and look straight forward. Exhale while moving the left foot one step to the left front drawing an arc with the foot, as if wading through mud, imagining an impeding force pulling the legs. But keep the weight on the right foot. Extend the arms forward and outward in a small curve pushing and pressing downwards, grasp the ground with the toes, calm the mind and regulate respiration, standing in a lunge in a half sitting position with the weight on the right foot. Now draw in the right foot to the inner side of the left foot which now bears the body weight and relax the body when exhaling. This completes the left-sided movement. (Figs. 284 to 287.)

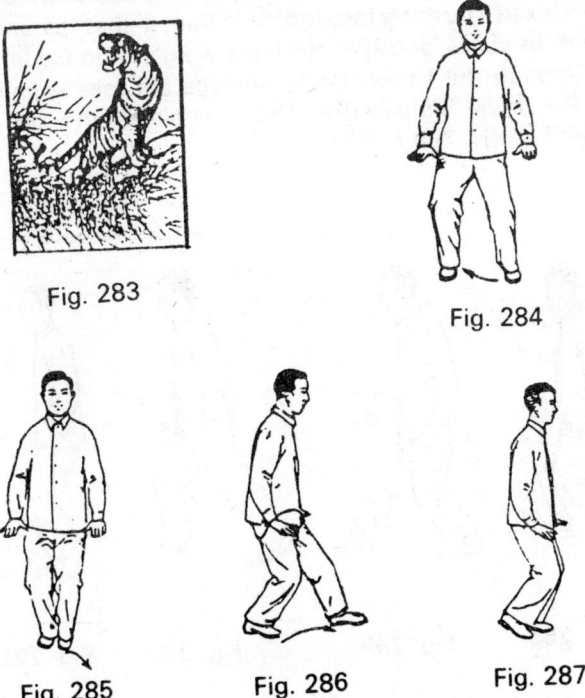

Fig. 283

Fig. 284

Fig. 285

Fig. 286

Fig. 287

Continuing from the previous exercise, shift the body weight to the left foot, draw in the right foot to the inner side of the left foot and take one step right-forward with the right foot while exhaling. With the body weight on the left foot form the half sitting bow step. This is the right-sided posture. Do the exercise as directed, changing the sides. Repeat the left and right exercises alternately.

(2) **Tiger Power** Continuing with body weight on the right foot, draw in the left foot to the inner side of the right foot; make an arc with both hands, pushing forward, outward and then back, stopping about one fist from the hips. While exhaling, move the left foot one step to the left front and gather all the strength to yell the word "Ha" silently. Flex the knees to form the left-sided small stride of the tiger, with the upper body tilted forward, back and spine held erect, eyes looking straight forward, and the left tiptoe and the left knee in alignment. Stretch the hands downward along a curve to exert a pushing force a little in front of the hips, as a tiger does with its claws, and shift the body weight onto the left foot. Inhale through the closed teeth, turn the left toes inward and rotate the body rightwards. This completes the left-sided movement. (Figs. 288 to 291.)

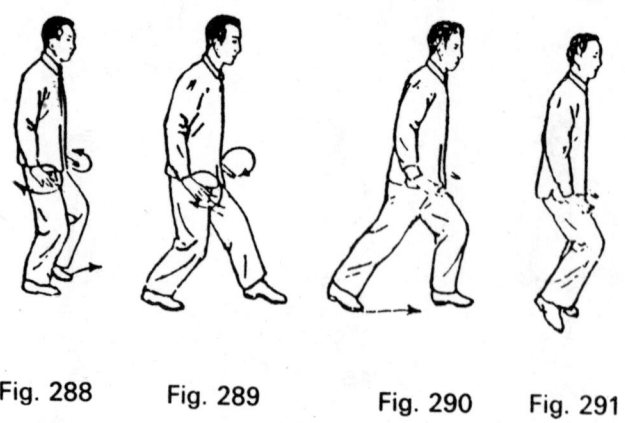

Fig. 288   Fig. 289   Fig. 290   Fig. 291

Continuing with body weight on the left foot, draw in the right foot to the inner side of the left foot and make forward then outward arcs with both hands. Move the right foot one step to the right front to form a small stride of the tiger and shift the body weight onto the right foot. Complete the right-sided movement according to the instructions changing left to right. Repeat, alternating left and right exercises.

(3) Coming out of the Den Continuing with body weight on the right foot, bring the left foot to the inner side of the right foot, hands drawing arcs by moving backward before moving upwards and forwards stopping beside the hips, pause. While exhaling, gather strength to yell "Ha" silently. Move the left foot one step to the left front with knees flexed to form a "tiger stride;" shift the body weight onto the left foot, with the upper body tilting forward, back and spine held erect, and left knee in line with the left toes. Extend both hands shoulder-width apart to breast level to draw arcs with arms flexed like bows and elbowing outward, and palms facing forward and exerting a triangular pushing force. Relax the chest and contract the abdomen with neck and spine held erect, eyes looking forward and toes of both feet grasping the ground. Inhale through the closed teeth, turn the left foot toes inward and rotate the body leftwards a little. Bring in the right foot, toes touching the ground, to the inner side of the left foot. This completes the left-sided movement. (Figs. 292 to 295.)

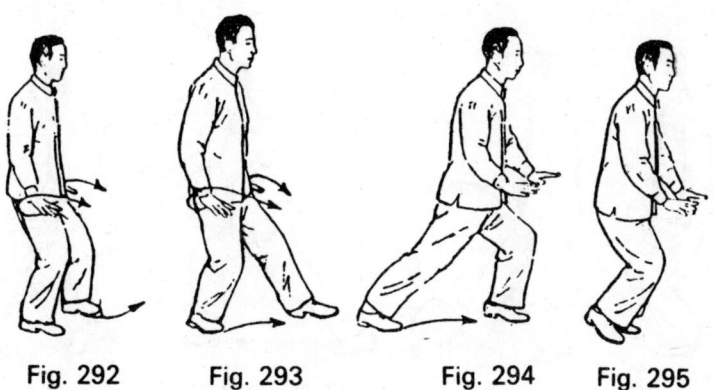

Fig. 292   Fig. 293   Fig. 294   Fig. 295

Continuing the left-sided posture, move the right foot one step to the right front to form the tiger stride, shift the body weight onto the right foot, and complete the exercise as directed, changing left to right. Repeat, alternating left and right exercises.

(4) Preying Movement Continuing from the previous exercise, place the body weight on the right foot, draw in the left foot to the inner side of the right foot, both hands drawing backward circles before stopping by the hips. Pause a while, move the left foot one step to the left front while exhaling and gather strength to yell "Ha" silently, slightly flex the knees to form the left-sided tiger stride and shift the body weight onto the left foot. Tilt forward, the spine and waist held erect and both hands drawing forward and outward arcs, leaving a fist's distance between the downward-facing palms which are barely at breast level, just like a tiger preying upon a game and pressing it firmly on the ground. The eyes looking forward and knees turned inwards, grasp the ground with both feet. While inhaling through the closed teeth, turn the left toes inward, draw in the right foot, toes touching the ground, to the inner side of the left foot, reach out the hands along a curve backwards, and stop them beside the hips. Slightly rotate the body rightwards. This completes the left-sided movement. (Figs. 296 to 299.)

Continuing in the left-sided posture with body weight on the left foot, draw the right foot to the inner side of the left foot, and

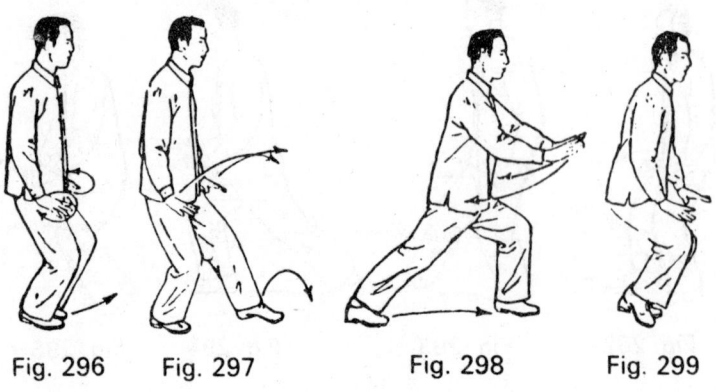

Fig. 296　　Fig. 297　　　　Fig. 298　　　　Fig. 299

move it one step to the right front while exhaling to form the right-sided tiger stride. Shift the body weight onto the right foot. Using both hands, draw forward and outward arcs, and complete the right-sided movement according to the directions changing left to right. Repeat, alternating left and right exercises.

(5) **Tiger Combat** Continuing in the previous posture with body weight on the right foot, the left foot is drawn to the inner side of the the right foot; the hands draw arcs forward and outward, stopping in front of the hips. Pause a moment. While exhaling, gather strength to yell "Ha" silently. Move the left foot one step to the left front and flex the knees to form a tiger stride, shifting the body weight onto the left foot, tilt forward with waist and spine erect, lower the chin with a backwards force and lips weighted down, chest relaxed and abdomen contracted. While raising both hands, fiercely thrust them forward and outward palms facing down, just like a tiger in combat. Leading with the left hand in the front, stop the arms and elbows at the forehead level with force going outwards. The palm faces obliquely downwards and lines with the left toes. Keep the right hand about three fists in front of the shoulder as if in protection and line it up with the left knee. Now, inhaling through the closed teeth, turn the left toes inwards and slightly rotate the body leftwards. Bring up the right foot, toes touching the ground, to the inner side of the left foot. Bring the hands in arcs down to the hips. This completes the left-sided movement. (Figs. 300 to 304.)

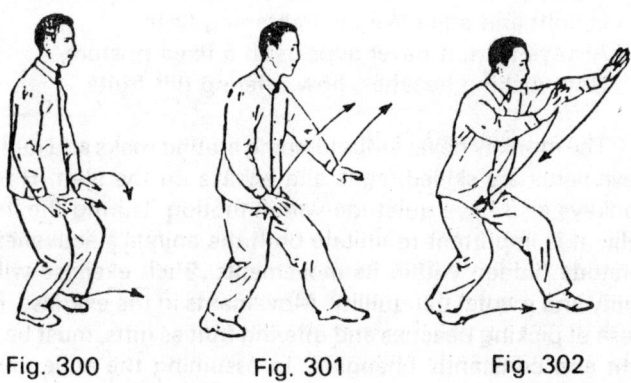

Fig. 300   Fig. 301   Fig. 302

Continuing with body weight on the left foot and right foot taken back to the inner side of the left foot, exhale while moving the right foot one step to the right front to form the right-sided tiger stride, shift the body weight onto the right foot, protect the lower jaw with the right hand and the heart with the left hand, both arms elbowing outward and pressing downward, and complete the exercise as described changing left for the right. Repeat both exercises alternating left and right.

Fig. 303   Fig. 304

5 Monkey Frolic

< Key points > Fond of movements by nature, the monkey Is light and agile like the lightening flash.
Always alert, it never appears in a fixed posture,
Now picking peaches, now offering gift fruits.

The monkey never stops jumping around rocks and gullies. Its movements are skilled, agile and always on the alert. However, monkeys also have quietude within motion. During the monkey frolic, it is important to imitate both the animal's activeness and quietude hidden within its movements. Such exercise will train agility and mental tranquillity. Movements in the exercise, mainly those of picking peaches and offering fruit as gifts, must be quick, light and constantly changing. In assuming the agile and alert appearance of the monkey, the slightest sign of stiffness is forbidden during practice. Another important point is to act monkey as vividly as possible. This is often difficult because man is the dignified monarch. But impersonation is the only approach to success in this exercise. So, the practitioner should not only show the minor actions, such as peeping and escaping, but also keep in mind the legendary Monkey King's power in wielding the golden cudgel. This last key point is important for all the animal frolics, except that it is more obvious in the monkey frolic.

(1) **Monkey Footwork** After the beginning exercise, draw the left foot, toes touching the ground, to the inner side of the right foot; turn the right foot toes inward while slightly rotating the body leftwards. While inhaling, move the left foot half a step to the left front toes touching the ground; slightly flex the knees and half sit down to form the right-sided small lunge. Simultaneously, push both hands forward and outward drawing arcs and turn the hands into hooks, move the left hand along a curve to stop about three fists in front of the left hip, elbow flexed and sinking and hand hooked downward, and move the right hand along a curve to stop about one fist to the side of the right hip, elbow flexed and pushing backwards. Relax the chest, shrink the neck and search ahead with the eyes. While exhaling, draw up the right foot, toes touching the ground, to the inner side of the left foot, and turn the left toes inwards. Slightly rotate the body rightwards. Draw arcs with the hands pressing them above the outer sides of the hips. This completes the left movement. (Figs. 306 to 309.)

Fig. 305

Fig. 306   Fig. 307

Fig. 308   Fig. 309

Continuing with body weight on the left foot and the right foot drawn up to the inner side of the left foot, move the right foot half a step to the right front, forming a right-sided small lunge; revolve the right hand to stop in front of the right hip and revolve the left hand to stop oeside the left hip. Now continue as directed, substituting left for right. Repeat both exercises alternating left and right.

(2) Peeping While Sitting Continuing with body weight on the right foot and the left foot drawn back to the inner side of the right foot, move the left foot half a step to the left front while inhaling through the closed teeth; flex the knees and half sit with the right toes turning inward, and slightly rotate the head rightwards, forming the right-sided small lunge in the half sitting position. Change the left hooked hand to a flat palm and raise it along a curve in front of the chest to stop above the right eye. Change the left palm into a hook again and rotate the head to look vigilantly rightwards; the right hooked hand draws a backward arc to stop a little behind the right hip, elbow flexed and pushing backward. Now, when exhaling, open the teeth slightly to gather strength to yell the word "Hai" silently. Lower the left hand along a curve from the eye's outer front to the outer front of the left hip and change the hooked hand to a flat palm. Simultaneously, revolve the right hooked hand forward and outward to stop in the outer front of the right hip and change it to a flat palm. Meanwhile, bring in the right foot, toes touching the ground, to the inner side of left foot, and slightly rotate the body leftwards. This completes the left-sided posture. (Figs. 310 to 313.)

Continuing with body weight on the left foot and the right foot brought in to the inner side of the left foot, move the right foot half a step to the right front while exhaling and turn the left toes inwards and slightly rotate the head and body leftwards. Raise the right hand along a curve in front of the chest to stop above the left eye and turn the head leftwards. Reach the left hooked hand forward and outward along a curve to remain hooked a little behind the left hip. Complete the right- sided exercise as directed changing left for right. Repeat, alternating left and right exercises.

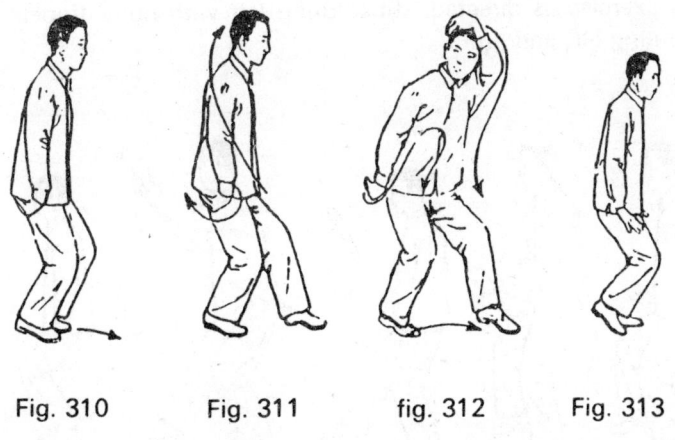

Fig. 310   Fig. 311   fig. 312   Fig. 313

(3) Offering Fruit Gifts Continuing with body weight on the right foot and the left foot drawn up to the inner side of the right foot, change both hands to hooks and push them forward along a curve to stop in front of the lower abdomen. While inhaling through the closed teeth, move the left foot one step to the left front; flex the knees and sit down, forming a right- sided large lunge in a half sitting position. Change both hooked hands to flat palms and revolve them from the lower abdomen to the front of the hips; then revolve both hands forward and outward and turn the palms to face upward with fingers slightly parted and bent; flex the elbows and raise the palms, stop the left hand at head level and the right hand at shoulder level with forearms tending inward, as if offering fruits. While holding the hands upward, lower the body with head turned upwards, neck shrunk and eyes looking at the upper front of the hands. After a pause, while exhaling by opening the teeth, gather strength to yell "Hai" silently. Turn the hands to draw downward arcs to the outer sides of the hips, bring up the right foot, toes touching the ground, to the inner side of the left foot, and slightly rotate the body rightwards. This completes the left-sided movement. (Figs. 314 to 318.)

Continuing with body weight on the left foot and the right foot brought to the inner side of the left foot, move the right foot one step to the right front while inhaling, and complete the right-sided exercise as directed, substituting left with right. Repeat, alternating left and right.

Fig. 314   Fig. 315   Fig. 316   Fig. 317   Fig. 318

(4) Picking Peaches Continuing with body weight on the right foot and the left foot brought up to the inner side of the right foot, change both hands to hooks and revolve them to the front of the lower abdomen. While inhaling through the closed teeth, move the left foot one step to the left front; flex the knees and half sit, forming a right-sided big lunge; change both hooked hands to flat palms and revolve them from the lower abdomen to the hip

224

sides. Now push both hands forwards and upwards, the left hand becoming hooked and stopping at head level with forearm flexed; in the meantime, the right arm has become hooked and is at eye level about two fists' distance from the head with elbow flexed and palm facing downwards obliquely. Vertically line up the left hand with the left foot, and the right hand with a point about one fist from the inner side of the right knee; keep the right hand behind and below the left hand with a distance of about two fists between the left elbow and the right hand; turn the head upward, shrink the neck and look over the left thumb into the distance, as if picking peaches. While exhaling by opening the teeth slightly to let air pass through them, gather strength to yell "Hai" silently. Lower both hands to the hip sides; draw up the right foot, toes touching the ground, to the inner side of the left foot; turn the left toes inward, and rotate the body rightwards. This completes the left-sided movement. (Figs. 319 to 322.)

Continuing with body weight on the left foot and the right ioot brought up to the inner side of the left foot, move the right foot one step to the right front while inhaling. Raise the right hand forward to head level; raise the left hand to shoulder level, complete the right-sided movement as directed, changing left for right. Repeat, alternating left and right exercises.

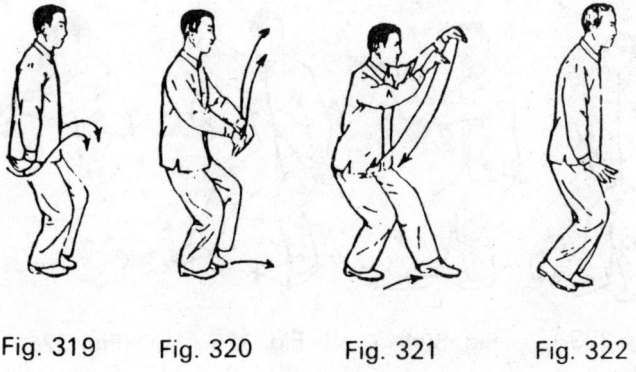

Fig. 319   Fig. 320   Fig. 321   Fig. 322

(5) Escaping and Hiding Continuing with body weight on the right foot and the left foot brought up to the inner side of the right foot, press both hands down beside the hips. When inhaling through the closed teeth, move the left foot half a step to the left front; flex the knees and weigh down the hips to form a right-sided lunge with hands hooked and crossed in front of the lower abdomen. While exhaling, push the hands forward from the sides to draw inward arcs; place the hands about one fist apart in front of the chest on breast level, elbow flexed and fingers held together, upper arms slightly pushing outward and eyes searching ahead. After a pause, move the left foot half a step forward while inhaling and lowering the body position to form a low lunge in a half sitting posture. Change the left hand into a hook and push it about four fists to the front of the left ribs, with forearm pushing outward and the hooked hand tending inwards; look rightwards and back. Pause, while inhaling, revolve the hands forward and stop them beside the hips. Move the right foot one step forward to the inner side of the left foot, form a right-weighted squatting posture, and rotate the body to face the front. This completes the left-sided movement. (Figs. 323 to 326.)

Continuing with body weight on the left foot, move the right foot half a step to the right front while inhaling to form a left-weighted small lunge in a half sitting posture. Change the hands into hooks and cross them in front of the lower abdomen, and complete the right-sided exercise as directed, substituting left for right. Repeat, alternating left and right exercises.

Fig. 323   Fig. 324   Fig. 325   Fig. 326

(V) Free Practice of the Frolics of Five Animals

The free exercises are variations of the basic methods and postures of the Frolics of Five Animals designed by the practitioners themselves. The basic methods and postures provide the necessary foundation without which, if one over eagerly goes on with free practice, the movements and Qi may become unstable resulting in wrong postures and skills. Free practice not only demands serious observance of requirements for the basic postures, but also goes beyond the basics. Only with this understanding, can one expect to integrate form and mind, maintain energy, carry out the movements freely and naturally and finally enter a state where the body and mind become an organic whole.

Besides the basic skills, the practitioner of free exercises must first concentrate and calm the mind, regulate respiration and conduct Qi to Dantian. Then, when Internal Qi is mobilized and creates momentum, the free exercises can be practised by combining the requirements for the basic forms with the observing and thinking method. Repeated observation of the animals imitated make deeper impressions on us and analysis of their movements imitated are necessary.

Key points in performing the free exercises of the Frolics of Five Animals include doing the beginning exercise well, calming the mind to regulate respiration, conducting Qi to Dantian and remaining in a tranquil state despite distractions. After entering into a state of quietude, concentrate on the appearance, nature and characteristics, movements and natural habitat of the animal being imitated. The cerebral activity becomes more and more concentrated and the impression of the animal more clear and true to life. When well focused, the cerebral cortex is fully conscious and can exclude some disturbances. This is called entering a quiescent state by substituting one idea for ten thousand. It produces good effects in relieving fatigue, stimulating physiological functions and increases the effects and interest in exercise.

Described below are specific methods of the Frolics of Five

Animals for free exercise.

1. Bear Frolic

After successful completion of the beginning exercise, regulate respiration, calm the mind, conduct Qi to Dantian, and think of a group of white bears slowly and steadily walking along a vast seashore. The bears' movements are bulky, firm, a little awkward and full of vigor. Imagine yourself walking and playing among bears.

Sometimes stroll and rock,
Now press and play,
Sometimes lean back to train the shoulders,
Now push to forge ahead,
Sometimes wash the face like a giant panda,
Now squat and press downwards,
Sometimes hurriedly prowl for food,
Now turn back to watch.

Do the exercise varying it with a myriad of changes.

2. Crane Frolic

After successful completion of the beginning exercise, regulate respiration, calm the mind, conduct Qi to Dantian and think of a flock of cranes resting in shady tranquillity beside a pond. The cranes' postures are graceful and their movements elegant and refined. Imagine yourself joining them on the scene.

Sometimes they land on the sandy beach,
Now spread their white wings,
Sometimes touch down on the water surface, Now peck at grain like golden cockerels,
Sometimes fly freely like the phoenix,
Now flutter the wings like swans,
Sometimes display the feathers like peacocks,
Now stand in perfect balance on one leg.

Do the exercise with a myriad of changes.

3. Dear Frolic

After successful completion of the beginning exercise, regulate respiration, calm the mind, conduct Qi to Dantian, and think of a flock of deer strolling on the boundless grassland. The deers' movements are graceful and casual. Imagine yourself roaming as they do.

Sometimes they roam on the grassland,
Now they spurt forward,
Sometimes stop to look back,
Now jump and leap forward,
Sometimes gallop across the grassland,
Now run into the forest,
Sometimes they swim,
Now stand peacefully by the forest.

Do the exercise with a myriad of changes.

4. Tiger Frolic

After successful completion of the beginning exercise, regulate respiration, calm the mind, conduct Qi to Dantian, and think of a fierce tiger suddenly appearing in the mountains with majestic and powerful magnificence. Stalking in the distance. Imagine you are that tiger, standing majestically and roaming the mountains.

Sometimes the tiger roams the mountains,
Now plays with the cubs,
Sometimes comes out of the den with hunger,
Now combats another tiger,
Sometimes loses its temper and raves furiously,
Now pounces on its prey,
Sometimes lies down and watches the moon,
Now prowls hills angrily.

Do the exercise with a myriad of changes.

5. Monkey Frolic

229

After successful completion of the beginning exercise, regulate respiration, calm the mind, conduct Qi to Dantian, and think of a group of monkeys jumping over rocks and leaping through the tree branches deep in the forest. Their movements are agile and alert. Imagine yourself playing among the monkeys.

Sometimes monkeys peep carefully around,
Now become terrified and run away,
Sometimes offer fruit gifts,
Now pull the head of the golden cudgel,
Sometimes pick peaches,
Now wield swards,
Sometimes learn to sit on the ground,
Now use fans imitating the princesses.

(VI) Walking Exercise for the Frolics of Five Animals

The Frolics of Five Animals was created by Hua Tuo who was an outstanding doctor of the Han dynasty. It is five sets of prophylactic exercises, combining imitations of the actions of five animals--tiger, bear, deer, monkey and bird. Hua Tuo said, "One should avoid overstraining when taking part in physical labor or exercise. But an appropriate amount of movement may aid in promoting digestion and and absorption of food, and blood circulation, thus preventing illness. A door hinge never gets worm-riddled. Prevention of premature aging can be accomplished by means of moving the body and all the joints. I have an art of healing which is called the Frolics of Five Animals-- tiger, deer, bear, monkey and bird. It can be used for curing certain kinds of diseases and building up the constitution. If one feels a bit unfit, take one set of the five animal frolics and one may sweat, feel a comfortable sensation throughout the body, and get an improved appetite." The Frolics of Five Animals is the earliest prophylactic exercise known in China.

The walking exercise of the five animal frolics presented is simplified from the Frolics of Five Animals. These exercises can be subdivided into five sets. Practise only one set each time. No matter which set is used, practise the beginning exercise first. The walking exercise should be followed by the ending exercise. The beginning and ending exercises basically train vital energy. So they must be done earnestly.

The walking exercises are used mainly for the prevention and treatment of chronic diseases and for building up the constitution. To cure diseases, we should relax the whole body, set aside disturbing thoughts and carry out the exercises slowly and gently. They are indicated in some chronic diseases such as neurasthenia, ulcers, chronic hepatitis, chronic bronchitis, lumbago, leg pain, hypertension or coronary heart disease. It is advisable for patients with the last two diseases to do the bear- walking exercise described for its training of relaxed but stable movement. As for building up the constitution, the amount of exercise should be properly increased according to the individual's conditions. The movement should always be gentle, slow and relaxed. Natural respiration and focusing the mind at Middle Dantian should be done during the exercise, and deep abdominal respiration can be gradually instituted.

Beginning Exercise

Stand naturally with feet parallel and shoulder-width apart; slightly rotate the knees inwards, adduct the hip joints, and half sit back on the buttocks. Straighten the spine, relax the chest and contract the abdomen. Relax the shoulder joints and press down both hands with palms facing downward, as if pressing a floating ball in the water. Keep the head level with the eyes looking ahead; gently close the mouth with the tongue naturally placed inside; inhale with the nose and exhale with the mouth, or breathe with both the mouth and nose; calm the mind, regulate respiration, and mentally conduct Qi to Dantian. Push the hands along a forward and outward curve, and turn the palms face upwards and cross them in front of the lower abdomen. After a short pause, slowly raise the the hands to breast level while inhaling, and turn the palms face downward; lower the hands to the lower abdomen while exhaling, and turn the palms face upwards. Do this set eight times, and lower to the sides.

1. Tiger Walk

Stand naturally as in the beginning exercise and focus the

231

mind at Middle Dantian. Draw in the left foot to the inner side of the right foot, forming a pseudo T gait with body weight on the right foot (Fig. 327). Move the left foot half a step to the left front and slightly flex the right knee with the right foot completely touching the ground, forming a lunge. Shape the hands like the claws of a tiger, and revolve them inward to stop beside the hips (Fig. 328). After a pause, shift the body weight onto the right foot, forming a small sitting stance; rotate the left toes inward to bear the body weight. Bring the right foot to the inner side of the left foot, forming a pseudo T gait; revolve the hands forward and outward to the lateral sides of the hips, the elbows flexed, claw-shaped fingers relaxed and the body gently rising (Fig. 329). After a pause, move the right foot half a step to the right front and repeat according to the directions.

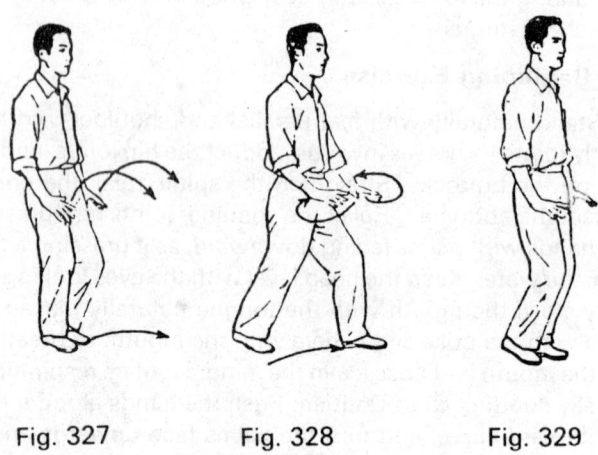

Fig. 327   Fig. 328   Fig. 329

2. Deer Walk

Stand naturally with the mind focused at Middle Dantian. Draw in the left foot to the inner side of the right foot, forming a pseudo T gait with body weight on the right foot (Fig. 330). Without stopping, move the left foot half a step to the left front; slightly flex the right knee with the right foot completely touching the ground to form a lunge; close the fingers and push the hands forward and outward along an arc to place them beside the hips, exerting force from the base of the palms (Fig. 331). After a pause, shift the body weight onto the right foot, forming a half sitting stance; turn the left toes inward to bear the body weight, forming a small lunge, and bring in the right foot to the inner side of the left foot, forming a pseudo T gait; move the hands forward, out and then inward in a small circle, pressing them downward still beside the hips, elbows straightened, the base of both palms exerting force but the fingers relaxed, and the body held erect (Fig. 332). After a pause, move the right foot half a step to the right front and repeat the exercise as directed.

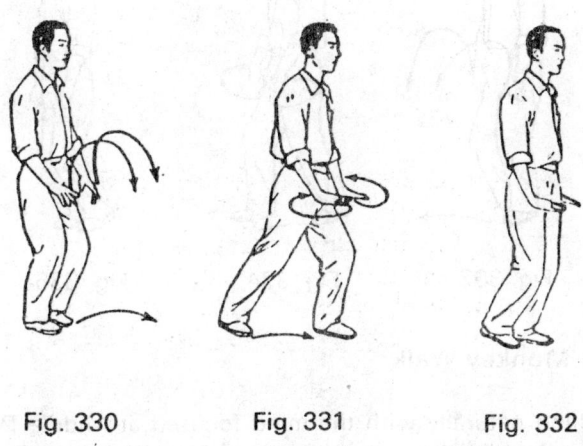

Fig. 330   Fig. 331   Fig. 332

3. Bear Walk

Stand naturally with the mind at Middle Dantian. Bring the left foot to the inner side of the right foot, forming a pseudo T gait with body weight on the right foot and press the hands downwards in front of the thighs, palms facing downwards (Fig. 333) and move the left foot half a step to the left front to form a lunge. Slightly flex the left knee with the left foot completely touching the ground. Raise the fists to breast level, and then lower them along a forward and downward curve to stop in front of the hips (Fig. 334). After a pause, shift the body weight onto the right foot, forming a small half sitting gait; rotate the left foot inwards and move the body weight to the left foot, forming a small lunge. Now draw in the right foot to the inner side of the left foot, forming a pseudo T gait; revolve the fists forward and inward to stop in front of the lower abdomen and slightly lower the whole body (Fig. 335). After a short pause, move the right foot half a step to the right front, and repeat as directed.

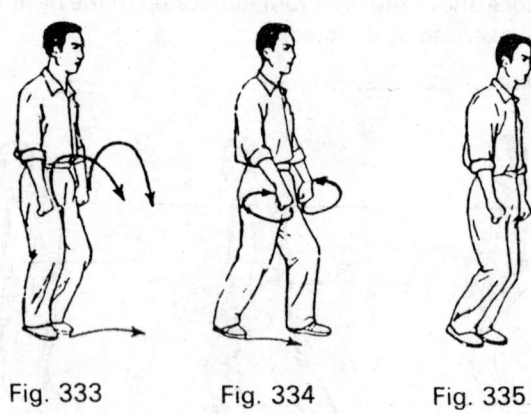

| Fig. 333 | Fig. 334 | Fig. 335 |

4. Monkey Walk

Stand naturally with the mind focused at Middle Dantian. Bring in the left foot to the inner side of the right foot, forming a pseudo T gait with body weight on the right foot; press the hands downwards in front of the thighs, palms facing downwards (Fig. 336). Move the left foot half a step to the left front to form a small lunge. Slightly flex the right knee with the foot flat on the ground. Shape the hands like hooks, wrists forwards, then raise them to chest level and lower them bilaterally to the sides of the hips. Meanwhile, turn the head right (Fig. 337). Pause, then shift the body weight onto the right foot to form a small half sitting gait; meanwhile, return the head to the central position; raise the hooked hands by flexing the elbows from 110 degrees to 70 degrees, and turn the left foot toes inward to bear the body weight,

234

forming a small lunge. Bring the right foot to the inner side of the left foot to form a pseudo T gait; simultaneously, raise the hooked hands to chest level before lowering them along a forward and downward curve to press downwards, palms flat beside the hips (Fig. 338). Pause, then move the right foot half a step to the right front and repeat as directed.

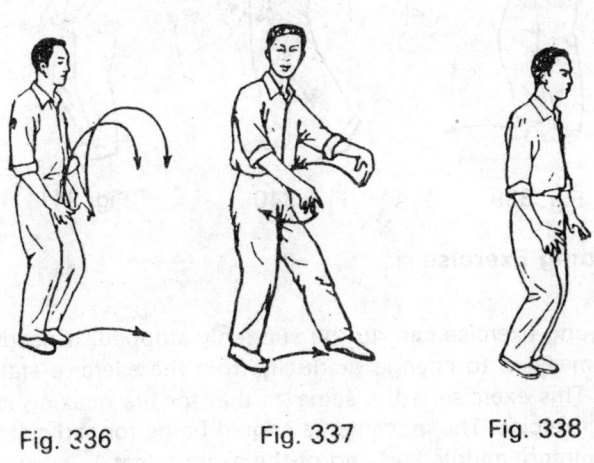

Fig. 336   Fig. 337   Fig. 338

5. Crane Walk

Stand naturally with the mind focused at Middle Dantian. Draw up the left foot to the inner side of the right foot, forming a pseudo T gait with body weight on the right foot. Place the hands beside the hips (Fig. 339). Without stopping, move the left foot half a step to the left front to form a small lunge; straighten the upper body with head, chest and the tip of the left foot in a line; lift the heels; turn the palms outwards and move them to the front of the hips. Keep the head level with eyes looking forward (Fig. 340). After a pause, shift the body weight onto the right foot with the foot flat on the ground to form a small sitting gait; turn the palms downwards; turn the left toes inwards and shift the weight onto the left foot, and bring the right foot to the inner side of the left foot to form a pseudo T gait (Fig. 341). After a pause, move the right foot half a step to the right front and repeat as directed.

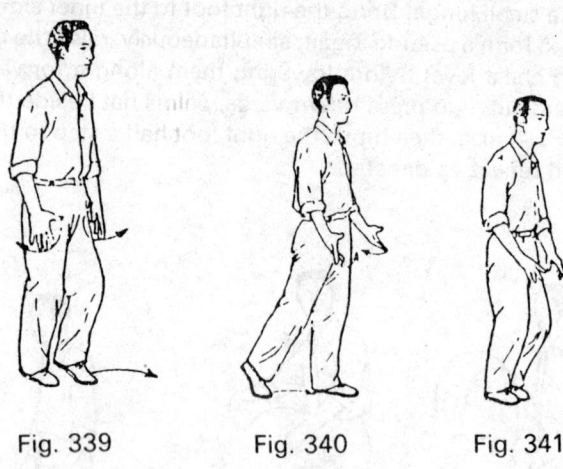

| Fig. 339 | Fig. 340 | Fig. 341 |

Ending Exercise

Qigong exercise can not be suddenly stopped. It needs an interim measure to change gradually from the exercise state to normal. This exercise is the same as that for the relaxing static Qigong exercise. The movements should be performed stably at the beginning, middle and end of the exercise set.

VI. Internal Qigong Self-massage

The simplified name of Internal Qigong Self-massage is self-massage. It is done by oneself and has good effects in curing diseases and preserving health. It is limited to points which one can reach. It is not only prophylactic but also curative in diseases suitable for self-massage under the guidance of a doctor.

Self-massage can be done before sleep, or at other times. For massage before sleep, the coat should be taken off and a shirt worn only. This is helpful to dredging channels and collaterals, dynamic equilibrium of Yin and Yang, harmonization of Qi and blood, and acceleration of blood circulation.

Self-massage depends on the TCM theory of massaging

acupoints along the channels and collaterals and employs a set of unique technics which can be applied by the practitioner himself. When self-massage is carried out in combination with Qigong exercise, self-massage (or external movement of Qi) and the internal movement of Qi/breath can be organically combined to be doubly effective, enhancing the efficiency of both exercises.

Self-massage's main effects are the dredging of the channels and harmonization of Qi and blood.

(I) The Main Technics of Self-massage

1. Patting Massage This method is conducted with the pads of the forefinger, middle finger, ring finger and little finger which pat the massage area. During massage, the four finger tips can be held together or slightly parted to pat and beat rhythmically with a bouncing force. This method can be applied to the four extremities.

2. Tapping Massage Curve all five fingers, their tips close together or slightly parted to become fan-shaped or shaped like a plum blossom. Using the wrist's spring force, tap the massage area with the fingertips. This exercise is rather powerful and the force rather concentrated. Fingernails should be clipped before employing this method, which is mainly applied to the four extremities.

3. Stroking Massage Use the palms or sides of the palms to stroke the massage area slowly and rhythmically. Although the force varies in intensity, it is in general rather light. Gentle stroking is mainly applied to the head, and quick-stroking mainly on the four extremities and trunk. Quick stroking uses the force of the whole body.

4. Twisting Massage This method is conducted with the pads of the forefinger, middle finger, ring finger and small finger or the palm and its side. The force of the former is rather concentrated, whereas the latter employs a rather even force on the superficial parts of the body. This massage is circular in motion. The fingertips are suitable for the extremities and the palm for the abdomen.

5. Poking and Pressing Massage Poke the acupoint and press it with the fingertips. Any of the the five fingertips with nails clipped can be used. It is done with either hand or both hands. The intensity of massage varies according to the massage point. This method is called the finger needle method in TCM and is used on major acupoints.

6. Finger Kneading The points are kneaded in circles with the finger pads. It is done by one or all of the five fingers with the nails clipped, and by one hand or both hands. The intensity of movement varies according to the massage point. This massage is applied on the main acupoints.

7. Kneading With the Heel of the Palm Use the heel of the palm (wrist force) to knead the acupoints in circles. This is more powerful than finger kneading and affects deep soft tissue. It is mainly applied to the joints and fleshy parts of the extremities.

8. Finger Pinching Extend the thumb and use the forefinger, middle finger, ring finger and little finger in opposition. The tips of the thumb, index and middle fingers pressed together from a crane's beak, open and close this "beak" to massage points on the upper extremities.

9. Palm Rubbing Use the side of the palm to rub in one direction or backwards and forwards. It is used on the abdomen and four limbs.

10. Hand Chopping Use the side of the palm to chop the acupoint, using wrist strength. Separate the fingers for more bounce. Use one hand or both hands. It is used on limbs where muscles are thick.

11. Pressing With the Palm Heels One hand is used or both, one on top of the other for heavy pressure. It is used on the four limbs and back of the waist.

12. Grabbing Using all fingers and the thumbs, grab up the muscle, lift and massage. For acupoints with muscle. This massage stimulates the circulation.

13 Hand Pounding Use the outer side of the palm to pound the acupoints lightly. It is used on the torso and four limbs.

(II) Order of Massage, Acupoints and Effects

Self-massage is done on the faces, head, arms, legs, lumbosacral region and chest, in that order.

1. The Face

(1) Using Both Hands to Wash the Face Wash the face, rubbing the hands over the entire face 10 times. This softens the face and makes it more wind and cold resistant.

(2) Massaging Yintang This is the midpoint between the eyebrows (Fig. 342). It cures headaches, dizziness, head tightness, insomnia, eye disease, neurasthenia, etc. Poke-massage with the thumb, forefinger or middle finger. Both middle fingers used together are correct, too. Poke 10 times.

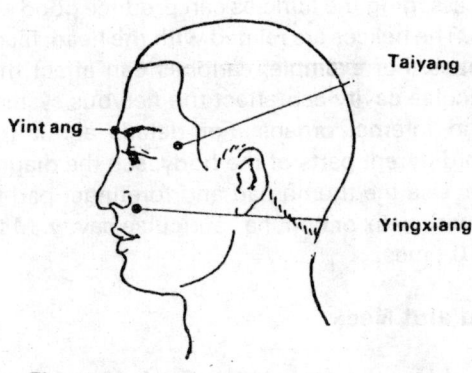

Fig 342

(3) Massaging Taiyang

Location: The two points are symmetrically located in the temple depressions about 3 centimeters from the midpoint between the eyebrow canthus (Fig. 342).

Indication: headache and eye pain.

Process: Use the pads of the thumbs, forefingers or middle fingers to apply massage or finger kneading. Practise this 10 times.

(4) Massaging Yingxiang

Location: The two symmetrical points are located in the nasolabial groove at the base of the nostrils.

Indication: rhinitis, smell disorder, colds and stuffed nose.

Process: Use the pads of the forefingers or middle fingers to apply kneading massage or use the backs of the second thumb joint to apply up-and-down massage along the nasolabial grooves 10 times using the "stroking method."

(5) Massaging the Auricles

According to the TCM theory of channels and collaterals and ear acupuncture, the auricle is closely related with the entire body. Therefore, massaging the auricles can produce good effect on the related parts. The helices are related with the head, face, trunk and four extremities. For example, earlobes can affect the eyes; the concha-auriculae cavity can affect the nervous systems, internal secretion and internal organs. For details about the auricles' relation with different parts of the body, see the diagrams for ear acupuncture. Use the thumb pad and forefinger pad to massage the auricles with helix or concha- auriculae cavity. Massage each part about 10 times.

2. Head and Neck

(1) Combing the Hair With Both Hands

Use the sides of both palms to smooth the hair from the hairline backwards 20 to 30 times. Women may use a wooden comb.

(2) Massaging Yuzhen

Location: The two symmetrical points are located about 2 centimeters to the sides of the protuberance of the occipital bone (Fig. 343).

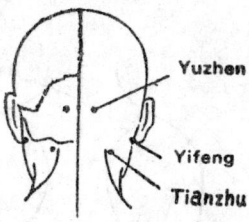

Fig. 343

Indication: insomnia, headache, neurasthenia, etc.

Process: Place both hands with thumb downwards a little above the Yuzhen points. Using the thumb pads to massage the points horizontally with moderate force. Massage 10 times leftwards and 10 times rightwards.

(3) Massaging Fengchi

Location: This pair is in the depression between the upper ends of m. sternocleidomastoideus and m. trapezius on the back of the neck below the occipital bone bilateraly (Fig. 343).

Indication: red and painful eyes, tinnitus, headache, insomnia, neurasthenia and colds.

Process: Massage 10 times by the point-poking method or finger kneading.

(4) Massaging Yifeng

Location: These points are located in the depression between the mandible and mastoid process posterior to the ear lobe on a horizontal line lateral of Fengchi (Fig. 343).

Indication: tinnitus, deafness, etc.

Process: Use the tip of the forefinger or finger to massage 10 times.

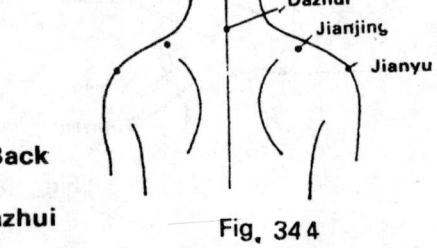

Fig. 344

3. Shoulder and Back

(1) Massaging Dazhui

Location: between the spinous processes of the seventh cervical vertebra and the first thoracic vertebra nearly at shoulder level (Fig. 344).

Indication: Stiffness of the back, headache, neurasthenia, and chronic bronchitis. It is the health preservation point that strengthens the body. Puncturing this point can cure many diseases.

Process: Place the ends of the forefinger and ring finger on the middle finger in order to increase the strength of stimulation. Use poking or poking and kneading massage. Or use the thumb, forefinger and middle finger to pinch 10 times the part between the center of the posterior hairline and the Shenzhu points along the spine.

(2) Grabbing and Pinching Jianjing

Location: These two symmetrical points are located at the highest point of the shoulder midway between Dazhui and the acromion (Fig. 344.)

Indication: pains in the shoulder and back, motor impairment of the hand and arm, neurosis and neuralgia of upper extremities.

Process: Place one hand on the opposite Jianjing point and massage 10 times by finger kneading or use the middle finger to press on Jianjing and shake the shoulder joint, letting the shoulder muscle movement and the finger pressure form a rhythmic stimulation; or pinch Jianjing point with the palm base and the forefinger, middle finger, ring finger, and little finger. Repeat the process 10 times alternating hands.

4. Upper Extremities

(1) Massaging Jianyu

Location: These two symmetrical points are located in the depression below the acromion and in the middle of the upper portion of m. deltoideus at the outer shoulder (Fig. 344).

Indication: Its effects are similar to those of the Jianjing acupoint.

Process: Place one hand on its opposite Jianyu point and use the middle finger to massage it 10 times by poking and kneading; or press Jianyu with the middle finger and shake the shoulder joint, letting the shoulder's muscle movement and the finger's pressure form rhythmic stimulation. After alternating hands, repeat the process 10 times.

(2) Massaging Quchi and Shaohai

Location: When the elbow is flexed, the Quchi point is located in the depression at the lateral end of the transverse cubital crease, midway between Chize and the lateral epicondyle of the humerus; Shaohai, when the elbow is flexed, is at the medial end of the transverse cubital crease in the depression anterior to the medial epicondyle of the humerus. (Figs. 345 and 346.)

Indication: elbow and arm pain and motor impairment of the

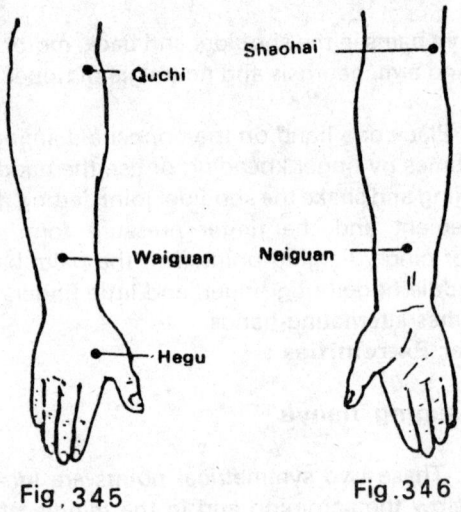

Fig. 345   Fig. 346

arms. Massaging Quchi point also expands diaphragm, preventing and curing chronic bronchitis. Massaging Shaohai also regulates heart Qi.

Process: Place the thumb of one hand on the opposite Shaohai point and its middle finger on Quchi point, slightly flex the elbow, massage the points 10 times. Alternating hands, massage these points on the other arm 10 times.

(3) Massaging Neiguan and Waiguan

Location: Neiguan, about 6 centimeters above the transcerse crease of the wrist, is between the tendons of m. palmaris longus and m. flexor carpi radialis. Waiguan, 6 centimeters above Yangchi, is between the radius and ulna (Figs. 345 and 346).

Indications: finger or arm pain, and motor impairment of the elbow and arm. Massaging Neiguan also treats headache, dizziness, insomnia, nausea, emesis, cold extremities, breakdown of balance between the spleen and stomach, and angina; massaging Waiguan also treats headache, dizziness, tinnitus and nerve deafness as well as regulating the circulation of Qi and blood.

Process: Raise one hand to chest level palm facing the chest, and use the thumb of another hand to press Neiguan and the forefinger to press Waiguan. Massage 10 times. After alternating hands, again massage the points 10 times.

(4) Massaging Hegu

Location: Between the first and second metacarpal bones, approximately in the middle of the second metacarpal bone on the radial side (Fig. 345)

Indication: eye diseases, headache, sore throat, tooth aches, odontopathy, insomnia, dizziness and neurasthenia.

Process: Press the thumb on the Hegu point and support the point on its palmar side with the forefinger; massage the point 10 times by poking and pressing; or, press the thumb on Hegu and the other four fingers on the side of the fifth metacarpal bone to do the massage. After alternating hands, massage it another 10 times.

(5) Massaging the Upper Extremities

After massaging the above points (or some of the points), massage the arms starting with the pinching method. Stretch out the arm to be massaged and keep its palm face up. Make a crane's beak of the thumb and four fingers and pinch massage the arm from the armpit down three to five times. It is also correct to use tapping message, chopping massage or stroking massage. Select the method according to the intensity of stimulation required. Massage the other arm, too.

5. Lower Extremities

(1) Massaging Futu

Location: Futu, about 18 centimeters above the knee, is on the line connecting the anterior iliac spine and the lateral border of the knee (Fig. 347). Each thigh has one of these points.

Indication: pain in the lumbar and iliac region, coldness of the knee, and fatigue in the lower extremities.

Process: The massage can be done with one hand or both hands by tapping, rubbing, chopping, cudgeling, or grabbing. The selection of method is decided by the intensity of stimulation required. Massage each thigh 10 times with each of the hands.

(2) Massaging Heding

Location: These points are in the centers of the knee caps' upper edges (Fig. 348).

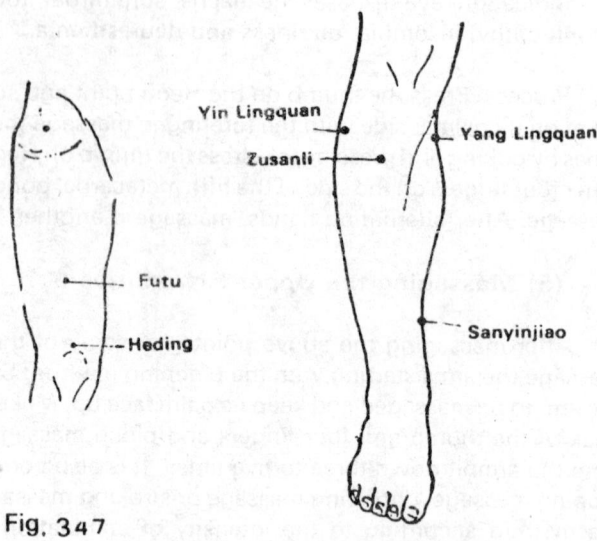

Fig. 347

Fig. 348

Indication: knee joint pain and motor impairment.

Process: Massage the points with one or both hands by finger kneading or chopping. Massage each side 10 times.

Location: Yin Lingquan is in the depression below the interior side of the knee joint head on the interior side of the lower leg. Yang Lingquan is in the in the depression opposite to Yin Lingquan (Fig. 348).

Indication: knee pain, knee motor impairment and knee joint fatigue. In addition, massaging Yin Lingquan treats indigestion, and deficiency of the spleen and stomach. Massaging Yang Lingquan treats lumbago, neurasthenia, and gall bladder functional disorder.

Process: Massage the two points simultaneously for 10 times with the thumbs by poking or finger kneading.

(4) Massaging Zusanli

Location: About 10 centimeters below the patella and about two fingers in width from the anterior crest of the tibia (Fig. 348).

Indication: Improving functions of the digestive system, respiratory system, cardiovascular system and urinary system. It is especially effective in treating indigestion, hypertension, neurasthenia, and habitual constipation. This is also a major acupoint. In ancient times, it was stated that if one wants to keep fit, moxibustion of Zusanli is indispensable. Therefore, frequent massage of this point can preserve health.

Process: Massage the two symmetrical points simultaneously 10 times by finger kneading.

(5) Massaging Sanyinjiao

Location: About 10 centimeters directly above the tip of the medial malleolus, is located on the border of the tibia and on the line connecting the medial malleolus to Yin Lingquan (Fig. 348).

Indication: abdominal pain motor impairment of the lower extremities, and some diseases of the urinary system, nervous system and cardiovascular system and, in particular, menalgia, irregular menses and hypertension.

Process: Massage the points simultaneously by finger kneading.

(6) Massaging Yongquan

Location: In the depression that appears on the sole when the foot is in plantar flexion, approximately at the junction of the anterior and middle third of the sole.

Indication: headache, dizziness, tinnitus, palpitation, amnesia, neurasthenia, and hypertension.

Process: Use the left hand to massage the right point, and the right hand the left point. Massage the points 10 times and exchange hands for another 10 times.

(7) Massaging the Lower Extremities

After massaging the leg points (or some of the points), massage the whole legs from the top of the thigh to the toes using both hands to pinch two to three times, then massage by chopping, patting, tapping, palm heel rubbing, palm heel pressing, grabbing, or cudgeling depending on the amount of stimulation required. Alternate the hands during practice.

6. Lumbar and Sacral Region

(1) Poking Shenshu

Location: These symmetrical points are about 5 centimeters lateral to the lower border of the spinous process of the second lumbar vertebra (Fig. 349), in the small of the back over the kidneys.

Indication: Pain in the knee, kidney deficiency, night emissions, impotence, menalgia, irregular menses, headache, dizziness, tinnitus, fatigue and neurasthenia.

Process: Clench both fists and place them against the lumbar region, use the second metacarpal joint to press and circularly rub the points 10 times. Or massage the points by light pounding with the other sides of the palms or palm heel rubbing and pressing.

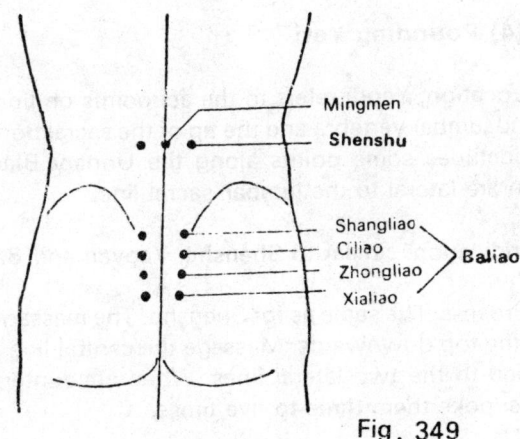

Fig. 349

(2) Poking Yaoyan

Location: In the depression lateral to the space between the spinous processes of the fourth and fifth lumbar vertebrae. The point can be located when the body is in a prone position.

Indication: lumbar muscle strain, senile lumbago, etc.

Process: Clench both fists and place their backs against the Yaoyan points, use the second metacarpal joint to press and rub in circles 10 times.

(3) Poking Baliao

Location: Baliao is the general term for Shangliao, Xialiao, Ciliao, and Zhongliao, four pairs of points individually located on the four pairs of sacral bone holes (Fig. 349).

Indication: sacral bone region pain, lumbago, emissions, irregular menses, enuresis, and senile enuresis.

Process: Massage the points by poking and pressing. As the muscle of this region are relatively thick, massaging circularly while pressing and poking can produce wide-spread diffuse sensations. The massage can be done from the top downwards.

(4) Pounding Yeti

Location: Yaodi refers to the acupoints on line between the second lumbar vertebra and the tip of the sacral bone. This region also includes some points along the Urinary Bladder Channel which are lateral to the lumbar-sacral line.

Indication: similar to Shenshu, Yaoyan and Baliao.

Process: The same as for Shenshu. The massage can be done from the top downwards. Massage the central line first, and then proceed to the two lateral lines. When encountering the major points, poke them three to five times.

7. Chest-abdomen Region

(1) **Massaging the Abdomen Sides** This region includes the upper line of the crista-iliaca, the soft waist, lateral waist, and lateral abdomen. The main acupoints in this region are Jingmen, Zhengmen, and Daimai.

Indication: It relieves pain in the waist and abdomen and regulates spleen and kidney Qi and blood.

Process: Pinch the waist with both hands, the thumb on the back side and the four fingers in the front, empty palms pressing on the crista-iliaca line. Use the pinching method. Apply on both sides of the waist simultaneously 10 times.

(2) Massaging the Ren Channel

The Ren Channel is one of the Eight Extra Channels, it runs down the anterior midline. The main points include Tanzhong, Jiuwei, Sanwan, Qizhong, Qihai, and Guanyuan (Fig. 350)

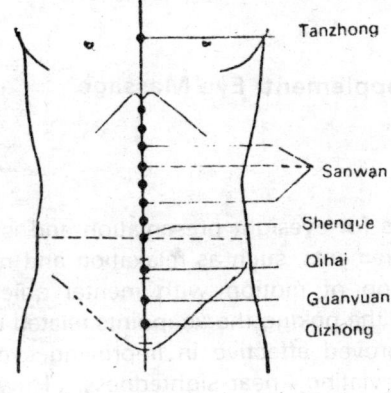

Fig.350

Indication: Massaging Tanzhong treats chest pain and palpitation, regulates chest Qi, and prevents and treats bronchitis. Massaging Jiuwei, Sanwan and Qizhong treats stomach extension and pain and reinforces gastric function. Qihai and Guanyuan treat diseases of the genitourinary system, nervous system and digestive system; Qihai and Guanyuan are also important health preservation points. Shenque is located in Front Dantian.

Process: Patients with hypertension and excessiveness in the upper organs (TCM terminology) should be massaged along this channel from Tanzhong downwards by light pounding with the sides of the palms. Patients with visceroptosis are advised to massage the main points with circular finger massage.

A Supplement: Eye Massage

This massage is for eyesight preservation and is based on some Qigong requirements, such as relaxation and naturalness and the combination of motion with mental quietude. The massage is done by the poking the acupoints related with sight. This method has proved effective in improving eyesight and preventing or alleviating near-sightedness. However, for preventing near sightedness, the more active way is to cultivate good habits of eye use.

1. Main Massage Acupoints

(1) **Jinmin**: in the depressions at the bridge of the nose just above the inner corner of the eyes.

(2) **Yangbai**: above the arch (center) of the eyebrow.

(3) **Yintang**: midway between the inner ends of the eyebrows on the midline.

(4) **Zanzhu**: on the eye socket bone depressions just above the two inner ends of the eyebrows.

(5) **Yuyao**: depression on the eye socket's lower edge above the pupil.

(6) **Sizhukong:** above the eye socket depression at the outer end of the eyebrow

(7) **Tongziliao:** above the eye socket depression at the tail (outer) end of the eye.

(8) **Taiyang**: the skull depressions at the temples

(9) Sibai: below Chengqi in the depression at the infraorbital foramen.

(10) Fengchi: bilateral acupoints on the back of the head below the occipital bone, in the depression between the upper portion of m. sternocleidomastoideus and m. trapezius.

(11) Binao: on the radial side of the humerus, superior to the lower end of m. deltoideus, on the line connecting Quchi and Jianyu points.

(12) Hegu: between the first and second metacarpal bones, beside approximately the middle of the second metacarpal bone on the radial side.

2. Directions for Eye Massage

Eye massage can be practised in the sitting or standing postures. When massaging Jingming, the hands should be clean and the finger nails clipped to avoid eye pollution. Place one thumb and one forefinger on both Jingming points, press towards the bridge of the nose, and then use the tips of both middle fingers to press and squeeze Yangbai--Zanzhu--Yuyao--Sizhukong--Tongziliao and Taiyang with relatively stronger force on the Taiyang points. Then, press Sibai and Fengchi points. Finally, massage Binao and Hegu points as described in the technics sections of self-massage. Each point should be massaged about 10 times. A complete massage requires a minimum of three to four minutes. Massage twice or three times a day. For better effect, some requirements for Qigong should be followed, such as conducting Qi to Dantian and inducing the cerebral cortex into a state of quietude.

Chronological Table of Chinese History

Primitive Society	Remote antiquity-4,000 years ago
Xia	Around 21st-16th century B.C.
Shang	Around 16th-11th century B.C.
Western Zhou	Around 11th century-770 B.C.
Spring and Autumn Period	770-476 B.C.
Warring States Period	475-221 B.C.
Qin	221-207 B.C.
Western Han	206 B.C.-A.D. 24
Eastern Han	25-220
Three Kingdoms	220-280
Western Jin	265-316
Eastern Jin	317-420
Sui	581-618
Tang	618-907
Five Dynasties	907-960
Song (Northern and Southern)	960-1279
Southern and Northern Dynasties	420-589
Yuan	1271-1368
Ming	1368-1644
Qing	1644-1911

About
the Author

The author, Mr. Jiao Guorui, is a renowned specialist in traditional Chinese medicine (TCM), acupuncture and Qigong for prophylaxis. The posts which he holds currently show his prestige and versatile expertise: professor and chief physician, member of the Academic Evaluation Committee, member of the Experts Committee, Professor of Graduate Studies, and Director of the Qigong Program; Vice Chairman, Board of Directors of the All-China Clinical Qigong Research Institute; Honorary Advisor of the Xinhua Society for the Promotion of TCM; member of the Hong Kong Traditional Chinese Medical Science and Medicine Association, and Visiting Professor of the Institute of Chinese Medicine in Japan.

A native of Fengren county, Hebei province, Professor Jiao was born in 1923 into a family famous for its TCM practice. He graduated from the North China College of Chinese Medicine. Although he had started Qigong as an 8-year-old under a famous teacher named Wang Tong, he did not begin serious studies of Qigong until in his middle age when he became a student of Hu Yaozhen, Zhou Qianchuan and then Wang Fangzhai and inherited much of the three Qigong masters' theory as well as exercise methods. In ensuing years, Dr. Jiao persisted in Qigong exercise, read extensively on the subject, visited Qigong masters throughout China and in general, devoted himself to the learning and practice of Qigong under TCM guidance. These efforts in seeking a new method of health care finally made Dr. Jiao an erudite scholar in this field. He systematized 10 sets of quiescent and dynamic exercise and created the system of mental and physical health prophylaxis through Qigong. Dr. Jiao's theory and exercises, including main principles and specific skills, are marked by special characteristics of of his own forming his own original style.

Academic activities at home and international exchanges have been increasing dramatically in recent years, which is greatly helps propagate this new prophylactic program. Due to the reform in the national public health system, assisted by the Ministry of Health, Dr. Jiao has established the Research Institute of the Science of Prophylaxis Through Qigong. Composed mainly of scientists, the institute is the first of its kind in China and specializes in the research and promotion of Qigong.

His main works include *The Teaching Notes of Acupuncture* (1953); *Ten Lectures on Acupuncture* (1955); *An Acupuncturist's Summary of Clinical Experiences* (1981); *Medical Encyclopedia: Acupuncture Section* (co-author); *An Outline of Lectures on Qigong* (1961); *Hua Tuo's Frolics of Five Animals* (1963); *Methods of Preserving Health Through Qigong* (1964); *Demonstration, Origin and Development of the Inductive Gong* (1983); *Essentials of the Science of Health Promotion Through Qigong* (1984), and *Qigong Essentials for Health Promotion* (1986).

中国气功养生学概要(英)

焦国瑞　著

＊

今日中国出版社出版

（原中国建设出版社）

（中国北京百万庄路24号）

世界知识印刷厂印刷

中国国际图书贸易总公司发行

（中国北京车公庄西路21号）

北京邮政信箱第399号　　邮政编码100044

1990年第一版　第二次印刷

ISBN 7-5072-0100-7/Z·23

01100

14-E-2338S

Qiging Essentials for Health Promotion

By Jiao Guorui

Published by China Today Press

(formerly China Reconstructs Press)

(24 Baiwanzhuang Road, Beijing, China)

Printed by World Knowledge Printing House

Distributed by China International Book Trading Corporation

(21 Chegongzhuang Xilu, Beijing, China)

P.O. Box 399 Beijing, China Postal Zone: 100044

2nd Edition 1990

ISBN 7-5072-0100-7/Z·23

01100

14-E-2338S